C++ IOStreams Handbook

Steve Teale

Addison-Wesley Publishing Company

Reading, Massachusetts • Menlo Park, California • New York
Don Mills, Ontario • Wokingham, England • Amsterdam • Bonn
Sydney • Singapore • Tokyo • Madrid • San Juan • Milan • Paris

Library of Congress Cataloging-in-Publication Data

Teale, Steve.
    C++ IOStreams handbook / Steve Teale.
        p.   cm.
    Includes index.
    ISBN 0-201-59641-5
    1. C++ (Computer program language)   I. Title.
    QA76.73.C153T43   1993
    005.7'11--dc20   93-12480
                                                                          CIP

The procedures and applications presented in this book have been included for their instructional value. They have been tested with care but are not guaranteed for any particular purpose. The publisher does not offer any warranties or representations, nor does it accept any liabilities with respect to the programs or applications.

Reprinted with corrections February, 1994

4 5 6 7 8 9 10-CRS-97 96 95

Preface

Books are like computer software. After cycles of writing and testing they reach a state where they are nearly finished, and that state then persists for the rest of their lives. It's always possible to find points that could be better stated, sentences that could be better structured, and topics that could be added or expanded.

Despite any misgivings, the time has arrived to finish this book and have it fixed in print. The idea was originally conceived because of the rather striking absence of published information on C++ IOStreams. In that sense the book is long overdue. I know from numerous conversations that many C++ users are interested in IOStreams, and can vaguely see its potential, but have more or less given up on the idea through lack of documentation. This book is for those C++ programmers; users who are already familiar with the language, but who want to extend their view of its idioms and areas of application.

The intention of the book, quite probably an overambitious one, is that it should cover the whole spectrum of requirements for those who need information on the subject. So there are a number of elements which I have tried to cover:

- An attempt to explain *why* IOStreams
- A basic road map for the structure of the IOStreams system
- Examples of straightforward and more devious usage of IOStreams in cookbook chapters

- Manual page style material which can be used for reference
- The mysteries of manipulators
- Implementation details to provoke future implementors into doing things better.
- Strategies, examples, and guidelines for the provision of IOStreams facilities for user defined types.

There are a number of people who should share the credit for the *C++ IOStreams Handbook*. The first is Jerry Schwarz, who created the IOStreams system, and was then too busy to do the book. I thank him for the opportunity even if only by default. Next, I should acknowledge the roles of Paul Leathers and Walter Bright of Zortech Inc. They gave me a deadline date for a working version of IOStreams, and thus made me find out what the system was supposed to do. I must also thank the language group of Symantec Corporation, who gave me yet another opportunity to try out my ideas on a real product.

The next is my wife Lynn. If I hadn't met her I would probably not have ended up as a long-term visitor to the United States with enough time on my hands to record the resulting expertise. The next is Debbie Lafferty of Addison-Wesley's computer science division, who has supported the project throughout, and who recruited my formidable array of reviewers. Both Lynn and Debbie were kind enough to assume that I could actually come up with the book given an appropriate combination of encouragement and arm-twisting.

The reviewers, Stephen D. Clamage, Jim Coplien, Margaret A. Ellis, Stanley Lippman, Jerry Schwarz, Steve Vinoski, and Nancy Wilkinson all clearly spent a good deal of time and effort in their contribution to the book. My thanks to all of them.

I'd also like to thank Helen Wythe for coordinating the production of the book. My copy editor was Laura Michaels, and I thank Laura for her patient work. The cover was the brain-child of Peter Blaiwas, and I want to thank him for his sense of frivolity. Perceptive collectors of Addison-Wesley computer science books will notice that this book is participating in a trend or fashion, the *creatures* series. You've seen the Dragon book, and the Teddy Bear book, to name just a couple— well this is the Fish book. I have to say that this is more of a pun than an attempt at association. Both the Dragon book and the Teddy Bear book are objects of my greatest respect.

Hackettstown, New Jersey   S.S.T.

Contents

FTP Access to Source Code

The sample programs presented in this book are available on line for your personal, noncommercial use. These programs have been compiled and run under MS-DOS using version 3.1 of the Symantec (Zortech) compiler. They should run with most C++ implementations with the caveats regarding their outcome that are noted in Chapter 21.

The files are available on the internet on host world.std.com via anonymous FTP. To access the files from an Internet host, enter the following commands:

```
% ftp world.std.com
Name: anonymous
331 Guest login ok, send email address as password.
Password: <your email address>
230-
230-Hello
...
ftp> cd AW/iostreams
250 CWD command successful.
ftp> ls
ftp> get README
```

You may use the FTP get command to retrieve additional files.

A 5 1/4 inch disk is also available. To order the disk, call Addison-Wesley at 617-944-3700, extension 2262.

1

Introduction

The C++ language and the object-oriented paradigm were developed to improve the productivity of programmers and to enable them to deal with greater complexity. This is to be accomplished by the following three approaches:

1. Through stronger type checking, which captures more errors at compile and link time, rather than leaving them to be eliminated by time consuming application debugging and maintenance.

2. By providing comprehensive support for data abstraction, encouraging the definition of user-defined types as reuseable components, and their specialization or incremental development through inheritance.

3. By providing for data types that have abstract properties and for hierarchies of derived types that implement those properties specifically but which can be manipulated with generality.

The IOStreams system is a proposed library component of the C++ language that supports these strategies with respect to input/output (IO). the most common

1

introduction to the IOStreams C++ class library takes the form

```
#include <iostream.h>

main()
{
  cout << "Hello World!";
}
```

which contrasts with the equivalent C program

```
#include <stdio.h>
main()
{
  printf("Hello World!");
}
```

Many programmers making the transition from C to C++ have noted, with the inclination toward economy typical of C programmers, that the C++ program contains three more characters than the second. Some have continued to use `printf`, maintaining that there is no obvious advantage in abandoning the familiar for the unfamiliar. There are good arguments against this view, however, which we explore in more detail in Chapter 3. Suppose that function `foo` is somewhat complex (we simplify it for our example) and was originally designed with two 16-bit `short` or `int` arguments, `i` and `j`, as follows:

```
void foo(int i, int j)
{
  // complexity
  printf("i = %d, j = %d\n", i, j);
}
```

As `foo` is developed, 32-bit `long` arguments become more appropriate than `int`, so the function `foo` is changed as follows; however, the `printf` statement is overlooked:

```
void foo(long i, long j)
{
  // complexity
  printf("i = %d, j = %d\n", i, j);
}
```

The function still compiles without comment, but when the code runs, it either prints garbage or provokes a memory protection fault. If the IOStreams alternative had been used instead, as shown below,

```
cout  << "i = " << i << " j = " << j << endl;
```

and no change had been made to this line either, then the function still would have compiled correctly. More importantly, however, because the IOStreams IO mechanism is type-safe, it would have produced the correct output. If a change in the code had been required, the compiler would have produced an error message.

Taking the example further, the function might not take integer arguments at all. It might be something like the following:

```
void foo(Coord a, Coord b);
```

The simple `printf` form would now be out of the question because it isn't possible to write

```
printf("a = %Coord, b = %Coord\n", a, b);
```

However, a normally designed implementation of the type `Coord` as a C++ class would provide the required IOStreams translator functions. Then the output line using `cout` could be used as it was with the integer arguments. In other words the IOStreams IO mechanism is extendable.

These particular examples might suggest only small advantages to using IOStreams. Remember though, that it is always a small bug that prevents a program from working properly. (Programmers should take any help that they can get.) In Chapter 3, we discuss in greater detail the reasons for a new IO system to accompany the new language. IOStreams supports the C++ strategies for productivity improvement and dealing with complexity. Its use shouldn't be rejected lightly, even though the existing alternatives are well tried and familiar.

IOStreams was first provided as part of the AT&T Cfront C++ Translator version 2.0 release in 1989, superceding the Streams library that had been supplied as part of earlier Cfront releases and with other inplementations of C++. Streams had been associated with the C++ language from its earliest days in much the same way as the `stdio` functions `printf`, `gets`, `puts`, etc., have been associated with C. Benefitting from users' experiences with the previous Streams library, IOStreams was designed using that most valuable of programming assets, hindsight, to give improved execution efficiency and convenience of use.

The AT&T IOStreams library was submitted to the ANSI C++ committee for inclusion in the standard. It seems likely to be accepted, albeit with considerable modification. At the time we finished this book, the ANSI IOStreams (Input/Output) document was at revision five and was still the subject of some unanswered questions.

Implementations of the IOStreams library have been licensed or separately developed by most other C++ vendors. What is still lacking, however, is a reasonably detailed and nonproprietary user handbook for IOStreams. Each supplier provides different documentation, with greater or lesser detail, but which unfortunately tends to be closer to a specification of the particular implementation than to an indication on how to use IOStreams in general. The familiarity of `printf` becomes even more appealing when the alternative is ill-defined and poorly documented.

This book is designed to fill that gap. Hopefully it will help during that awkward time when many new C++ programmers find the IOStreams approach unfamiliar and possibly somewhat verbose. It might also help established C++ users who previously have incompletely investigated Streams or IOStreams and subsequently reverted to using the more familiar stdio functions. This is what happened to us, before the necessity of implementing a version of IOStreams provided us with the required familiarity. We suspect that when the ANSI standardization process is more advanced or completed, a second edition of this book will be required. However, delays in this process didn't seem a good reason to put off writing this edition. It could be quite some time before the standard is completed and all the compiler vendors have caught up with it.

The IOStreams library is substantially different from the original Streams library in both its structure and implementation. However, they are sufficiently compatible that it should rarely be difficult to convert existing programs using Streams. Only a small, and presumably rapidly diminishing, number of C++ users are still constrained to using the original Streams system. Consequently, as its title implies, this book does not set out to describe it.

We have assumed that the reader is quite familiar with both C and C++ but not necessarily with IOStreams. If you are a C++ beginner this is the wrong book for you now! We suggest you instead try references 1 through 3 in the list in Appendix 3. There you'll find a small sampling of the many C++ books available.

For IOStreams beginners, some simple examples of the use of its IO facilities are provided in Chapter 2, the first "cookbook" chapter. These are intended to provide ready reference information. We follow in Chapter 3 with some further explanation of why a system like IOStreams should be regarded by programmers, or by their managers, as necessary or desirable. Beginners to IOStreams should find this chapter more comprehensible if they first read Chapter 1.

In Chapter 4 we describe the structure of the IOStreams system, with skeleton class outlines to give a broad overall picture of the sytem. In Chapters 5 through 14, each class that comprises IOStreams is then discussed, with examples of how to use their public interfaces included.

Some examples of how manipulators improve the economy of use of IOStreams are then presented in Chapter 15. We feel that IOStreams' capability to define manipulators should be more than enough to counter the criticism that IOStreams is verbose when compared to the facilities of the C stdio library. We expect that the number of predefined manipulators in vendors' implementations will increase sharply as their utility becomes more appreciated. Chapter 16 deals with the use of the stdio and IOStreams facilities simultaneously.

Chapters 17 and 18 offer examples of the derivation of new classes from the base classes in the IOStreams library. These include a good deal of implementation detail and illustrate the use of the protected interfaces of the base classes, where these exist. Users of the UNIX operating system may detect a bias towards the PC operating systems, MS-DOS and OS/2, in this discussion. IOStreams was designed and originally implemented under UNIX, and its design and conventions are consequently a good match to that operating system. Other operating systems with large user bases, however, don't do things in quite the same way. For example, newline translation in text mode is the norm in C and C++ implementations for MS-DOS and OS/2, which makes implementations significantly more complicated. Therefore we felt it appropriate to present implementation details for the more demanding of the two cases.

Chapters 19 and 20 deal with some techniques for developing IOStreams inserters and extractors for both built-in and user-defined types. This is currently something of a black art and is possibly an area where a standard for IOStreams might provide beneficial guidelines. Inserters and extractors implemented in several different ways are presented as illustrations.

We offer in Chapter 21 a second set of "recipes." The programs presented there probe limiting conditions and generally investigate the properties and behavior of IOStreams that were described in the preceding chapters. Some of these programs do not currently have well-defined results. Such examples may be useful to C++ users in encouraging their compiler vendors to achieve timely uniformity of interpretation and implementation. Because of the general purpose nature and flexibility of C++ libraries like IOStreams, a set of examples like this can't be exhaustive; there are simply too many permutations and combinations involved to illustrate all possible uses of such a system. However, the programs in this section do provide several further examples of how the IOStreams library can be used.

This book doesn't purport to describe any particular implementation of IO-Streams. Neither does it attempt to censor features or behavior that the user might find in current implementations but which might not make it to the ANSI standard. Also our own prejudices might be visible at times and the word "probably" occurs more often than it should in a reference book. After all, IOStreams is a system in a state of change.

IOStreams Cookbook–
Simple Input and Output

This chapter provides a simple guide to using IOStreams facilities for the built-in types of C++. For users migrating from C, equivalent usages of `stdio` facilities are shown where appropriate.

There are four topic areas: Output to the standard output, input from the standard input, output to and input from a file, and output to and input from an arbitrary memory area. In each case we deal with IO of the built-in types. Because IOStreams was designed to be extended to deal with user-defined types, you should expect to be able to use it for them by analogy with the operations presented for the built-in types.

Little, if any, understanding of how IOStreams works is assumed or required. Use the material in this chapter like recipes from a cookbook. If you need to know how they work, read on.

2.1 Output to the Standard Output

Displaying a character

In C you can use the following statements to display a single character on a line by itself:

```
#include <stdio.h>
```

```
char c;
printf("%c\n", c);
```

The analogous IOStreams usage is

```
#include <iostream.h>

char c;
cout << c << endl;
```

Here, the operation cout << c is called inserting c into cout. The entity cout is an instance of a class called an ostream, which will be described in detail in the chapters that follow.

Using C you might be able to get by without including stdio.h, depending how fussy your C compiler is about functions being declared. In C++, however, all functions must be declared before they are used. With IOStreams, the header file iostream.h or some other IOStreams header file must be included. The naming of these C++ header files is not yet standardized, so depending on which compiler you are using, the name might be any of the following:

```
#include <iostream.h>
#include <iostream.hpp>
#include <iostream.hxx>
```

We use the .h extension for header files in this book.

In a loop in a C program, you could use the statement

```
for (i = 0; i < n; ++i)
    putchar(c);
```

The IOStreams equivalent is

```
for (i = 0; i < n; ++i)
    cout.put(c);
```

C++ supports char, signed char, and unsigned char as distinct types. However, these are all output by IOStreams as though they are simply char.

The following C statements deal with the output of character constants:

```
printf("%c%c\n", '\t', c);
printf("\t%c\n", c);      /* more common */
putchar('\t');
```

Equivalent statements using IOStreams are

```
cout << '\t' << c << endl;
cout.put('\t');
```

Note in the first example the use of end1 rather than the alternative '\n' which ultimately has much the same effect. The two alternatives differ in that using end1 immediately flushes the output to its destination, whereas using '\n' the output is buffered until there are several kilobytes of characters to write to the screen.

Suppose the following program has a bug:

```
void c();    // contains the bug that terminates the program
void d();

void main()
{
  cout << 'c' << '\n';
  c();
  cout << 'd' << '\n';
  d();
}
```

The bug is in the function c(). Because of it, the program won't get past the second line; that is, it won't display any intended output. Instead it terminates before the output buffer is full, and you won't know which function was responsible, c() or d(). If you had used end1 instead of '\n', the program would have displayed 'c' before it died.

You get the same diagnostic effect using

```
cerr << 'c' << '\n';
```

Items sent to the standard error output in this way are always displayed immediately, because the buffer for the cerr stream is flushed automatically after each insertion.

Rather than using end1 to achieve immediate output—that is, flushing of the buffer—you can use either flush in the same way as end1 or a specific call to the cout member function flush as shown in the following:

```
cout << c << flush;
// or
cout << c;
cout.flush();
```

In either event, the output is displayed immediately, before the next program statement is executed.

Note, however, that buffering is used to improve performance. Flushing each line of output using either end1 or flush decreases efficiency. Therefore if speed is a consideration, use end1 or flush only when the output must be up-to-date.

Field width and justification setting

In preceding examples a tab character was sent before the output character in order to position the output correctly. However, you can position the output more flexibly by using the manipulator setw( ) to set the field width in which the output is to be printed. A *manipulator* is a data object of a type known to IOStreams that allows a user to change the state of a stream. In this case, include the header file iomanip.h. This will include iostream.h for you. Then use the following:

```
#include <iomanip.h>


c = '+';
cout << '[' << setw(10) << c << ']' << endl;
// similar to printf("%10c.\n", c);
```

which will give the output

```
[         +]
```

Note that inserting an object of this kind into a stream might or might not produce output. For example, the setw manipulator does not, while the endl manipulator does by outputting a newline before it flushes the stream.

The position at which the padding appears in the output produced by a call to printf is controlled by the sign of the padding digit string in the format specifier for each individual variable. In the IOStreams system, the position is controlled by the state of the stream. Such a state, or mode, is persistent and is represented by an internal flag value that is set by a function call. For example

```
cout.setf(ios::left);
cout << '[' << setw(10) << c << ']' << endl;
// similar to printf("[%-10c]\n", c);
```

produces the output

```
[+        ]
```

Here, ios::left produces output that is left justified. To return to the original (default) state of affairs, which is right justification, use

```
cout.unsetf(ios::left);
```

The flags that control padding are called ios::adjustfield. The cout.setf() function can also be called with two arguments: The first argu- s flags to be set, the second specifies flags that are to be first cleared kample, calling setf( ) with a second argument value of ios::ad- , as follows:

```
os::left,ios::adjustfield);
```

ensures that all existing settings of the padding control flags are cleared before the selected value is set.

If none of the `ios::adjustfield` flags are set, output within a field is right justified.

Padding is a consideration only if the field width has been set to something other than its default value of 0. This default value specifies that only as wide a field as is required will be used. Consequently if the field width is 0 or if the number of characters representing the item exceeds the specified field width, the item is output using the number of characters required to represent the item.

As an alternative to the `setw()` manipulator, an explicit `cout` member function call can set the field width, as follows:

```
cout.width(10);
```

Regardless of how the field width is set, padding is applied only to the next output item. After that, the width setting reverts to the default value of 0. This result is unusual in IOStreams; most adjustments to the stream state persist until specifically cancelled.

String output

Output of a `char*` value output closely resembles single character output. The pointer is assumed to point at a null-terminated array of characters, and the null terminator byte is not sent to the output. An example is:

```
char *string = "The quick brown fox";
cout << string << endl;
```

The other character pointer types

```
const char *
signed char *
const signed char *
unsigned char *
const unsigned char *
```

behave the same way.

IOStreams pads strings within a field width in the same way that it pads characters, so

```
cout.width(24);
cout << string << '.' << endl;
```

gives output

```
     The quick brown fox.
```

Alternatively

```
cout.setf(ios::left,ios::adjustfield);
cout.setw(24);
cout << string << '.' << endl;
```

gives

```
The quick brown fox      .
```

Specifying a field width that is less than the string length produces no effect. For example,

```
cout.setw(5);
cout << string << "." << endl;
```

produces the same output as would be obtained without any field width setting, that is,

```
The quick brown fox.
```

Integer output

Output of an integral type, such as short, int, unsigned, long, etc., takes exactly the same form as it does for a single character or a string. This consistency is one of the strengths of the IOStreams system. For example,

```
int n = 10;
count << n << endl;
```

In C the printf function call specifies how an integer value is displayed, as in

```
printf("%d\n", n);        /* similar to the C++ above */
printf("%i\n", n);        /* same as %d */
```

where the %d or %i notations specify that output should be as a decimal integer, such as

```
10
```

Alternatively, using printf we can have

```
printf("%o\n", n);
```

where %o specifies that output should be as an octal integer, and n gets displayed as

```
12
```

The %x or %X notations specify hexadecimal output with alpha characters in lowercase or uppercase, as in

```
printf("%x\n", n);
```

which produces the output

a

and

```
printf("%X\n", n);
```

which produces the output

A

Using the different forms in sequence, as in

```
printf("%d %o %x\n", n, n, n);
```

thus produces the output

10 12 a

In IOStreams there is always a current mode for integer output. Switching to octal or hexadecimal mode is accomplished using one of the manipulators oct and hex. Once a base or radix mode is set, it persists until another explicit change is made. The analogous sequence of operations is

```
cout << n << endl;
```

which produces the output

10

Next,

```
cout << oct << n << endl;
```

produces the output

12

And finally,

```
cout << hex << n << endl;
```

which produces the output

a

Using each successively, as follows:

```
cout << dec << n << ' ' << oct << n << ' ' << hex << n << endl;
```

produces the output

`10 12 a`

Notice that in the last statement it's necessary to use `<< dec`. Recall that the modes are persistent. Because the display base was previously set to hex, without the explicit resetting to decimal base, the output would have been

`a 12 a`

The flags that control the radix of the representation are called collectively `ios::basefield`. As already noted, the `cout.setf()` function can be called with two arguments: The first specifies a flag to be set, the second allows a group of flags to be cleared. It's best to ensure that no more than one bit is set. Do this by using `setf()` with two arguments. For example, to ensure that all existing settings of the basefield flags are cleared before your selected value is set, use

`cout.setf(ios::dec,ios::basefield);`

The manipulators `dec`, `oct`, and `hex` used as part of an output statement do this automatically. If none or more than one `adjustfield` flag is set, IOStreams assumes decimal conversion is required; none is the default state of affairs. If changes have been made, it can be restored using

`cout.unsetf(ios::basefield);`

To force the hexadecimal alpha characters to uppercase (the equivalent of `printf("%X...`), use

```
cout.setf(ios::uppercase);
// set the standard output flag for upper case
```

Once again the effects of this setting persist until you remove the setting with the following statement:

`cout.unsetf(ios::uppercase);`

Integer values can also be output with a more specific indication of their radix. In C this is done for each variable output, in the same way as it's done for the radix specification, that is,

```
n = 7;
printf("%#x  %#o  %#d\n", n, n, n);
```

which produces the output

`0x7 07 7`

In C++, however, the setting is persistent. Hence the statement

`cout.setf(ios::showbase);`

```
cout << hex << n << ' ' <<   oct << n
          << ' ' <<   dec << n << endl;
cout.unsetf(ios::showbase);
```

produces the output

```
0x7 07 7
```

Note that in a case like this it might be more convenient to use the manipulators `setiosflags()` and `resetiosflags()` than the separate function calls to `setf()` and `unsetf()`, as follows:

```
cout << setiosflags(ios::showbase) << hex << n
      << resetiosflags(ios::showbase) << endl;
```

   Padding integer values into a specified field width is accomplished in much the same way as it is for character output. For example, the statements

```
cout << setw(10) << n << '.' << endl;
cout.setf(ios::left);
cout << setw(10) << n << '.' << endl;
cout.unsetf(ios::left);
cout << setw(10) << n << '.' << endl;
```

produce output

```
         7.
7         .
         7.
```

There is another option, however, which is not supported by C `printf` style output: The padding can be placed *internal* to the representation of whatever is being output. In the case of a character, doing this leaves things just as they were, with padding on the left or right. But with a negative integer, the effect can be seen as in the following:

```
cout.setf(ios::internal,ios::adjustfield);
int m = -n;
cout << setw(10) << m << '.' << endl;
cout << setw(10) << n << '.' << endl;
```

which produces the output

```
-        7.
         7.
```

It is also possible to force the usually redundant plus sign to appear. Do this with

```
cout.setf(ios::showpos);     // show positive sign
cout << setw(10) << m << '.' << endl;
```

```
cout << setw(10) << n << '.' << endl;
```

which produces the output

```
–          7.
+          7.
```

The results are similar to those when using `printf("%+10d\n", n)` except for the internal padding. If either hexadecimal or octal output has been set, all integer values are output as unsigned values. For example, -1 will appear as `ffff` or `177777` (16 bit), or `ffffffff` or `37777777777` (32 bit).

Floating-point output

Output of floating point numbers using IOStreams takes a now familiar form. The output syntax is identical to that which we saw for character, string, and integer variables, as follows:

```
double d = 10.0;          // or float, or long double
count << d << endl;
```

which is more or less equivalent to

```
printf("%f\n", d)
```

either of these should output

```
10.000000
```

It is possible, however, that your version of IOStreams will output

```
10
```

This ambiguity arises because, at the time of this writing, no agreement exists as to which should be the default behavior for floating-point output. There are two options. The first, which could be described as informal, produces from the statements

```
double a = 10, b = 10.1, c = 10.11
cout << a << ',' << b <<   ','   << c << endl;
```

the output

```
10,10.1,10.11
```

The second more formal option uses a fixed precision (number of places after the decimal point) regardless of whether doing so adds any extra information. The corresponding output is

```
10.000000,10.100000,10.110000
```

Presumably one of these behaviors will be written into the standard as the default.
The first option can be forced by

```
cout.unsetf(ios::showpoint);
```

and the second by

```
cout.setf(ios::showpoint);
```

The default value for the precision—that is, the number of digits shown after the decimal point if ios::showpoint is set, or if the digits are nonzero—is 6. If the decimal exponent of the value is less than −4 or greater than the precision, the form of the value output will convert to scientific notation. For example, 0.000011 would be output as 1.1e−05 and 10000000.1 as 1.0e+07.

The fixed or scientific notations can be forced by setting one of the internal flags, ios::fixed or ios::scientific. These two fields are known collectively as ios::floatfield. They are used as in

```
cout.setf(ios::fixed);
```

to ensure output of

```
0.000011
```

or

```
cout.setf(ios::scientific);
```

to ensure that 1.1 gets output as

```
1.1e+00.
```

If the output format you want is actually 1.1E+00, the ios::uppercase flag forces this, too, as well as the 0x to 0X in hex integer representations (cout.setf(ios::uppercase);).

As we noted earlier in this chapter on discussions of padding and of integer representations, defensive programming dictates using the two-argument form of setf() for the multi-bit fields ios::floatfield, ios::basefield and ios::adjustfield. You might "know" that only one bit in a field is set until someone modifies a function somewhere or you insert some debugging code, at which point what you "know" turns out to be false.

So far we've assumed that the precision is set to the default value of six places after the decimal point. However, the precision is adjustable. Two methods are available to do this. It can be set by an explicit funcion call, as follows:

```
cout.precision(10);
```

or by a manipulator that can be used as part of an output statement, as in

```
d = 1.0/3;
cout << setprecision(10) << d << endl;
```

with the resulting output

```
0.3333333333
```

Another feature of floating-point IO that is not yet covered in the ANSI discussion document is worth noting here. Some floating-point implementations might conform to ANSI C NCEG (Numerical C Extensions Group) standards. These extensions introduce, among other things, the concepts of NANs (not a number) and INFINITIES, that is, floating point numbers with distinct representations that do not correspond to numbers in the specified range of the floating-point types. When such values are encountered, the IOStreams implementations for such systems should display appropriate values such as NAN or INFINITY or –INFINITY. Such NCEG implementations might also support plus and minus values for floating-point 0.

Pointer value output

A variable of type `void*`, a pointer type for which output is not specifically defined or any other pointer type explicitly cast to a void pointer, is output as a representation of the address corresponding to the pointer value. The exact representation is implementation dependent, but the ANSI discussion document requires that it be presented in hexadecimal. For example,

```
void *p;
class Thing;   // unknown to IOStreams
Thing *tp;
char *s = "some string";

cout << p << ' ' << tp << ' ' << << (void *) s << endl;
// pointer value is output in each case
```

In a PC environment, pointers in some of the memory usage models are represented as a segment and offset pair of 16-bit values. In such cases, expect a pointer representation of a form such as

```
12aa:123f
```

Otherwise a pointer will probably be just a four-digit hex number in a 16-bit implementation or an eight-digit hex number in a 32-bit implementation.

2.2 Input from the Standard Input

IOStreams input has potential difficulty for newcomers. The IOStreams input facilities are designed so that experienced users can use them quite casually to write interactive command line programs for their own use or to input debugging information. This sort of usage is often seen in C++ textbook examples, where the input process is only of subsidiary importance to some feature that is being demonstrated. However, if an application is to be delivered to end users, the IOStream facilities need to be used in quite a different way.

Common difficulties with iostreams input

Difficulties typically arise for three reasons:

1. The IOStreams input system, by default, ignores whitespace on input.
2. The standard input is usually line buffered.
3. IOStreams input stream class objects set themselves into a safe, do-nothing state if they detect an error.

The input process is, in principle, very simple. The layout of an input statement is exactly analogous to an output statement. For example,

```
int n;
cout << n;          // output the value of n
cin >> n;           // input a value for n
```

The input from the stream `cin` to a variable such as `n` using the `>>` operator is called an *extraction*.

We deal with the details of the input process in Section 2.9 and what follows. For the moment, it's important to explain the common difficulties. First, the input operation doesn't announce itself to the user in any way. If you have forgotten that you included an input statement in a program, it's easy to conclude that the program has hung up, that is, halted or entered some perpetual loop. So always announce in some way that input is required, and remember that the output needs to be flushed to guarantee the user will see the announcement. This is not an IOStreams feature; it is equally true in the case of the `stdio` facilities if, for example, you are using `scanf`. The precursor for input of `n` therefore should be

```
cout << "Enter a value for n: " << endl;
```

or better still

```
cout << "Enter a value for n: " << flush;
```

The second form leaves the input cursor, if there is one, positioned immediately after the request rather than on the next line.

The second difficulty is that typing in digits doesn't get you anywhere. In this case, the beginner then might enter the digits 1 and 2 and wait forever for some result. The wait would ensue because input is probably processed one line at a time; therefore the application that uses `cin >> n;` doesn't receive any input until the [Return] or [Enter] key is pressed. Accordingly the prompt line for input should be, for example,

```
cout << "Enter a value for n, then press [Enter]: " << flush;
```

If [Enter] is pressed after the two digits, the value 12 should be transferred successfully to the variable n. If on the other hand the user panics and is unwilling to commit to a number and simply presses [Enter] instead, the application receives a newline character, which is whitespace and, given the default behavior of IOStreams, is ignored. No amount of pressing [Enter] will get the user anywhere. By now the user is probably even more panicked and might never revert to the option of entering the integer number.

Should the user be perverse and enter something like "NO" followed quite properly by [Enter], IOStreams will determine that there are no characters that match an integer value and so set itself into a fail state. If the application was written by a programmer who did not check the state of the input stream, its progress will then be doomed.

From this we can conclude that interactive input using IOStreams is as potentially difficult as any other form of interactive input. Following is a remedial approach to the scenario just sketched:

```
#include<limits.h>
int n;
cin.unsetf(ios::skipws);
                    // turn off white space skipping
cout << "Enter a value for n, followed by [Enter]: " << flush;
for (;;) {
  cin >> n;
  if (cin) {         // cin is in good state, input was ok
    cin.ignore(INT_MAX,'\n');
                    // flush away the unwanted
                    // newline character
    break;
  }
  cin.clear();       // clear the error state
  cin.ignore(INT_MAX,'\n');
                    // get rid of the garbage characters
  cout << "That was no good, try again: " << flush;

}
```

We notice that we can set control flags in the standard input stream `cin` just as we could in the standard output stream `cout`. This facility is used to turn off white-space skipping. Once this has been done, a newline character entered when the required sequence is digits will be treated as an error rather than as just some preliminary space to skip like input of any other non-digit character.

An IOStreams feature introduced here is the test on `cin` — `if (cin)`. All streams, both input and output, have this capability. We can test the stream to check if it is in a good state using either

```
if (cin)...
if (cin.good()) ...
 // was good
if (!cin) ...
 // was bad
```

If the input stream is "bad" in this sense, it will not participate in input activities until its error state is cleared. Again, any stream can be cleared. In this case, we do it using

```
cin.clear();
```

We discuss error states in detail in Chapter 6.

Whether the input was good or bad, using `cin.ignore(INT_MAX,'\n');` eliminates any extraneous characters that were entered by removing up to `INT_MAX` characters from the input stream until it finds and removes a newline character. Note that this example suffices if input is from the standard input. However, if the input is actually redirected from a file, input of the integer value could fail because the file is empty. We can handle this possibility by adding another error state test before the `cin.clear()`, as follows:

```
if (cin.eof()) {    // test explicitly for end-of-file
  cerr << "End of file on cin\n";
  exit(-1);          // or whatever is appropriate
}
cin.clear();
...
```

Input of characters and strings

The code fragment above could use any of the built-in types as its input target. With two of them though, `char` and `char*`, some slightly different checking or program logic would be required.

In the case of `char` with whitespace skipping turned off, the newline character is perfectly acceptable input. If the newline is not a value we want to consider, we can include a test as follows:

```
if (c != '\n') {
  cin.ignore(INT_MAX,'\n');
  // ignore all but the first character on the line
  // OK - process the character
} else {
  // user pressed [Enter] - request reentry
  ...
}
```

In the case of extraction into a char* variable, whitespace skipping should be turned on. This done, leading whitespace characters are skipped until some nonwhitespace character is found. Input is then terminated by the next whitespace character encountered. The previous code fragments can be modified as follows to input an array of characters

```
char buf[80];
cout << "Surname followed by [Enter]: "
cin >> buf;
cin.ignore(INT_MAX,'\n');
if (*buf) {
  // got a string - process it
  ...
} else {
  // user pressed [Enter] - request reentry
  ...
}
```

This fragment is fine for inputs of a single word, for example "   Smith". (The leading spaces are ignored.) However, if the user mistakenly enters "Fred Smith", the name Fred is recorded and Smith is flushed away by the cin.ignore(). In these circumstances or where multiple word inputs are required, use the input functions cin.get(buf), or cin.getline(buf). These are described in detail when input streams are discussed later in Chapter 9. However, for now, to get a whole line of input use

```
char buf[80]
cin.getline(buf,80);
```

The effect here is to read a line of input, provided it comprises fewer than 80 characters. The string read into buf is null terminated, and the newline character is removed from the stream but not stored in buf.

Field width setting for string input

Field width setting is meaningful only for the extraction of strings. It indicates the size of the array into which the characters are to be stored, taking into account the requirement for a null terminator byte. If the width is set to n, then at most n−1 characters will be read from cin to the array. A null terminating character is always stored in the array even if no characters are extracted. For example,

```
char buf[8];
cin.width(8);
cin >> buf;
// puts no more than 7 characters from the input into buf
```

Using the setw( ) manipulator is generally more convenient than using the width function, and it works in this context also, as in

```
cin >> setw(8) >> buf;
```

The field width setting used in this way doesn't alter the fact that leading white-space is skipped and that extraction of the string is terminated by the next whitespace character.

Radix (base) setting for integer input

Another setting that affects input is the radix for integer input. The manipulators hex, oct, and dec can be used with input streams as well as with output streams, as follows:

```
cin >> oct >> n;
// input of "10" leaves n with decimal value 8
cin >> hex >> n;
// input of "10" leaves n with decimal value 16
```

If no radix or base flag is set, the input process interprets numbers as decimal, unless they start with a '0', in which case they are translated as octal, or with "0x" or "0X", in which cases they are translated as hexadecimal. In the hex instance, of course, the translated sequence can include the hex digits 'A' through 'F' and 'a' through 'f' as well as '0' through '9'.

2.3 Output to a File

The recipes so far have been for input from and output to the standard input or output. Because IOStreams attempts be a completely general facility, it's possible to use IOStream input or output with a file or some other file-like device. When files are involved you must include the header file `fstream.h` in your program. You can include `iostream.h` as well, but this isn't necessary. The `fstream.h` header file includes it for you.

You probably won't be surprised to learn that the statements to write an integer, a double, and a string to a single line of a text file are

```
#include <fstream.h>

...
int n;
double d;
char *s;
fout << n << ' ' << d << ' ' << s << endl;
```

Note that this sequence is analogous to that for sending the same output to `cout`. The only difference is that here a stream called `fout` is used, and while `cout`, the standard output stream, is provided to any program that includes the header file `iostream.h`, you as the programmer, must set up stream `fout` before you can use it. This is simple to do; it involves only a declaration with an initialization, as follows:

```
ofstream fout("filename.txt");
```

This statement declares an object of type `ofstream`—an output file stream—and initializes it to use file `filename.txt`. The defaults for this constructor are such that if the file `filename.txt` exists, it is *truncated,* that is, the existing contents are discarded. If you want to avoid this, you can use

```
ofstream fout("filename.txt", ios::noreplace);
```

This initialization will fail if the file already exists. You can then subsequently test the status of `fout` as follows:

```
if (!fout) {    // state of fout not good
  cerr << "File open failed ...
```

If the operation does fail, however, all is not lost. Presently `fout` is useless—that is, in a fail state—but we can revive it by using the `fout.open()` function to try another file name, again with or without the precaution for an existing file, as follows:

```
fout.open("another.txt", ios::noreplace);
```

In fact we could have used this route at the outset. Class `ofstream` has a default constructor designed to create an `ofstream` in a bad (unusable) state. The resulting useless `ofstream` then can be made functional by using the `open` function or by attaching it to a file descriptor that has been obtained independently, as in

```
ofstream fout;    // state of fout not good
fout.open("filename.txt");
```

```
// or
```

```
ofstream fout;
int fd = open("filename.txt",O_WRONLY);
fout.attach(fd);
```

Using `open(...)` to get a file descriptor here is appropriate for UNIX, DOS, or OS/2 filesystems but doesn't correspond to standard C and might not be applicable in other environments. After employing either of these options, you should test the state of the stream to ensure that all went well.

If the target output file already exists and you need to attach the new output to the end of the existing file, create or open the `ofstream` using a second argument of `ios::ate` (short for at-end), as follows:

```
ofstream fout("filename.txt", ios::ate);
      // tag new output on the end
```

Unless you provide a file descriptor, the file attached to an `ofstream` object is closed by the `ofstream` destructor when the object goes out of scope. If you did provide the file descriptor, it's your responsibility to close the file.

In the output examples presented so far, no testing has been done on the state of the output stream. Noncritical programs that send their output to `cout` are often written in this way, and generally this arrangement is adequate if the user of such a program is its author. However, in more robust applications whose output might be redirected or when programs deal with files explicitly, the user should be told if there is a problem with an output file, as follows:

```
if (!fout) {
 cerr <<
    "The output file is not functioning properly" << endl;
 ...
}
```

Output file streams should therefore be checked periodically to ensure they are functional. The most critical time to do this is when the `ofstream` object has just been created. After that the state of the stream might typically be checked at each loop iteration.

2.4 Input from a File

We can define a file input stream `fin` analogous to the preceding output file stream `fout`. Input processing code then takes the same form as it did with `cin`, as follows:

```
int n;
double d;
char buf[80];
fin >> n >> d >> buf;
```

As with input from the standard input, we stress the importance of checking the state of the input stream when using a file also.

Setting up a stream for input follows the same general form as setting up one for output:

```
#include <fstream.h>

ifstream fin("filename.txt");   // create fin and open a file
// or
ifstream fin;                   // create fin
fin.open("filename.txt");       // then open a file

// or
ifstream fin;                   // create fin
int fd = open("filename.txt", O_RDONLY);
                                // open a file
fin.attach(fd);                 // get the two together
```

It is usually not necessary to use a second argument. The file is expected to exist, and reading from the end of the file is not likely to be productive, so the default open mode, `ios::in`, is quite adequate.

At this point, we note a somewhat more advanced technique: a characteristic IOStreams idiom that is sufficiently terse that the intended effect might not be clear to the beginner. We illustrate it by showing the C and C++ IOStreams styles of writing a program to copy a file to the standard output. First the C style:

```
#include <stdio.h>

int main(int argc, char *argv[])
{
    FILE *fp;
    int c;
    if (argc < 2) return -1;
    fp = fopen(argv[1], "r");
```

```
    if (!fp) return -1;
    while ((c = getc(fp)) != EOF)
        putchar(c);
    return 0;
}
```

Next the C++ IOStream paradigm:

```
#include <fstream.h>

int main(int argc, char *argv[])
{
    if (argc < 2) return -1;
    ifstream ifs(argv[1]);
    if (!ifs) return -1;
    cout << ifs.rdbuf();
    return 0;
}
```

The two programs are essentially parallel until the stage at which both files have been opened and the outcome checked. At this point, IOStreams provides a considerable simplification. Both input systems are buffered, but in the IOStreams system the input buffer, or more specifically a pointer to the input buffer, is itself a data object that can be sent to the standard output. The input file stream, in this case ifs, has a function that returns a pointer to its buffer object, so all we have to do is send the contents of the buffer to the output, as follows:

```
cout << ifs.rdbuf();
```

This process conveniently terminates when the input is exhausted.

2.5 Formatted Output to a Memory Buffer

The IOStreams system also provides the capability to send formatted output to an arbitrary area of memory. This facility is useful, for example, when the output is to be sent either to some block structured device or to some device where individual output transactions are expensive. It can also be useful simply for constructing messages to pass to functions which require a single char* argument.

An output stream can be mapped to a specified area of memory as follows:

```
char buf[256];
ostrstream os(buf,256);
```

Output can then be sent to the `ostrstream` `os` as follows, just as it can to any other output stream:

```
int wincount, modified;
os << wincount << " windows are active, and " << modified
    << " have been edited - do you wish to proceed?" << ends;
```

Notice the use of `ends` to send a null character string to a stream. Including it leaves a properly null terminated string in the character array `buf`, which can then be used, for example, as an argument to a Microsoft Windows message box function, as in:

```
int winhandle;
MessageBox(winhandle,buf,"ACTIVE WINDOWS",MB_YESNOCANCEL);
```

It's not necessary for the user of an `ostrstream` to provide the memory. If an `ostrstream` is declared without constructor arguments, it will allocate memory as required. So instead of the preceding sequence, we could substitute the following:

```
ostrstream os;
os << wincount << " windows are active, and " << modified
    << " have been edited - do you wish to proceed?" << ends;
char *s = os.str():
MessageBox(winhandle, s, "ACTIVE WINDOWS", MB_YESNOCANCEL);
```

In this example, the `ostrstream::str` function returns the address of the dynamically allocated memory to which the formatted output was written. Once it has been called, it becomes the user's responsibility to free the memory. So the sequence with a dynamic `ostrstream` needs the following addition:

```
delete[] s;
```

Call `str` as many times as you like for a particular dynamic `ostrstream` object, but delete the memory only once!

2.6 Input from a Memory Buffer

It's also possible to use an arbitrary area of memory as the source for formatted input. An input stream can be set up using either a null terminated string or a buffer of specified size. The first example below translates a string representing a binary number into an integer value and conveniently ignores the spaces that separate the two bytes:

```
istrstream is = "11001100   11000110"
```

```
unsigned n = 0;
for (char c; is << c;)
  n = (n << 1) | (c != '0');
cout << n << endl;
```

The following example shows the use of an arbitrary buffer as a source:

```
char *p = new char[512];
istrstream is(p,512);
is.unsetf(ios::skipws); // make all characters significant
int alpha = 0;
for (char c; is << c;)
    // count alpha characters in allocated memory
  if (isalpha(c)) alpha++;
```

2.7 Summary

In this chapter, we've presented much of the IOStreams usage required to write conventional command line interactive programs in C++, to read from and write to text files, and to manipulate text in memory buffers.

The examples focused on the built-in types. However, the usage should not be restricted. Well-designed user-defined types will have IOStreams extractor and inserter functions. In familiarizing yourself with these types, you should investigate their IO behavior. Check their justification in a specified field width. See what happens when you modify the format flags. Output some extreme or improbable values and input some values with syntax errors while making appropriate error checks. If these experiments don't work at all or don't work in a manner that seems consistent with the way the built-in types work, notify the class designer.

3

Why Use IOStreams

The C programming language has a well-established IO system that has served well in a vast number of applications. C++ is, to a close approximation, a superset of C, and in particular, the C input-output system can be used as is in C++ programs. Therefore you might wonder why a new IO system for C++ is necessary. The reasons can be summarized as follows:

- Improved type safety
- Modularity and reusability through user-defined types
- Generality and extendability through abstract types and polymorphism

3.1 Improved Type Safety

Improved type safety is a substantial motivation for the IOStreams approach. An example was mentioned briefly in the introduction, and most C programmers will recognize the trap. For those who don't, it might be useful to elaborate here.

The standard C `printf` function takes an indefinite number of arguments. Its prototype is

```
int printf(const char *, ...);
```

The format string is examined at run time for embedded indications of the types of objects to be printed. There is no compile-time checking of the arguments other than the first char* argument. For example,

```
printf("%d %d %d\n");
```

has no arguments corresponding to the three type specifications ("%d") in the format string. At run time, either the three integer values that happen to be on the stack will be printed or the operating system will object to an unauthorized memory access. This case is relatively easy to spot. More insidious, however, is the case in which the arguments are present, but are of the wrong type, as in the following:

```
long a = 0x0010ffff, b = 0;
printf("%d\t%d\n", a, b);
```

In an implementation where sizeof(int) is two bytes and sizeof(long) is four bytes, this will probably print as

–1   16

or

16   –1

depending on whether the least-significant bit in a multi-byte integer representation is at the low or the high memory end. In either case, this result is probably not what was intended.

The type safety situation on input is worse. In a situation like

```
void crashdive()
{
  char c;

  ...
  scanf("%ld", &c);
}
```

an attempt is made at run time to read a long value into a char variable. In many operating systems, this will provoke a memory protection fault. In others it will overwrite the function's return address on the stack and crash the system with potentially dangerous results.

3.2 Modularity and Reuseability through User-defined Types

The IO mechanisms in C provide for the built-in types. However, input and output of more complicated data types can be provided for, since the elementary components of such types are always available. For example,

```
typedef struct {
   double re, im;
} Complex;
Complex v;
printf("(%f: %f)\n", v.re, v.im);
```

This is not the place for a detailed discussion of the virtues of data abstraction and encapsulation. (There is already copious literature on the subject. See for instance reference 4, page 169; reference 5, page 56, and reference 6, page 74.) We will say, however, that in a C++ implementation of type `Complex`, this violates a principal requirement of the object-oriented approach, namely information hiding. The internal variables `re` and `im` should not be directly accessible to a user of type `Complex`. The `printf` approach will then not work:

```
class Complex {
public:
  ...
private:
  double re, im;
};

Complex v;

printf("(%f: %f)\n", v.re, v.im);
     // error v.re and v.im are private
```

It's possible to use `printf` in this way only if information hiding is broken by making the state variables of a class public, or by providing explicit access functions for some or all of the state variables. The first alternative throws away almost all the advantages of the object-oriented approach. The second is moderately safe but will destroy the freedom of the type implementor to change and improve the internal workings of the type, since users will have become dependent on its being implemented in a particular way.

A workaround is to give class `Complex` a format function, as in the following:

```
class Complex {
```

```
public:
  enum format_style { normal, fixed, scientific };
   ...
  const char *format(format_style style = normal,
                     int fieldwidth = 0);
   ...
};
```

Here the format function is intended to return a pointer to a string representing the value of a Complex; then of course it's possible to write

```
printf("%s\n", v.format());
```

This solution seems fine. It doesn't seem a lot to ask for the designer of a class to provide such a function, and using a function in this way doesn't restrict the details of the implementation. However, there is a problem. What about

```
Complex v, w;
printf("%s %s\n", v.format(), w.format());
```

Usage like this restricts the implementation of Complex::format() in that it can't use a static buffer, as in:

```
const char *Complex::format(format_style style, int fieldwidth)
{
  static char buf[BIG_ENOUGH];
  switch (style) {
  default:
    sprintf(buf,"(%f: %f)",re,im);
   ...
  return buf;
}
```

With this implementation, both calls to format in the preceding printf example would return a pointer to the same string; which string—(v.format() or w.format())—would be undefined, since the compiler is allowed to evaluate arguments in any order. More generally, Complex::format() would not be re-entrant. The format function would probably have to allocate the buffer it needed dynamically. At that point, it also becomes necessary either to decide who will clean up afterwards or to insist on one Complex::format() call per printf(). The latter rule is unenforceable, however, and in any case, the notational convenience of printf(), already eroded by the need to call Complex::format(), is completely gone. The sequence

```
printf("%s ", v.format());
printf("%s\n", w.format());
```

is now much less attractive than is

```
cout << v << ' ' << w << endl;
```

But the case where the format buffers are allocated dynamically is even worse, as in the following:

```
printf("%s %s\n", v.format(), w.format());
v.format_cleanup();
w.format_cleanup();
```

IOStreams provides notational convenience for output by overloading the << operator. This means that there is a separate function call, or its semantic equivalent, for each item sent to the output stream. The operator functions return a reference to the stream; therefore

```
cout << v << w;
```

is equivalent to

```
(cout.operator<<(v)).operator<<(w);
```

Because there are two separate operations, even if a format function is used as an implementation mechanism, any buffering problem disappears.

In the case of input of a Complex value using the stdio facilities, we would have to use the scanf() function to collect a set of values. These could then be used to construct a Complex object, as shown in the following:

```
Complex v;
double real, imag = 0;
scanf("(%f,%f)",&real,&imag);
v = Complex(real,imag);
```

These operations would probably be made into an input function for the type, as in

```
class Complex {
public:
    ...
    int get(FILE*);
};

Complex v, w;
FILE *fp;
...
v.get(fp);
w.get(fp);
```

This approach is type-safe and can be comprehensive. It is not particularly expressive, however, and it forces a discrimination between the way things are done for user-defined types and for the built-in types.

3.3 Generality and Extendability through Abstraction and Polymorphism

If we accept the restrictions already described, object-oriented programs can certainly be written using the `stdio` facilities. Consider for example:

```
class A  {
public:
  ...
  virtual const char *format() const = 0;
};

class B : public A {
public:
  ...
  const char *format() const;
};

class C : public A {
public:
  ...
  const char *format() const;
};
```

This simple class hierarchy has an abstract base class that requires its concrete derived classes to provide a `format()` function, thus making it possible for a loop using `printf()` to scan and properly output an arbitrary collection of B and C objects, as in the following:

```
A *collection[10];

...     // initialize collection
for (int i = 0; i < 10; ++i)
  printf("%s\n", collection[i]->format());
```

IOStreams can achieve the same result more elegantly and across a broad spectrum of input-output devices because abstraction and polymorphism are used in the implementation of the IO system itself.

The C output facilities distinguish between input and output operations on file-like devices and on memory, using functions such as the following for the two different circumstances:

```
fprintf(FILE *, const char *, ...);
sprintf(char *, const char *, ...);
fscanf(FILE *, const char *, ...);
sscanf(const char *, const char *, ...);
```

Having functions tied to a particular type of source or destination constrains the generality and flexibility with which IO operations can be treated. For example, using the stdio facilities, a function that reads from and writes to sources to be determined at run time, must be written in a way similar to the following:

```
enum io_option { file, memory };

int function_does_IO(io_option in_option, io_option out_option,
                 char *msource, char *mdest,
                 FILE *fsource, FILE *fdest)
{
  int a, b, inv, outcc;
  if (in_option == file) {
    if (!fsource)
      return ERROR;
    inv = fscanf(fsource,"%d %d", &a, &b);
  } else {
    if (!msource)
      return ERROR;
    inv = sscanf(msource,"%d %d", &a, &b);
  }
  if (inv < 2)
    return ERROR;
  ...
  if (out_option == file) {
    if (!fdest)
      return ERROR;
    outcc = fprintf(fdest,"%d %d",a,b);
  } else {
    if (!mdest)
      return ERROR;
    outcc = sprintf(mdest,"%d %d",a,b);
  }
  if (outcc < 0)
    return ERROR;
```

```
    return 0;
}
```

In the IOStreams paradigm, the function doesn't have to concern itself with the nature of the source or the destination at all. IO is dealt with as an abstraction. The exact details of the process for different devices are delegated to virtual functions and dealt with using polymorphism. For example,

```
int function_does_IO(istream &is, ostream &os)
{
    int a, b;
    is >> a >> b;
    if (!is)
        return ERROR;
    ...
    os << a << b;
    if (!os)
        return ERROR;
    return 0;
}
```

The `stdio` discrimination between files and memory would also require separate IO functions be provided for each user-defined type. For instance in class `Complex`, we would need to provide two or three input functions along with the equivalent set of functions for output, as the following shows:

```
class Complex {
public:
    int get();                  // from stdin
    int fget(FILE *);           // from a buffered file
    int sget(const char *);     // from memory
    ...
};
```

Input and output streams themselves can behave in a way that is essentially polymorphic. Suppose for instance that a new output stream class has been derived from the one we have assumed so far. The new stream works with an ANSI display terminal. Some extra manipulators that allow us to position output on the screen and change the color of the output have been defined. Assume then we can write

```
ansiterm atout;
atout << blue << screenpos(12,31) << "Centered on screen";
```

We can design the new stream class, `ansiterm`, and the manipulators so that if the same sequence is used with `cout`, as in

```
cout << blue << screenpos(12,31) << "Centered on screen";
```

the `blue` manipulator will be ignored and the `screenpos` manipulator will have the same effect as `endl`.

3.4 Who Needs `printf` Anyway?

It could be argued that programmers don't use functions like `printf` anymore, so why devise a substitute for it? In current applications being written with a graphical user interface (GUI), the programmer has to use some window function to do output. Unfortunately, however, this is not a solution, but rather another problem. Yet more to learn! Perhaps it would be better if GUI system designers adopted the IOStreams way of doing things. Then, using a now familiar analogy, it would be possible to write

```
GUI_window_ostream os(window_handle);

os << bold << new_times_roman << "Hello world";
```

3.5 Summary

IOStreams for C++ has three areas of advantage over C input-output systems: It is type safe. Given

```
class T {
   ...
};

T t;
cout << t;
cin >> t;
```

the compiler will produce an error message if output is not defined for T or there is no user-defined conversion from T to a type that has a defined output operation. Similarly, the compiler will produce an error message if input is not defined for T.

It is extendable in terms of data types. As implied by the previous paragraph, conforming IO operations can be implemented for user-defined types.

It provides uniform operations over varying IO contexts and is extendable in this respect also. The IOStreams classes provide a base from which new types can be derived to provide standardized IO behavior for a new context.

4

The Structure of the
IOStreams System

As with many books on computing, it's difficult to avoid making forward references. We could have presented this chapter at the end of the book after all the
component parts had been described. However, then there would have been no
justification for the components. Hence, we have elected to discuss overall structure first.

In its simplest configurations, an IOStreams consists of three parts, as follows:

- A buffer, which acts as an intermediary between the generalized input-
  output system and some particular source or sink for characters

- A specification system responsible for reporting errors and controlling
  formats

- A translation system that converts C++ language typed objects to or from
  sequences of characters

We first describe a simple input-output system in terms of C++ classes. Then we
show how the IOStreams structure builds on these simple ideas.

4.1 C++ Classes for IO

Buffer class

The buffer class provides a uniform set of primitive operations. These operations decouple the other classes from the actual details of the device from which input is being received or to which output is being sent, as in

```
class buffer {
public:
  put(char);                // put a character
  put(const char *, int);   // put n characters
  get(char &);              // get a character
  get(char *, int);         // get n characters
  ...
};
```

Specification Class

The specification class provides functions that allow format control and error checking. It can also conveniently hold the link (pointer or reference) to an associated buffer object. Following is an illustration:

```
class specification {
public:
  set_state_flags();        // set state control bits
  set_width();              // set state control variables
  set_representation();
  read_errors();            // error functions
  clear_errors();
  ...;
private:
  buffer *bp;               // pointer or reference to
                            // an associated buffer
};
```

Translator classes

The translator class used here as an example is an output_translator. It provides formatted output operations for the built-in types. It also provides lower-level output capabilities, reflecting those of its embedded buffer, for implement-ing output operations for user-defined types. `Translator` classes for both input and output are derived from the `specification` class so that format information and error control can be applied uniformly and to avoid code duplication.

```
class output_translator : public specification {
public:
  output_operator(char);
  output_operator(const char *);
  output_operator(int);
  output_operator(double);
  // etc

  put(char);
  put(const char *, int);
  ...;
};
```

An IO operation can be viewed as a binary operation between a type and a translator. Built-in types have their IO operations provided by `translator` class member functions with a single argument, as in

```
output_translator::output_operator(T&);
        // Built-in types use a translator member function
```

User-defined types have their IO operations provided by a global function with a translator object as the first of two arguments, as follows:

```
output_operator(output_translator&, T&);
        // User-defined types use a regular function
```

4.2 The IOStreams Classes

The names used in Section 4.1 are not those given to the corresponding classes or their member functions by the original AT&T implementors. They called the buffer element a `streambuf`, the specification element an `ios` (they did not state how this term was derived, but we can suppose that it is an acronym for input-output specification), and the translation element either an `istream` (an input stream) or an `ostream` (an output stream). A composite element that allowed bidirectional IO was called an `iostream`, which was both an `istream` and an `ostream` and was implemented using the multiple inheritance feature of the C++ language.

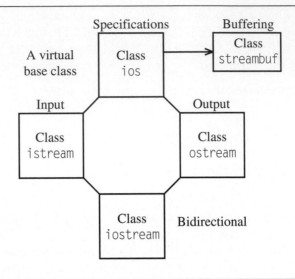

FIGURE 4.1
Relationship between the component parts of IOStreams

Following are the corresponding classes in IOStreams:

```
class streambuf { ... };   // the buffer class

class ios {                // the specification class
public:
  ...;
private:
  streambuf *sb;           // an ios has a private pointer
                           // to a streambuf
};

class istream : virtual public ios { ... };
class ostream : virtual public ios { ... };
                           // translators

class iostream : public istream, public ostream { ... };
                           // bidirectional translator
```

If you are not familiar with multiple inheritance, you might find useful an explanation of the `virtual` keyword as used in this context. A *virtual base class* is a base class of which there is only one instance in a composite-derived class. In the IOStreams class system, both `istream` and `ostream` are an `ios`. An `iostream` is both an `istream` and an `ostream`, but the virtual keyword ensures that an `iostream` contains only one `ios` object, that is shared by its component `istream` and `ostream`. This relationship is illustrated in Fig. 4.1.

4.3 Location of IOStreams Class Descriptions

We have based the descriptions of the IOStreams classes on a 1989 version of the AT&T IOStreams documentation and on ANSI discussion documents (see references 7, 8, and 9 in the list at the end of the book).

The concept of a `streambuf` is essentially abstract. Most, if not all, real-life `streambuf` type objects are objects of derived classes. Two principal derived classes are normally included in an IOStreams system: the `filebuf` and the `strstreambuf`. Class `streambuf` is described in Chapter 5, `filebuf` in Chapter 11, and `strstreambuf` in Chapter 14. Class `ios`, the specification element, is common to all of the other `IOstream` classes and is described in Chapter 6. Chapter 7 introduces the translator elements by presenting an example that illustrates how these facilities might be provided.

The real situation, as distinct from the example, is as shown by the preceding class declarations and by Fig. 4.1. Input translators—`istreams`—and output translators—`ostreams`—contain an embedded `ios` object (an IO specification). An `ios` contains a pointer to a `streambuf`, which is a buffer between the translator and the initial source of the input characters or the final destination of the output characters. Class `iostream` is derived from both class `istream` and class `ostream`. Class `ostream`, the output translator, which is the customary introduction, is discussed in Chapter 8, class `istream` in Chapter 9, and class `iostream` in Chapter 10.

The base versions of these classes in the AT&T variety of IOStreams do not support assignment or copy initialization. It's not immediately obvious how to specify these operations for the translator classes. Derived `translator` classes that support a well-defined interpretation of assignment and copying are provided, specifically

```
istream_withassign
ostream_withassign
iostream_withassign
```

These classes are described in Chapter 11. The ANSI discussion document bundles assignment and copy initialization with the regular classes.

4.4 A Buffer for Files and the Standard Streams

We can specialize the system described so far by substituting types derived from `streambuf` for the `streambuf` element. The best-known example uses a `filebuf`, which, not surprisingly, is a `streambuf` specialized to deal with a file as its ultimate source and/or sink for characters. The C++ standard IO streams are provided by combinations similar to those shown in Fig 4.1 but using a `filebuf` as the `streambuf`. They also use the input and output translators that support assignment. Their structure is depicted in Fig 4.2.

The standard output and error streams are provided by an `ostream` of this kind, and the standard input is provided by an analogous structure using an `istream`. The standard streams are set up as follows, where the integer arguments to the `filebuf` constructors are file descriptors:

```
filebuf fb0(0);                    // filebuf tied to console
                                   // input
istream_withassign cin(&fb0);      // standard input istream

filebuf fb1(1);                    // filebuf tied to console
                                   // output
ostream_withassign cout(&fb1);     // standard output ostream

filebuf fb2(2);                    // filebuf tied to error output
ostream_withassign cerr(&fb2);     // standard error ostream
```

That is, a `filebuf` constructor takes a file descriptor as its argument, and the translators take a pointer to a `streambuf` as an argument to their constructor. In this example, the `streambuf` happens to be a `filebuf`.

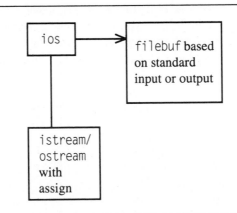

FIGURE 4.2
General structure of the standard streams.

4.5 File-oriented Translators

The `filebuf` buffer class is also packaged into further translator classes derived from `istream` and `ostream`. These translator classes are `ifstream`, `ofstream`, and `fstream`. They allow convenient one-line instantiation of streams for file IO; for example,

```
ifstream infile("infile.dat");
ofstream outfile("outfile.dat");
fstream bothways("somefile.dat");
```

These file-oriented classes are derived as follows. Each may use an intermediary class (`fstream_common` in this illustration) to factor out commonality in its behavior. However, there is nothing in the ANSI discussion documents to say that the file-oriented translators must be implemented in that way.

```
class fstream_common: virtual public ios {
public:
  ...;
private:
  filebuf fb;      // fstream_common includes a filebuf,
  ...              // which is required by all three
                   // fstream classes
};

class ifstream : public fstream_common, public istream { ... };
class ofstream : public fstream_common, public ostream { ... };
class fstream : public fstream_common, public iostream { ... };
```

In these cases, `ifstream`, `iostream`, and `fstream`, which intrinsically deal with files, the `streambuf` element, a `filebuf`, is actually incorporated either in the derived translator classes or in their common base class. The `streambuf` pointer in the embedded `ios` object points at another part of the composite object. This structure is shown in Fig. 4.3. The file-oriented translators are described in Chapter 12.

4.6 A Buffer and Translators Specialized for Memory

IOStreams also contains specializations of the base stream types to deal with in-memory formatting. These specializations use class `strstreambuf`, which is derived from `streambuf`, and is described in Chapter 13. It allows input from and output to arbitrary character arrays. Such arrays may be static or dynamic. The translator classes that provide these facilities are `istrstream`, `ostrstream`,

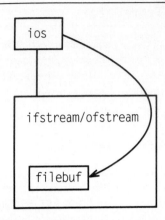

FIGURE 4.3
Structure of a file oriented translator

and `strstream`. The last class, like an `iostream`, is both an `istream` and an `ostream`.

```
                                // set up a scratch output
ostrstream dynamic;             // stream
ostrstream fixed (somewhere, 80); // provide for output of up
                                // to 80 characters into the
                                // array somewhere
```

The structure of this system is shown in Fig. 4.4. The `istrstream`, `ostrstream`, and `strstream` classes are derived as follows, or similarly, and are described in Chapter 14:

```
class istrstream : public istream { ... };
class ostrstream : public ostream { ... };
class strstream : public istream, public ostream { ... };
```

4.7 A Buffer Linked to `stdio`

A buffer class `stdiobuf` is derived from `streambuf`. This class employs the facilities of the standard C `stdio` package and it is designed for use when IO using `stdio` and IOStreams must be intermixed.

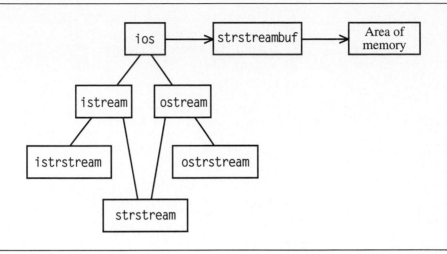

FIGURE 4.4
Translators specialized for in-memory formatting

4.8 Summary

The IOStreams system consists of the following three computer types:

- Buffer types–These act as intermediaries between the IO system and actual devices or locations.

```
streambuf       // an abstract base class (Chapter 5)
filebuf         // buffer for files (Chapter 11)
strstreambuf    // buffer in memory (Chapter 13)
stdiobuf        // use stdio facilities (Chapter 16)
```

- Specification type–This logs errors and controls formats.

```
ios             // (Chapter 6)
```

- Translator types–These convert sequences of characters to typed data and typed data to character sequences.

```
istream         // input (Chapters 7 and 8)
ostream         // output (Chapter 9)
iostream        // bidirectional (Chapter 9)
ifstream        // file input (Chapter 12)
ofstream        // file output (Chapter 12)
```

```
fstream          // file bidirectional (Chapter 12)
istrstream       // input from memory (Chapter 14)
ostrstream       // output to memory (Chapter 14)
strstream        // memory bidirectional (Chapter 14)
```

5

The Buffer Component–
streambuf

The `streambuf` is an abstraction of a *conceptually* unlimited linear character array from which it is possible to get characters from a current getting position or to put characters to a current putting position. The get and put positions can be moved about. At any time, there is actually some position in the array that is the limit of the get area and another position that is the limit of the put area.

According to the specification in the ANSI IOStreams discussion document, `streambuf` objects and the streams that utilize them are able to deal with wide characters (objects of type `wchar_t`) to address international requirements. How this is to be done is not yet well defined; therefore we restrict the following discussion to the plain `char` case.

We might visualize a `streambuf` as shown in Fig. 5.1.

In this figure, the get position, referred to hereafter as the get pointer and symbolized by the "G", has just passed the character `'a'` and is just before the character `'b'`. This means the last character we got was `'a'` and the next one we will get, all other things being equal, is `'b'`. The last character put into the `streambuf` was an `'E'`. This is shown by the arrow and the "P", which indicate the put position, or, as we call it hereafter, the put pointer. Notice that the put pointer was advanced to the next free position *after* the `'E'` was deposited. The put pointer always points to the position where the next character is to be placed.

Clearly, in any real situation the get and put areas cannot be unlimited, nor can they have persistence, which is a feature usually desired in IO systems. In most

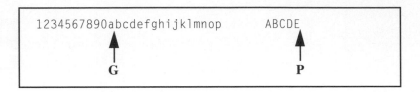

FIGURE 5.1
Example of a `streambuf`

cases it is no use to have the results of output in memory. Output needs to be either displayed, printed, or stored in a form where it can subsequently be reused as input. However, in practice the appearance of being unlimited is achieved by refilling an empty get area from some external source and by sending the contents of a full put area to some external sink. The external source and/or sink can be assumed to handle the need for permanence.

Real external sources and sinks usually also embody the concept of sequence. The `streambuf` class therefore provides facilities to request repositioning, or seeking, in the external source or sink.

5.1 The Public Interface

We describe the public interface of class `streambuf` in detail because its operations are fundamental to the working of the whole IOStreams system, to the derivation of new classes related to the IOStreams system, and to the implementation of facilities for the input and output of user-defined types. The public member functions of class `streambuf` are listed next in groups according to what they do. The comments are action summaries that don't always indicate what happens on boundary conditions. A more detailed description of the member functions follows in Section 5.3.

```
#ifndef EOF
const int EOF = -1;
#endif

class streampos;   // describes an absolute byte position
                   // in a stream.
class streamoff;   // describes a byte offset in a stream
                   // these are usually defined in the header
                   // file for class ios.
```

```
class streambuf {
public:
// Operations to get characters
   int sgetc();     // Returns current character in get area
                    // without moving the get pointer.

   int sbumpc();    // Moves the get pointer along one place
                    // returning the character it moved past.

   void stossc();   // Advances the get pointer; if already at
                    // end of get area, does nothing.

   int snextc();    // Moves the get pointer forward one and
                    // returns the character at the new position.

   int sgetn(char *m, int n);
                    // Attempts to get n characters from the get
                    // area, and to place them at m; returns
                    // the number it actually got.

// Replace a character in the get area
   int sputbackc(char);
                    // Backs up the get pointer by one position.

// Operations to put characters
   int sputc(int c);
                    // Puts c in the put area and advances the
                    // put pointer.

   int sputn(const char *m, int n);
                    // Attempts to put n characters taken from
                    // location m; returns the number it
                    // actually put.

// Reset the position of the get and put pointers
   virtual streampos seekpos(streampos,
                    int = ios::in|ios::out);
                    // Sets pointer(s) to an absolute position in
                    // the overall character stream.

   virtual streampos seekoff(streamoff, seek_dir,
                    int = ios::in|ios::out);
                    // Sets pointers relative to start, current
```

```
                    // position, or end of overall character
                    // stream.
virtual int underflow();
virtual int overflow(int=EOF);

// Synchronize the streambuf state with the external
// source/sink
  virtual int sync();

// Constructors and setup function
  streambuf();    // Default constructor (dynamic allocation).
  streambuf(char *m, int len);
                    // Explicit constructor; can be used to force
                    // unbuffered operation if m == 0 or len <= 0.
  virtual~streambuf();
  virtual streambuf *setbuf(char *m, int len);
                    // Fix up an existing streambuf to use a
                    // specified buffer; can be used to force
                    // unbuffered operation if m == 0 or len <= 0.
};
```

5.2 Function Descriptions

The operations that can be performed on a streambuf can be conveniently described by referring to the schematic in Fig. 5.1. We describe first the operations on the get area and then those on the put area. Note that users of this class must include file iostream.h.

Future versions of IOStreams will provide for member functions to participate in the exception handling mechanisms that are a proposed part of the ANSI C++ standard. This change will probably not affect the public interface of the streambuf class, however, as it seems unlikely there will be any restriction on the kind of exception a class derived from streambuf can throw. In that case, no exception specifications will be required. The virtual functions and some protected member functions of this class, however, may throw exceptions. In the case of the protected member functions, the exceptions either will not be caught by the public member functions or will be caught and rethrown. Consequently, any exceptions thrown by streambuf member functions will be propagated to the translator class using the streambuf.

Operations on the get area.

The following functions apply to the get area.

```
int sgetc();
```

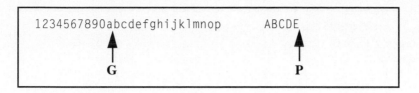

FIGURE 5.2
sgetc() **example context**

The sgetc function provides the capability to look at the next character available from the get area. For example, in Fig. 5.2, it is a 'b', the character immediately after the get pointer. The sgetc function returns an int rather than a char, because like most streambuf functions it can return the special end-of-file value, EOF, when no next character is available.

A call to sgetc for our example streambuf returns an int with value 'b', leaving the streambuf unchanged.

int sbumpc();

The sbumpc function moves the get pointer right one character and *returns the value of the character it just moved past.* For example, in Fig. 5.2 a call to sbumpc returns an int with value 'b', as does sgetc. However, it also simultaneously advances the get pointer, leaving the streambuf as shown in Fig. 5.3, with the get pointer just before the 'c'.

If the pointer has nowhere to go—that is, it is already pointing just after the 'p' in our example—sbumpc returns the EOF value.

void stossc();

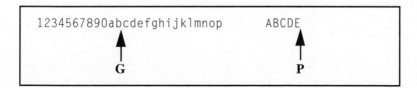

FIGURE 5.3
State after sbumpc

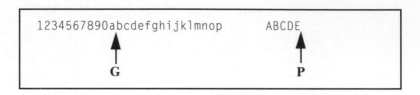

FIGURE 5.4
streambuf example restored to starting condition

The stossc function moves the pointer right one character, *provided the pointer is not already at the position just past the end of the get area.* For example, in Fig. 5.4 stossc would advance the get pointer by one character unless the pointer is past the 'p', that is, beyond the get area. If the get pointer is already beyond the end, the stossc function does nothing.

The stossc does not return a value. It can be used with sgetc to make up a type of conditional sbumpc. For instance, we could use

```
if (sgetc() == whatever)
  stossc();  // not interested in this character
```

This would work as follows. In Fig. 5.4, an sgetc() call returns the 'b' and leaves the get pointer unchanged.

Then we decide we aren't interested in the 'b', so we call stossc. Doing this gets us to the same place that sbumpc would have, as shown in Fig. 5.5.

```
int snextc();
```

FIGURE 5.5
Result of sgetc / stossc

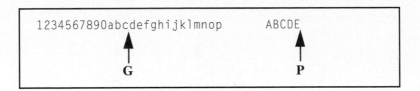

FIGURE 5.6
The streambuf after snextc

The snextc function moves the pointer right one character, and returns the value of the character *that is then immediately to the right of the new pointer position.*

Referring back to Fig. 5.5, we can see that a call to snextc advances the get pointer so it is just before the 'd' and returns the value 'd', leaving the streambuf as shown in Fig. 5.6. If there is nowhere for the get pointer to go—that is, it was already past the end of the get area, after the 'p' in the example, or it is in that position after it has moved—then snextc returns the EOF value because there is no character there to return.

```
int sgetn(char *dest, int n);
```

sgetn fetches multiple characters as a block. It returns the number of characters it managed to get. The characters taken are put in the area indicated by the char* argument, and sgetn attempts to fetch n characters. For example, starting from the state shown in Fig. 5.6, the call sgetn(buffer,4), where buffer is some suitable char*, moves "defg" into buffer, returns the value 4, and leaves the streambuf as shown in Fig. 5.7.

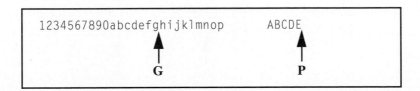

FIGURE 5.7
The streambuf after sgetn(buffer,4);

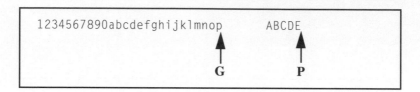

FIGURE 5.8
The `streambuf` after `sgetn(buffer,12);`

A further call `sgetn(buffer,12);` moves "hijklmnop" into `buffer` (over the "defg" contents), returns the value 9, and leaves the get pointer pointing after the 'p', that is, at the end of the get area, as shown in Fig. 5.8. Note that although the call was for 12 characters, there were only nine available.

Any of the previous operations carried out on this example `streambuf` now will fail: `sgetc`, `sbumpc`, and `snextc` will return EOF, and `sgetn` will return 0.

`int sputbackc(char c);`

The `sputbackc` function moves the get pointer back (left) one character. The single character argument must be the character we just got from a previous operation that moved the get pointer.

For example, referring back to Fig. 5.8, we see that the result of calling `sputbackc('p')` is to back up the get pointer so that it points to just before the 'p', with a return value that is something other than EOF. The `streambuf` will be left as shown in Fig. 5.9.

The effect of calling `sputback('z')` or some other character that is not 'p' under the same circumstances is not defined. However, it may not leave the

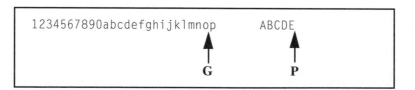

FIGURE 5.9
The `streambuf` after `sputbackc`

'z' in the place of the 'p'. If there is some error in pushing the character back, EOF is returned. In the simple streambuf of our examples, this result could occur because the get pointer was already at the first position in the get area; therefore there was no place to which it could back up.

Operations on the put area

Two operations can be requested for the put area.

```
int sputc(int c);
```

The sputc function takes an integer argument, so it's possible to give it the EOF value as an argument. Normally EOF would be ignored, though some derived classes might treat it specially. Usually this function gets a character argument that is put into the space just *after* the put pointer. The pointer is then advanced so it points to just after the added character. In Fig. 5.9, the pointer is just after the 'E'. After sputc('*') is called an '*' is added and the pointer advanced to just after the new character, as shown in Fig. 5.10. If the put pointer were already pointing at the position just beyond the end of the buffer, the call sputc(c) would return EOF.

```
int sputn(const char *s, int n);
```

The second operation on the put area, sputn, moves a block of characters into the area. Similar to sgetn, this function returns the number of characters it was able to place in the put area of the streambuf. Referring again to Fig. 5.10, we see that the call

```
sputn("FGHIJKLMNOPQRSTUVWXYZ", 9);
```

returns 9 and leaves the put area as shown in Fig. 5.11.

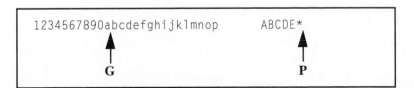

FIGURE 5.10
streambuf example after sputc('*')

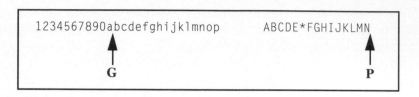

FIGURE 5.11
A block of 9 characters moved to the `streambuf`

A further call such as

`sputn("FGHIJKLMNOPQRSTUVWXYZ", 21);`

leaves the put area full and the put pointer just beyond the end of the area. It returns 4, the number of characters that fit into the remainder of the put area. The result is shown in Fig. 5.12.

5.3 Overflow and Underflow

The functions we described for the get and put areas can all encounter the situation in which the pointer in question has reached the limit of its buffer area. In the simple view of a `streambuf` that we have taken so far, once this happens that's the end of the matter. No more characters can be gotten or put. However, the `streambuf` abstraction is intended to describe conceptually unlimited get and put areas. Furthermore, it is not intended to be a stand-alone class. Rather it is specifically

FIGURE 5.12
The put area filled to capacity

designed as a general purpose abstraction of IO buffer behavior, which is intended as a base for the derivation of other classes with behavior more precisely related to actual IO requirements.

Functions like `sgetc` and `sputc` are specific operations on a `streambuf`. Although we described what they do in terms of the get and put areas, we now need to discuss the functions `overflow` and `underflow`. When a function that gets characters, such as `sgetc`, is called and the get pointer is at the position just beyond the end of the get area, the function does something before it returns the `EOF` value: It calls another function called `underflow`. Similarly, a call to a function that puts characters—`sputc` or `sputn`—when the put pointer is just beyond the end of the put area calls the function `overflow`.

The functions `underflow` and `overflow` represent abstract operations on a `streambuf`. They are general properties that are expected to be provided by all classes derived from `streambuf`, although their exact action will vary among such derived classes.

```
virtual int underflow();
```

This function is called by the get functions `sgetc`, `sbumpc`, `snextc`, and `sgetn` when there are no more characters to be had in the get area. In some current versions of IOStreams it's a public function that can also be called by a client at any time, although it's not clear what useful purpose doing this would serve. The tendency in IOStreams design thinking is to make both `underflow` and `overflow` pure virtual functions. When this is done, `streambuf` becomes an entirely abstract class.

The `underflow` function attempts to make more characters available from whatever source the `streambuf` is designed to deal with. It moves as many characters as will fit, or failing that, as many as are available, into the get area. It then sets the end of the get area to be just after the last character, positions the get pointer just before the first one, and returns the value of the new first character. Only if the function can't make characters available from the source does it return the `EOF` value.

Figure 5.13 mirrors where we left off in Fig. 5.8. Continuing from there, a call to `sgetc` results in a call to `underflow`. If there are no more characters to be had this call will return `EOF` and any further get operation carried out on this example `streambuf` will now fail.

If there are more characters to be had, however, the result might appear as in Fig. 5.14.

The get area is now a different length. Presumably only a limited number of further characters—`'q'` through `'z'`—were available. The `underflow` function leaves the get pointer pointing to just before the new first character—the `'q'`—and returns that character. The `sgetc` function then returns this same value.

```
virtual int overflow(int = EOF);
```

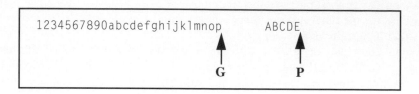

FIGURE 5.13
streambuf example with no characters available in get area

The overflow function works in a corresponding way, except that it gets passed to it the character for which sputc or sputn could find no room. The argument type is int, so that the EOF value can be passed; in this case, the overflow function ignores the argument value. Otherwise it must find somewhere to put the argument character as well as the characters already in the put area.

In Fig. 5.15, the put area is full; therefore a call to sputc('$') causes a call to overflow('$').

If overflow can't dispose of the put area full of characters, it returns an EOF, and this situation is unchanged. If it can dispose of the characters, the result will most likely be as shown in Fig. 5.16.

The put area was cleared out to some as yet unspecified destination by overflow('$'), then the '$' character was saved in the first available position in the put area and the put pointer positioned after it, ready for the next character to be put. It's also possible that some implementations of overflow will dispose of the '$' character to the final destination at the same time as it does the rest of the contents of the put area, leaving a completely empty put area.

FIGURE 5.14
The get area replenished with new characters

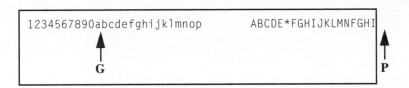

FIGURE 5.15
streambuf **example with the put area full**

The operation of the overflow and underflow functions is intended to be transparent as far as the user of a streambuf is concerned. The streambuf should behave like a character array that holds all the characters available from the source and any characters that are put into it. There should be no need for the user to call these functions. Forthcoming IOStreams designs therefore are likely to make overflow and underflow pure virtual functions in the base class and private (virtual) functions of derived classes.

The public implementations of overflow and underflow present in some implementations are leftovers from the older C++ Streams system. If such functions are present, then underflow should return EOF, and if the buffer area was user-specified, the overflow function should return the same. If no buffer area was specified, the original implementations of streambuf would have overflow dynamically allocate one on the assumption that this behavior could be used by all derived types. Because the tendency now is to consider streambuf purely a sequence abstraction, buffering behavior might now be left to the derived class. Note that in a version of IOStreams supporting exception handling, both overflow

FIGURE 5.16
streambuf **example after overflow**

and `underflow` might throw an exception. Such exceptions will be propagated by the get and put functions.

5.4 Repositioning the get and put Pointers

The operations we have discussed so far in this chapter are concerned principally with getting characters from or putting characters into the `streambuf`. (The `stossc` function is an exception, but it is almost always used as part of a conditional character get.) Other functions are provided whose sole purpose is to reposition the pointers.

You should consider repositioning pointers in the same context as you do the `overflow` and `underflow` functions, that is, assume there is some as yet unspecified source of characters from which the get area can be replenished and some sink into which the put area can be emptied.

Repositioning the get pointer to a position before the start of the get area should cause the get area to be filled at the next underflow with characters that logically precede its previous contents. For example, suppose we want the get pointer to move from where it is back (left) by a total of 16 characters. Figure 5.17 shows the pointer at its starting position.

Because there are no characters prior to the `'q'` at the get pointer, the repositioning function must "know" about the unspecified external source of characters and must be able to arrange for characters that had previously been gotten to be placed once more in the get area. The result needs to appear as in Fig. 5.18.

This does not necessarily have to be done as a single operation. It might be accomplished simply by adjusting the get area so that it has no contents and manipulating the external source so the next thing it regurgitates is the "`abcd...`" sequence. A subsequent call to one of the get functions would then cause `underflow` to be called, and the get area would be filled with the characters "`abcde...`".

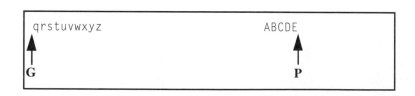

FIGURE 5.17
`streambuf` example before repositioning

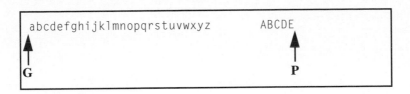

FIGURE 5.18
streambuf **example after repositioning**

Repositioning the put pointer disposes of the characters in the put area. This can be done by a call to overflow(EOF), the result of which leaves the put area empty with the pointer pointing at its first position. The external destination is then is adjusted so that the next batch of characters overflowed from the put area is placed at the required offset. Suppose the put pointer is positioned as shown in Fig. 5.18 and we want to move it back (left) three character positions. The characters "ABCDE" would be transferred to the final destination, leaving the put area empty. The external destination would then be adjusted so that any further characters it receives are written over the "CDE".

Because the nature of the external source and sink of characters remains unspecified, some unrestrictive data type is required to represent an arbitrary position in a stream. In current implementations, the type used is often a long, which is capable of representing an arbitrary position in a very large file while simultaneously representing the customary error value EOF. However, the eventual ANSI standard for IOStreams will probably define classes to represent both absolute positions and relative offsets within streams. This approach would allow for extremely large files or would, for instance, allow the source and sink to actually be sets of files, or disjoint sources. The classes will probably be something like the following:

```
class streampos {
public:
   streampos(long elem_no, size_t offset = 0,
                           size_t elemsize = 1);
   operator long();
private:
   ...;
};

class streamoff {
```

```
public:
  streamoff(long elem_no, size_t offset = 0,
                          size_t elemsize = 1);
  streamoff(const streampos&);
private:
  ...;
};
```

The constructor arguments allow expression of almost any conceivable byte offset into a stream. Class `streamoff` also has a constructor to convert from a `streampos` to a `streamoff`. Both classes are capable of casting the value 0 to the respective type, as follows:

```
streampos(0);
streamoff(0);
```

The `streampos` type also has a conversion operator to `long` that allows its use in a comparison with the `EOF` value, as in

```
streampos sp;
...
if (sp == EOF)
  ...;
```

If the `streampos` object stands for an error condition, the `operator long()` function returns `EOF` (-1); otherwise it returns some other long integer.

These operations—that is, construction from 0 and in the case of class `streampos`, comparison with `EOF`—are the only absolutely safe operations that can be performed to set or interrogate the value of these types. Otherwise the only guaranteed safe source is the return value of one of the following functions, which accomplish get and put pointer adjustments:

```
virtual streampos seekpos(streampos absolute_position, int which);
virtual streampos seekoff(streamoff, seek_dir, int which);
```

Both of these return a value of type `streampos`. If some error occurs, the returned `streampos` value will translate to `long(EOF)`. The `seekpos` function performs an *absolute* seek to a `streampos` relative to the start of the stream. `seekoff` performs a seek *relative to some specified position* in the stream, the options being the start of the stream, the current position in the stream, or the end of the stream.

The `seek_dir` type used in the following as an argument to `seekoff` is an enumeration type defined in the public interface of class `ios`.

```
class ios {
  enum seek_dir { beg, cur, end };
  enum open_mode { in, out, ... };
```

```
  ...
};
```

The name `seek_dir` was used in the AT&T version of IOStreams and is used in the ANSI discussion document. However, the name is misleading. The direction of the seek is determined by the value of the `streamoff` argument, which will in effect be negative or positive, not by the value of the `seek_dir` argument. A name such as `relative_to` would be more descriptive. The other enumeration, `open_mode`, defines bit values among which are bits that determine whether a stream is to be used for input or output.

Values of this sort can be combined, as in `ios::in | ios::out` to provide the final argument to `seekpos` and `seekoff`, the `which` argument. This final argument determines whether the get pointer, the put pointer, or both are to be moved. The `which` argument is in each case defaulted to move both pointers.

Notice that when given the preceding definitions for both `streampos` and `streamoff`, it's possible to define the absolute seek in terms of the relative one, as follows:

```
virtual streampos seekpos(streampos pos, int which)
        { return seekoff(streamoff(pos), ios::beg, which); }
```

So it's not necessary to implement more than the `seekoff` function. It might, however, be more efficient in some implementations to have two separate functions using different addressing techniques.

The safe way to use these functions follows:

```
streambuf sb;        // in practice this will be a derived class

// Note the current stream position
streampos sp = sb.seekoff(0, ios::cur, ios::in);

// Move get position to start of source,
// zero is a guaranteed valid argument
streampos start = sb.seekpos(0, ios::in);
if (start == EOF)
  // something seriously wrong

// Move to end of file
sb.seekoff(0, ios::end, ios::in);

// Move back to the noted position
sp = sb.seekpos(sp, ios::in);
if (sp == EOF)
  // also serious trouble
```

In these cases, we have used only the conversions from 0 to `streampos` and `streamoff`, and the conversion of `streampos` to `long` for comparison with `EOF`. Other `streampos` values used were obtained from calls to `seekpos` or `seekoff`. This safe technique is usually described as using the `streampos` and `streamoff` types as "magic cookies." However, if enough is known about the nature of the stream being manipulated, it might be possible to use the functions more adventurously, as follows

```
sp = sb.seekpos(HDRSIZE, ios::in);
                    // skip the file header
...
sp = sb.seekoff(sizeof(Thing), ios::cur, ios::in);
                    // move to next item
if (sp == EOF)
                    // whatever
```

These virtual functions should have implementations in the base class that return `EOF` to signify that their use is an error. The behavior of a derived class that neglects to provide an implementation will then be correct. Derived classes should give these functions whatever behavior is appropriate for that particular ultimate source and/or destination of characters.

5.5 Synchronization

A `streambuf` is an intermediary. It acts as a proxy for some external character stream or streams. It usually transfers characters to and from these external streams in blocks of some predetermined size. However, it then accepts or dispenses these characters either one at a time or in blocks of unknown size. Because of these different methods of handling characters, the external stream or streams and the `streambuf` can disagree as to how many characters have been supplied or received.

Suppose the contents of the `streambuf` are as shown in Fig. 5.19. The external source and sink streams are represented by Figs. 5.20 and 5.21.

Let's assume the characters 'l' through 'p' were previously supplied to the get area. Consequently the character source currency is at 'q' in the source sequence. However, the get pointer is only at 'b' in the get area, which so far has supplied only the characters 'l' through 'a'. On the other hand, the put area has received five characters while the character sink has not yet received any. The required synchronized state is that shown in Figs. 5.22, 5.23, and 5.24.

The characters that were in the get area have been returned to the source, whose currency is now at character 'b', and the get area is now empty. Any attempt to get a character will result in a call to `underflow`, which will place a block of

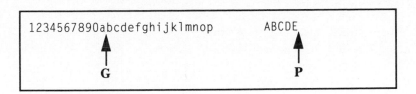

FIGURE 5.19
streambuf **example before synchronization**

characters starting from 'b' in the get area. So the source and the get area now agree on the next character. *Note:* This particular synchronized state is not unique. The source and the get area could be made to agree in another way, by simply moving the currency of the source back to 'b' and leaving the get area as it started.

All characters that were in the put area have been sent to the sink, and the currency of the sink is at its logical end, that is, at the position where any succeeding character should be put. As usual, the put pointer is at the position where the next character will be put. Therefore the put area and the sink agree.

The synchronization function, shown next, is virtual.

```
virtual int sync();
```

An implementation must be provided for each class derived from streambuf and that implementation must do whatever is appropriate to achieve the logical equivalent of synchronization as we described it.

In cases when the virtual sync function has an implementation in the base class, it should return 0 if the get and put areas are both empty and EOF otherwise. If streambuf is to be an abstract base class, sync can be a pure virtual function. In derived classes, the sync function should return EOF if an error occurs and some other value if it succeeds.

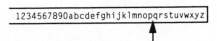

FIGURE 5.20
Source of characters

FIGURE 5.21
Sink (currently empty, end of sink unspecified)

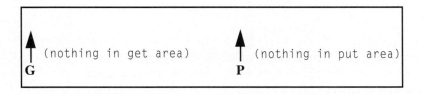

FIGURE 5.22
streambuf example after synchronization

FIGURE 5.23
Source after synchronization

FIGURE 5.24
Sink after synchronization (end of sink unspecified)

5.6 Inquiry Functions

The following pair of functions allows the user to determine whether there are characters in the get area waiting to be got or whether any characters have been put into the put area and are still held there:

```
int in_avail() const;
int out_waiting() const;
```

These functions might be useful in determining if flushing is desirable under some particular circumstance. Both are guaranteed to have no effect on the `streambuf` object.

5.7 Constructors and Setup Function

Class `streambuf` has two constructors—a default constructor—and a constructor that specifies an area of memory to be used for the get and put areas:

```
streambuf();
streambuf(char *buffer, int length);
```

The default constructor is used to instantiate a `streambuf` that will subsequently allocate its get and put areas dynamically. The other, used with either a `0 buffer` pointer or a `length` argument less than or equal to 0, prompts the `streambuf` to provide all the functions that have been described. However, characters won't be accumulated in either the get or put areas. Rather, they will be obtained from the external source as they are required and sent to the external sink directly instead of being queued in the put area. This state is known as unbuffered operation, and is used when it's important that the characters are obtained from and delivered to their final destination immediately.

The setup function, `setbuf`, can be used with an existing `streambuf` to request a particular area of memory be used for the get and put areas, as follows:

```
virtual streambuf *setbuf(char *buffer, int length);
```

Its action is similar to that of the explicit constructor. While not strictly necessary to the public interface, it's included for compatibility with the older Streams library. Classes derived from `streambuf` are not required to honor the `setbuf` request. However, if they do they should either return a pointer to the `streambuf` or otherwise return 0. Derived classes should generally honor a call to `setbuf` in two circumstances: when the arguments indicate that unbuffered operation is required, and unbuffered operation is appropriate to the derived class, or if the arguments specifies a suitably sized memory area, and no buffer already exists.

This virtual function might have an implementation in the base class whereby it acts on the request if no buffer area has already been set up. Therefore

```
char *memory;
int length;
streambuf sb1;
sb1.setbuf(memory, length);  // should be honored
                             // (returns &sb1)

streambuf sb2;
sb2.sputc('c');              // should cause dynamic allocation
sb2.setbuf(memory, length);  // will probably be declined
                             // (returns 0);

// but

sb2.setbuf(0,0);             // should be honored, it requests
                             // unbuffered operation
                             // (returns &sb2)
```

5.8 The Protected Interface

We discuss the protected interface of class streambuf in detail in Chapter 17 where we deal with implementation of the derived class filebuf.

5.9 Summary

Class streambuf is an abstraction of a sequence of characters. Facilities are provided to examine or fetch the next character available from the sequence, to skip characters in the sequence, and to combine these operations. A specified number of characters from the sequence can be fetched as a block. The position at which characters in the sequence are examined or copied can be arbitrarily adjusted (called *seeking*). A single character fetch can be undone with the fetched character, or possibly some other character being replaced in the sequence at the position from which the last fetch took place. Further, characters can be inserted into the sequence singly or in groups, and the position in the sequence at which such insertions take place can be arbitrarily adjusted.

In anticipation that the actual implementation of a `streambuf` will maintain temporary states, a synchronization operation is supported to force such temporary states to be reflected in the sequence.

Classes derived from `streambuf` can deal with sequences such as files, areas of memory (private or shared), communication channels, and windows in a GUI.

6

The IO Specification– Class *ios*

Class ios, as we noted in Chapter 4, can be thought of as a specification for input or output. An important part of such a specification is the state of the represented object with respect to errors.

An object of type ios is not a fixed specification. Errors can happen at any time, and any element comprising the specification can be changed as required. Class ios is also designed so that further descriptive elements can be added. This feature enables translator classes to be derived for streams that require more format information than is used by the standard streams. For example, a stream might maintain information about the current display color and/or font.

As with any well-designed class, the state variables are hidden and can't be changed haphazardly. The public interface includes a set of functions to allow appropriate adjustments to the specification, thus ensuring that the implementation details are not tied down by the interface specification. As is customary in C++ classes, such facilities are provided by inline functions in cases where it's appropriate so that, when possible, there is no speed or code size penalty.

The state variables that describe the IO specification comprise the following four groups:

- Error state
- Format state

- Format parameters
- Extended format parameters

We use these terms often in following chapters whenever we refer to the state of an `ios` object.

6.1 The Public Interface

The following public members are listed in groups according to what they do. The comments are brief summaries of their usage. The members are described in more detail in the sections that follow.

```
class ios {
public:
// Error state bits
  enum io_state { goodbit = 0, eofbit, failbit, badbit = 4 };

// Enumerators for controlling the opening of files
  enum open_mode {
    in, out, ate, app, trunc, nocreate, noreplace, binary
  };

// Enumerators for relative seeks
  enum seek_dir { beg, cur, end };

// Format control bits
  enum format_flags {
    skipws, left, right, internal,
    dec, oct, hex,
    showbase, showpoint, uppercase,
    showpos, scientific, fixed,
    unitbuf, stdio
  };

// Format control bit sets
    static const int basefield;   // dec | oct | hex;
    static const int adjustfield; // left | right | internal,
    static const int floatfield;  // scientific | fixed

// Functions to interrogate and set the error state
  int rdstate() const;    // Returns current error flags state
```

```
void clear(int = ios::goodbit);
                    // Sets error state flags, defaulted
                    // to no errors

int good() const;     // rdstate() == goodbit;
int eof() const;      // (rdstate() & eofbit);
int fail() const;     // (rdstate() & (failbit | badbit));
int bad() const;        // (rdstate() & badbit);
int operator!() const;    // fail();
operator void *() const; // fail()? 0:this; 0;

// Functions to interrogate and set format flags
long flags() const;       // Read the current flag word
long flags(long);         // Set the flag word absolutely
long setf(long bits);
                    // Set a specified group of bits
                    // Return the old value
long setf(long bits, long mask);
                    // Set a specified group of bits
                    // having first cleared a specified
                    // group (mask). Return the old
                    // value
long unsetf(long bits);
                    // Reset a specified group of flags.
                    // Return the old value.

// Functions to interrogate or set parameters
char fill() const;        // Return the current fill
                    // (padding) character
char fill(char);          // Set a new padding character,
                    // return the old one.

int precision() const;    // Returns the current floating
                    // point precision
int precision(int);       // Set a new value for floating
                    // point precision, returns the
                    // old value.

ostream *tie() const;     // Return a pointer to any ostream
                    // that is currently tied to this
                    // stream, zero if none.
ostream *tie(ostream *t);
                    // Tie the argument stream to
```

```
                              // this one, return the old tie.

  int width() const;          // Returns the current width setting
  int width(int);             // Set a new value for width, return
                              // the old one.

// Functions to get and use user-defined bits and parameters.
  static long bitalloc();     // Returns a long with one
                              // previously unused format bit set.
  static int xalloc();        // Returns an int index into an
                              // array of objects suitable for
                              // use as a long or a pointer. The
                              // index is of an entry that has
                              // not yet been used.

  long &iword(int i);         // Returns a reference to the i'th
                              // object as a long.
  void* &pword(int i);        // Returns a reference to the i'th
                              // object as a pointer

// Access the associated streambuf
  streambuf *rdbuf() const;

// stdio synchronization
  static void sync_with_stdio();

// Constructor and destructor
  ios(streambuf*);
  virtual ~ios();    // virtual because it will be used as a base
                     // class in derivation
private:
// These prohibit copying
  ios(const ios&);
  ios &operator=(const ios&);
  ...;
};
```

6.2 Implementation of State Variables

The error and the format states are usually implemented as bits in an int and a long private class variable respectively. This implementation detail is not particularly well hidden, and especially in the case of the format state, might restrict implementation portability. For instance, given an environment where an int and long are both 32 bits, then

```
enum flagbits { lowest = 1, another = 0x8000 };
long bitmap = 0;
bitmap |= another;
```

leaves one bit set in bitmap. If on the other hand, an int is 16 bits, and a long is 32, then the assignment

```
bitmap |= another;
```

ends up setting 17 bits in bitmap. The language specification requires the value of an enumerator to be an int; therefore the initializer (0x8000) sets flagbits::another to a negative value, which then gets sign-extended when it is promoted to a long.

An implementation like

```
class  Bitmap {
public:
  Bitmap(int);     // required number of bits specified
                   // to constructor
  int operator[](int i) const;
  void set(int i);
  void reset(int i);
  // etc
};

class ios {
private:
  Bitmap flags;
  ...;
};
```

might be more adaptable, although possibly less efficient. An approach similar to this has been proposed in the latest ANSI discussion document.

6.3 Error States

Input and output operations are notoriously error prone, whether the errors are caused by users or devices, so a "foolproof" IO system, if indeed one exists, must properly note and propagate errors. Error propagation is important because if an error indication is available only immediately after the operation that caused the error, then the error is likely to be ignored. Further, after it has been ignored, erroneous data may be read or written.

If an object of a class like ios goes into an error state, it must stay there until the user of the class explicitly does something about it. Classes derived from ios must ignore further requests for action if the associated ios object is in an error state. Of course errors can be of different natures and severities. In IOStreams they are described by one or more of the following enumerators:

```
class ios {
public:
  enum io_state { goodbit = 0, eofbit ,
                  failbit, badbit  = 4 };
  ...;
};
```

which stand for the bits of some internal state variable.

The first enumerator, goodbit, is not a bit; rather it represents the state when no error bits are set. The eofbit flag indicates that no further characters are available from the associated streambuf or that an attempt to output a character failed because the streambuf to which it was being sent couldn't accept more. EOF will be a normal condition on many streams, for example, when inputting from a file or outputting to a fixed-size memory buffer. In these cases, there is nothing wrong with the streambuf; it is behaving as expected. On the other hand, finding an end-of-file situation could indicate a real problem, such as a disk that is full, a printer with no paper, or a hardware error. While these cases might be viewed as more serious, they will also simply cause eofbit to be set, since a streambuf can only report that it has failed. When exception handling is available, it should be possible to make finer distinctions in failure handling.

The failbit flag signifies that there is not necessarily anything wrong with the streambuf but that a requested operation failed. The failure could result because of some translation issue or because of an EOF condition, in which case eofbit would also be set. The badbit flag classifies the streambuf associated with an ios object as being unuseable. It is set, for example, if the associated streambuf object has not been connected to some source or sink for characters.

These three flags can be combined to cover a spectrum of situations: for example,

Example Situation	Flag Combination
Stream contents "123"; requested input of an integer (hit EOF while still scanning legitimate digits)	eofbit
Stream contains only whitespace, requested input of an integer (no digits available before EOF)	failbit | eofbit

Stream contains `"zzz"`, requested input of an integer (next character is not whitespace and not a digit)	`failbit`
Stream set up without source or sink for characters	`badbit`
Input requested from stream set up without source/sink	`failbit	badbit`
Stream contains `1.234567e-a2`; input of a double requested	`failbit`

In the last example, the input translator could make no sense of the characters it encountered; that is, those characters could not be reconciled with the data type for which input was being attempted. Such situations have the following two manifestations:

1. The error state was detected before any characters were passed over and thus lost, so input from the same point could be restarted with other assumptions,
2. The error state was detected only after a number of characters had been processed; therefore some characters were lost.

Generally, we want to discriminate between these two conditions, and in the older Streams library, the first condition set `failbit`, while the second set `failbit` and `badbit`.

However, in current implementations of IOStreams this discrimination is barely documented (although it's likely to be implemented in some versions, since much of the code of translators will have carried over from the older streams library). In the present ANSI discussion document, this discrimination is not supported.

6.4 Error State Member Functions

Class `ios` provides eight member functions for reading and manipulating the error state. Strictly speaking, only the following two are required; however, all are very small inline functions, and their existence makes for more readable programs:

```
int rdstate() const;
void clear(int state = ios::goodbit);
```

`rdstate` returns an `int` with any appropriate error bits set. `clear` substitutes its argument value for the current error-flags word. To set a particular flag while leaving the others unaffected, use the form:

```
clear(ios::failbit | rdstate());
```

Any required manipulations can be done with these two functions. However, the following six alternatives to `rdstate()` are also available. Note that the equivalences are not intended to reflect the detail of the implementation.

```
int good() const;    // !rdstate() - true if no error bits set
int eof() const;     // (rdstate() & eofbit) - true if an end
```

```
                      // of file condition was encountered
int fail() const;     // (rdstate() & (failbit | badbit)) - true
                      // if either failbit or badbit set
int bad() const;      // (rdstate() & badbit) - true if badbit set
int operator!() const;
                      // (rdstate() & (failbit | badbit))
                      // - similar to fail()
operator void*() const;
                      // ((void *) (rdstate() & (failbit
                      //            | badbit)))? 0: this; )
```

The first five of these return `int` values. The final one is a conversion function to `void*` that allows testing of an `ios` object in a conditional statement. It's safer to provide this automatic conversion to `void*` than a conversion to another of the built-in types, such as `int`. It returns `(void *) 0` if either `ios::failbit` or `ios::badbit` is set and a nonzero value otherwise. The last two of these member functions are used in situations like the following:

```
ifstream infile("infile.dat");
if (!infile)       // uses operator!()
  // error set while opening file

while (infile)     // uses operator void*()
  // no failure, so continue with next operation
```

Future versions of IOStreams will support exception handling. The ANSI discussion document currently requires that `ios` objects can have exceptions enabled or disabled. It also specifies a class `failure`, as follows, nested within class `ios`, to signal exceptions peculiar to `ios` and the derived translator classes:

```
class ios {
  class failure {
  public:
     failure(const char *cause, ios *ios_instance);
     const char *cause() const;
     ios *rdios() const;
  ...
  }
  ...
};
```

However, it doesn't include exception specifications in the `ios` or the translator classes member function declarations. Many such exceptions will originate from the associated `streambuf`. Since in the ANSI discussion document `streambuf` is an abstract class, there is no unrestrictive way to specify the type of exceptions propagated by a client `ios` object.

The ANSI discussion document also provides an extra pair of error management functions to set the exception state of an `ios` object. The first of these specifies the circumstances under which exceptions will be thrown for the object, as follows:

```
int exceptions(int exception_mask);
```

The second reports the current exception state, as follows:

```
int exceptions() const;
```

The setting function takes an argument, `exception_mask`, which specifies the error flag bits that will cause an exception to be thrown. If a member function of `ios` or a derived class has to set any error state bit that corresponds to a bit in `exception_mask`, it must throw an exception. The exception `ios` throws could be `ios::failure`. This will be the case if the error doesn't originate from the associated `streambuf`. Alternatively it may propagate an exception thrown by the `streambuf`. Class `ios` objects must be initialized by their constructors to a state where exceptions are disabled.

6.5 Open Mode

Class `ios` also has enumerators for controlling the mode in which an associated `streambuf` is opened. However, it has no member function that utilizes these enumerators and no functions that use them as arguments. They are defined in class `ios` because `ios` is common to all stream objects.

The AT&T implementation defines

```
enum open_mode {
   in, out, ate, app, trunc, nocreate, noreplace
};
```

In this book the range is extended to

```
enum open_mode {
   in, out, ate, app, trunc, nocreate, noreplace, binary
};
```

Doing this provides for a distinction between text files, which are assumed to be the default file type used with IOStreams, and binary files. The most commonly encountered difference between these two file types is the treatment of end-of-line characters (`'\n'`). Under MS-DOS and OS/2 for example, the newline characters manipulated by C and C++ programs are customarily expanded to carriage return/ linefeed pairs when they are sent to text files and converted to single newline characters when they are gotten from them. Other operating systems will make different distinctions between text and binary files. The binary flag is included in the ANSI discussion document.

On the other hand, the ANSI discussion document proposes to reduce the number of open modes. They could end up as

```
enum open_mode {
   in, out, ate, binary
};
```

We describe the uses of the open mode enumerators in later chapters as they are encountered.

6.6 Format State

The following bit flags and bit sets are also defined by class ios. The initializers can vary from implementation to implementation.

```
class ios {
   ...
   enum format_flags {
      skipws = 1, left = 2, right = 4, internal = 8,
      dec = 0x10, oct = 0x20, hex = 0x40,
      showbase = 0x80, showpoint = 0x100, uppercase = 0x200,
      showpos = 0x400, scientific = 0x800, fixed = 0x1000,
      unitbuf = 0x2000, stdio = 0x4000
   };
   ...
   const int basefield = dec | oct | hex;
   const int adjustfield = left | right | internal;
   const int floatfield = scientific | fixed;    ,
```

We describe next the effect of these bit flags when they are set.

skipws   Leading whitespace is usually ignored during formatted input. This is the default state. For example, the same integer would be input from both of the following character streams:

```
"99"
"\n\n   99"
```

`left` The item being output is left justified. If any padding is required to make the required width, it is added *after* the item.

`right` The item being output is right justified. If any padding is required to make the required width, it is added *before* the item. This is the default state and the behavior if no justification flag is set.

`internal` If any padding is required to make the required width, it is added after any sign or radix base information but before the actual value.

    With a required field width of 6 and padding character '*', these bits, when set, result in the following:

```
-99***          // left
***-99          // right - the default if none of these
                // flags is set
-***99          // internal
```

    The set of flag bits `left | right | internal` is known collectively as `adjustfield`.

`dec` Specifies conversion base 10 for integers

`oct` Specifies octal conversion for integers

`hex` Specifies hexadecimal conversion for integers
    If none of these bits are set, output of integers is with decimal conversion but input conversion of a character stream follows the usual C++ conventions; for example,

```
77              // input as 77
077             // input as 63 - octal notation
0x77            // input as 119 - hex notation
```

The set of flag bits `dec | oct | hex` is known collectively as `basefield`.
`showbase` Output of integers includes a base indication according to the C++ conventions. The default state does not have this bit set.
    With `showbase` set output will be as follows:

```
77   -   77     with dec set (or with none of these set)
63   -   077    with oct set
119  -   0x77   with hex set
```

`showpos` A plus sign is included on output of a positive decimal number. Minus signs are included automatically, and so don't require a flag bit. The default condition omits plus signs. Octal and hex numbers are regarded as unsigned and therefore get neither.

uppercase The alphabetic characters that can appear in the following circumstances are output in uppercase:

- The hex digits 'a' – 'f' in hexadecimal integers
- The 'x' in a hexadecimal base indicator
- The 'e' in floating-point numbers when formatted in scientific notation.

The default is lowercase.

showpoint This bit controls the output of a decimal point and trailing zeroes
when floating-point numbers are translated. When it is set, the translation will have
a decimal point and will be padded out with 0's to the required precision in all
cases. If this bit isn't set and a floating-point number has a fractional part that is
0, no decimal point and no following zeroes are printed. Similarly, if it isn't set
and the fractional part has fewer significant digits than the required precision,
trailing 0's are omitted.

The bit set scientific/fixed is known collectively as floatfield.
(It's not clear why showpoint is not a member of floatfield, since it applies
only to floating-point numbers.)

scientific Floating-point output is converted to scientific notation; for example, possible sign, one digit, decimal point, N digits, 'e' or 'E' (depending on
the setting of the uppercase flag), exponent sign (+ or −), and digits representing
the exponent. N here represents the required precision, which defaults to six
decimal places.

fixed Floating-point output is converted to decimal notation with N digits after the
decimal point, where N is the currently set precision. The default is six decimal places.

If neither of these bits is set, floating-point output is translated to fixed point
format unless the exponent is less than −4 or greater than the required precision.
The following examples summarize how these bits work:

Default
```
1.2e-05      -> 1.2e-05
1.234567     -> 1.234567
1.2          -> 1.2
1.000000     -> 1
1.2e+07      -> 1.2e+07
```

Scientific bit set
```
1.2e-05      -> 1.2e-05
1.234567     -> 1.234567e+00
1.2          -> 1.2e+00
```

```
1.000000    -> 1e+00
1.2e+07     -> 1.2e+07
```

Fixed bit set
```
1.2e-05     -> 0.000001
1.234567    -> 1.234567
1.2         -> 1.2
1.000000    -> 1
1.2e+07     -> 12000000
```

The effect of setting both of these `floatfield` bits is implementation dependent and should be avoided.

The following flags are not strictly format flags because they don't change the format. They relate to the exact point at which characters get sent to their ultimate destination.

`unitbuf` The `streambuf` related to an `ostream` has its `sync()` function called after each item is translated and put into the `streambuf`. This ensures that at that point, the ultimate destination of the characters being output reflects what has just been done.

`stdio` Affects the interactions between output sent to the standard output and standard error streams by a program that mixes output from the `stdio` functions like `printf`, `puts`, and `fprintf`, with IOStreams output through `cout` and `cerr`. If the bit is set in an `ostream`, the `stdio` streams `stdout` and `stderr` are flushed after each item is translated.

6.7 Format State Member Functions

The format state flag bits we discussed in Section 6.6 are examined and manipulated using the following four functions:

```
long flags() const;
long setf(long bits_to_set);
long setf(long bits_to_set, long mask);
long unsetf(long bits_to_unset);
```

`flags` returns the current value of the class `ios` state variable, a 32 bit value.

`setf` sets the bits which correspond to the `bits_to_set` argument. The previous value of the flags is returned. The third function, an overload of `setf`, clears the group of bit flags corresponding to the `mask` argument and then sets the bits corresponding to the `bits_to_set` argument. The last three functions return a `long` representing the previous setting of the format flag bits. The second one is used, for example, to set a different floating-point output format, as follows:

```
long oldflags = setf(ios::scientific, ios::floatfield);
```

This works whether the current state is the default (neither `ios::scientific` or `ios::fixed` is set) or `ios::fixed` has previously been set, since both bits in `ios::floatfield` are cleared first.

The fourth function, `unsetf`, resets the bits specified by the `bits_to_unset` argument and returns the previous value of the flags; for example,

```
unsetf(ios::floatfield | ios::showpoint);
```

can be used to restore default floating-point output conditions.

Format state flags can also be changed by manipulators, which are discussed in Chapter 15.

6.8 Format Parameters

Some details of the required output format require more information than one bit can provide. The current padding character, precision of floating-point representations, a link to a related stream and the required field width must be stored by class `ios` in some other way. Just how these are stored is implementation dependent. However, a number of functions are provided to manipulate these values, which we discuss next.

Format parameter member functions

The `ios` class provides the following eight public functions to look at or modify format parameters:

```
char fill() const;
char fill(char);
```

These functions control the current filler or padding character; the default is the space. On output, if the required field width is not set to 0, padding characters are output according to the setting of the bits in `ios::adjustfield` (`ios::left | ios::right | ios::internal`).

The first fill function reports the current padding character. The second changes the padding character to that specified by its argument and reports the previous padding character.

```
int precision() const;
int precision(int);
```

These functions control the number of digits that are displayed after the decimal point in floating-point representations. The default value for precision is 6 digits. The first precision function reports the current setting. The second changes the precision to that specified by its argument and reports the previous value.

```
ostream *tie() const;
ostream *tie(ostream *)
```

These functions report or specify what, if any, `ostream` is to be flushed before an IO operation on the current stream. For example, the standard output stream, `cout`, is tied to the standard input stream `cin` and also to `cerr`. Therefore before `cin` attempts to get input from the console, it calls `cout.flush()` to ensure that any previous output is up to date. Only the `cout` stream is tied by default, to `cin` and `cerr`; in other cases, such ties must be set up explicitly.

The first tie function reports the current setting and returns a pointer to any currently tied `ostream` or 0 if there is none. The second changes the tie to that specified by its `ostream*` argument and reports the previous tie.

```
int width() const;
int width(int);
```

These functions control the setting of the width state variable, which is used in different ways by input and output operations; the default value is 0. The first `width` function reports the current setting. The second changes the width to that specified by its argument and reports the previous value. *Note:* The width setting is reset to 0 by each input or output operation.

6.9 User-defined Parameters

When extending IOStreams, you might need to use extra format flags, or extra format parameters, or both. Provision for such extensions is made within `ios`.

You can choose from three types of parameters: bit flags, long integers, or pointers. The number of these you can use isn't currently limited by the ANSI discussion document. Note that all extra format parameters should be set to 0 by the `ios` constructor (only the latest ANSI discussion document mentions this).

Each `ios` object notionally contains an anonymous array of available extra format parameters. Static member functions are provided to allocate array elements to classes which need them. Having the extra parameters in class `ios` allows the definition of manipulators that can be applied to translator class objects with generality. If a particular manipulator isn't relevant to a particular translator type, it can be ignored or its operation simplified.

In Chapter 18 we offer examples of how to use extra format parameters.

6.10 User-defined Parameter Functions

The functions that allocate the extra flags or parameters are static. Each allocation earmarks a flag or parameter from a reservoir that is built into class ios. The bit or parameter indices are allocated on a classwide basis; they are in effect static members of class ios. The returned flat value or parameter index should be kept in a static variable of a derived translator class.

```
long bitalloc();
```

This function is a static member function. The bit offered takes into account all previous user-requested bits in use by any ios object in the program. If no further format bits are available, bitalloc should probably return 0. Some ANSI discussion documents have it throwing an exception on failure, but none of the existing descriptions indicates what value should be returned if exceptions are not available or not enabled. In fact, the latest ANSI discussion document omits bitalloc altogether on the grounds that it's difficult to implement in a portable fashion and the same effects can be achieved using an extra long integer parameter.

```
int xalloc();
```

If a long integer format parameter or a pointer format parameter is required, current versions of IOStreams provide xalloc, also a static member function which returns an index into a general-purpose array of such entities. If no more parameters are available, the return value isn't specified; however, −1 would be an obvious choice.

Because this is a static member function, the index it returns applies to all instances of ios objects in the program. It can be used as follows:

```
class thingstream : public ostream {
friend ostream &dosomething(ostream&);
public:
  enum things { firstthing, secondthing };
  ...
private:
  static int inited, xindex;
};

int thingstream::inited = 0, thingstream::xindex = 0;
thingstream::thingstream()
```

```
{
  if (!inited) {
    xindex = xalloc();
    inited = 1;
    ...
  }
  ...
}
```

When exceptions are supported, `xalloc` must throw an exception if alloca-tion of an extended format parameter fails.

Given such an index, two functions allow actual access to the user-defined words.

```
long &iword(int index);
void* &pword(int index);
```

The first function, `iword`, returns a reference to a `long`; the second, `pword`, returns a reference to a `void*`. These are likely to be, in current versions of IOStreams, casts of a union type that is large enough to hold a `long` or a pointer. The indexing is into one array of this union type. The object referred to by `iword(n)` is the same as that for `pword(n)` except for the type coercion. The current ANSI discussion document requires separate and conceptually infinite arrays of pointers and integers respectively; therefore it follows that users shouldn't write code that makes assumptions about implementation.

Continuing the example we gave for `xalloc`, the constructor could allocate a value to the acquired format parameter, as follows:

```
thingstream::thingstream()
{
  if (!inited) {
    xindex = xalloc();
    inited = 1;
    pword(xindex)= this;
  }
  ...
}
```

A manipulator for class `thingstream` then could take the form

```
ostream &dosomething(ostream &os)
{
  if (!thingstream::inited)
    return os;        // not a thingstream object
  if (pword(thingstream::xindex)== &os) {
    // do something
```

```
} else
  // not a thingstream object
  return os;
}
```

Extra format flags allocated by `xalloc` and accessed using `iword` can also be used to control IO format for user defined types. For example, a `Money` type might allocate extra format parameters to control the currency symbol, and to control the delineation of thousands by commas, as in the different representations:

$1,000,000.00

and

$1000000.00

The `Money` class would have to make provision for these extra format parameters to be allocated and initialized before any use of the extraction and insertion operators for `Money`. This could be done by a static data member of the `Money` class that had a suitable constructor. For example:

```
class MoneyInit {
public:
  MoneyInit();
};

class Money {
friend ostream &operator<<(ostream &, const Money&);
public:
  enum format_flags { thousep = 1 };
  ...
  static int setsymbol(ostream &, char);
  static int setioflags(ostream &, int);
private:
  static MoneyInit setup;
  static int flagsindex, symbolindex;
  ...
};
```

The `MoneyInit` constructor would allocate suitable extended format parameters and give them default values.

```
MoneyInit::MoneyInit()
{
  Money::symbolindex = ios::xalloc();
  Money::flagsindex = ios::xalloc();
```

```
cout.iword(symbolindex) = '$';
cout.iword(flagsindex) = Money::thousep;
...
}
```

The extractor and inserter functions could then be written so as to observe the formatting conventions that had been set for any particular stream.

```
ostream &operator<<(ostream &os, const Money &m)
{
  os << char(os.iword(money:symbolindex));
  ...
  if (os.iword(money::flagsindex) & money::thousep)
    os << ',';
  ...
}
```

The money class would also have to provide functions to set the financial formatting requirements for a stream.

```
int Money::setsymbol(ostream &os, char s)
{
  int t = os.iword(symbolindex);
  os.iword(symbolindex) = s;
  return t;
}
```

6.11 **Synchronization with** `stdio`

The following static member function of class `ios` is provided to reset the IOStreams standard input and output streams to use the IO mechanisms of the `stdio` package in the standard C library. When this resetting is done, input and output using `stdio` and the IOStreams facilities can be freely mixed, although at some loss in efficiency.

```
static void ios::sync_with_stdio();
```

The `sync_with_stdio` function is located in class `ios` because that class is common to all IOStream structures. There, it has the member access privileges required for it to do its job.

```
for (int i = 2000; i--;) {
  cout << "Hello world C++ style";
```

```
  printf("Hello world C style");
}     // proper interleaving not guaranteed here

ios::sync_with_stdio();
     // mixed output will now be properly interleaved
for (i = 2000; i--;) {
  cout << "Hello world C++ style";
  printf("Hello world C style");
}
```

6.12 Constructor

Class ios has a single constructor that takes a streambuf pointer argument, as follows:

```
ios(streambuf *);
```

This constructor creates an ios object associated with the specified streambuf, with its flags and format parameters set to the default values and its extended format parameters set to 0.

6.13 Copying of ios Objects

Given two ios objects it would appear we can assign one to the other, as follows:

```
ios a;
ios b;

...;
a = b;
```

However, the semantics of copying ios objects are ill-defined. Does such an assignment mean that a should use its own streambuf but copy its state variables from b? Does it mean that it should keep its own state variables and use the same streambuf as b? Does it mean that it should use b's streambuf and copy b's state variables? Or does it mean that it should copy b's state variables and set up a streambuf just like b's?

If a sets up a streambuf like that of b, then the new streambuf will have to use the same external source and sink as does b's streambuf. Therefore it might just as well use b's streambuf, because the output is going to get mixed up anyway.

Because these questions don't have an overwhelmingly clear answer and because most of the effects desired from a can be had by using a pointer to b, class ios provides that the compiler will not permit copying of ios objects. This prohibition is enforced by the relatively common subterfuge of giving class ios a private copy constructor and assignment operator, as in

```
class ios {
  ...
private:
  ...
  ios(const ios&);
  ios &operator=(const ios&);
};
```

These functions don't even need to be implemented anywhere; the development process will never get as far as attempting to link a program that attempts copying because the compiler will produce error messages, such as

```
a = b;
  ^
"Operator= of class ios is not accessible";
ios c = b;
    ^
"Copy constructor for class ios is not accessible";
```

The ANSI discussion document proposes to define what copying does mean for ios objects and to provide the appropriate functions.

6.14 Summary

Class ios provides facilities to record errors and control format when objects of built-in types are input or output. The facilities can be extended to provide for other types of format information, or for the specific formatting requirements of user-defined types.

7

The Translator Classes–
An Illustrative Example

In Chapter 4, we introduced the concept of translators. The translator classes are derived from class `ios`. Input translators have member functions that convert to typed objects the character sequences obtained from the `streambuf` associated with the embedded `ios`. Output translators convert typed objects to character sequences in the `streambuf`.

The nature of the translator classes is probably best illustrated by sketching the implementation of a translator. In this example, the C standard library `stdio` facilities are used as source and sink for characters. For the purposes of this exercise let's suppose the comma operator acts as the IO operator. Two translator classes are required, one for input and one for output, which are defined as able to translate the types `int`, `double`, `char`, and `char*`. Each also has a constructor, leading to the following definitions:

```
#include <stdio.h>
#include <stdlib.h>
#include <ctype.h>
class in {
public:
    in(FILE *);             // constructor to link to a FILE*
    in &operator,(int&);    // input operator for int
    in &operator,(double&); // for double
```

```
    in &operator,(char *);    // for string
    in &operator,(char&);     // for single char
private:
    FILE *f;
};

class out {
public:
    out(FILE *);
    out &operator,(int);        // output operator for int
    out &operator,(double);     // for double
    out &operator,(const char *);  // for string
    out &operator,(char);       // for single char
private:
    FILE *f;
};
```

All that the constructors for these translators need do is remember which file they are associated with (attached to).

```
in::in(FILE *fp) : f(fp) {}  // constructors
out::out(FILE *fp) : f(fp) {}
```

The input operations can then use the low-level operations such as `fgetc` and `fscanf` provided by the `stdio` package, as shown in the following:

```
in &in::operator,(int &n)
{
  int v, got = fscanf(f,"%d",&v);
                          // use stdio to get an int
  if (got == 1) n = v;
  return *this;           // return a reference to the
                          // input object
}
```

Notice that the argument to these input functions is a nonconstant reference to the object into which the value is to be read. It can't be `const` because the reference is being used to affect the value of the argument object.

All of the input operator functions return a reference to the `in` object for which they were called, rather like an assignment operator. The input operation gives the `in` object a new state, and we want this new state to be available at the next use of the `in` object. A return value of the required type is obtained by dereferencing the `this` pointer.

```
in &in::operator,(double &d)
{
```

```
    double v;
    int got = fscanf(f,"%lf",&v);
    if (got == 1) d = v;
    return *this;
}
```

The input operator for a string takes a pointer rather than a reference argument, as follows:

```
in &in::operator,(char *s)
{
    fscanf(f,"%s",s);
    return *this;
}
```

```
in &in::operator,(char &c)
{
  for (int v = fgetc(f); isspace(v); v = fgetc(f)) ;
  if (v != EOF) c = v;
  return *this;
}
```

The output operators follow the same general pattern, except that the arguments are either passed by value or are references to const objects or pointers to const objects. There is no intention of modifying the object associated with the argument.

The output operator functions also return a reference to the object for which they were called, as shown in the following:

```
out &out::operator,(int n)
{
    fprintf(f, "%d ",n);    // use fprintf for actual output
    return *this;           // return reference to output object
}
```

```
out &out::operator,(double d)
{
    fprintf(f, "%f ",d);
    return *this;
}
```

```
out &out::operator,(const char *s)
{
    fprintf(f, "%s ",s);
    return *this;
}
```

```
out &out::operator,(char c)
{
    fputc(c, f);
    return *this;
}
```

To test this, we input some values then echo them back, using instances of the in and out classes:

```
void main()
{
// define instances of the in and out classes using the
// file handles for the standard input and standard output
    in is = stdin;
    out os = stdout;
    int n;
    double d;
    char c, buf[80];

// input an int, a double and a string
    is, n, d, buf;
// output a string constant, the int, the double,
// the input string and a character.
    os, "Hello world", n, d, buf, '\n';
}
```

This simple example works fine as far as it goes, which is in fact almost as far as some of the early implementations of the older Stream library.

The successive output operations illustrated resolve to

```
(((((os.operator,("Hello World)).operator,(n)).operator,(d)).
    operator,(buf)). operator,('\n')
```

a syntax that is type safe. The compiler won't allow us to output anything it can't convert to match an argument to one of the overloaded operator comma functions. Written like this, it's an impossible syntax for output; however, overloading the comma operator makes the syntax quite tractable and still type safe.

The input operations resolve to

```
((is.operator,(n)).operator,(d)).operator,(buf);
```

The associativity of the comma operator turns out to be what we want, left to right, so that in both input and output, the items get processed in a logical order.

The precedence of the comma operator is also exceedingly low, so we can write

```
os, n << 3;
```

which the operator precedences make the same as

```
os, (n << 3);
```

The translator prints out the value of n left-shifted by three bits. In fact to achieve output of any expression, only comma expressions need to be explicitly parenthesized in this context.

The only objection to using the comma operator is that it doesn't give any indication of whether it's being used as an input or output operator. This could be inconvenient in the case of multi-line output statements such as

```
os,
// page or screen break
    , d1
    , "% annually or\n"
    , d2
    , "% if calculated monthly\n";
```

In a case like this, it might not always be obvious whether a particular code line is dealing with input or output. A pair of operators with symmetry would be better.

The lowest precedence symmetrical pair of operators turns out to be << and >>, which is why they were used in the Stream library, and subsequently in IOStreams, in otherwise much the same way as we have used the comma operator in our example. The input and output functions providing these operations are dealt with in detail in Chapters 8 and 9.

8

Output Translation–
Class `ostream`

IOStreams provide translator classes for input and output, istream and ostream, respectively. We introduce the output-translator base class, ostream, first because it's the one users usually encounter first. Also, in some respects, output is easier to deal with and to describe than is input. We discuss the public interface of an ostream in two ways: first in the form in which it appears in the header file iostream.h—all the functions in the public interface are shown there—and second by describing the functions in more detail and in groups determined by their purpose.

8.1 The Public Interface

The ostream class is defined in the IOStreams header file iostream.h. The comments describe the groupings that are used in the detailed descriptions of member functions that follow beginning in Section 8.2.

```
class ostream : virtual public ios {
public:
// Constructor/ destructor
```

```
  ostream(streambuf *);
  virtual ~ostream();

// Functions to simplify design of user-defined inserters
  int opfx();
  void osfx();

// Overloads of <<  - these are called "Inserters"
  ostream &operator<<(const char*);
  ostream &operator<<(const signed char*);
  ostream &operator<<(const unsigned char*);

  ostream &operator<<(char c);

  ostream &operator<<(signed char);
  ostream &operator<<(short);
  ostream &operator<<(int);
  ostream &operator<<(long);

  ostream &operator<<(unsigned char);
  ostream &operator<<(unsigned short);
  ostream &operator<<(unsigned int);
  ostream &operator<<(unsigned long);
  ostream &operator<<(float);
  ostream &operator<<(double);
// possibly
// ostream &operator<<(long double);

  ostream &operator<<(void *);

  ostream &operator<<(streambuf *);

  ostream &operator<<(ostream &(*)(ostream &));
  ostream &operator<<(ios &(*)(ios &));

// Unformatted output functions
  ostream &put(char c);
  ostream &put(signed char c);
  ostream &put(unsigned char c);
  ostream &write(const char *data, int size);
  ostream &write(const signed char *data, int size);
  ostream &write(const unsigned char *data, int size);
```

```
// Synchronize the output device with what has been dispatched
   ostream &flush();

// Seek and tell functions
   ostream &seekp(streampos position);
   ostream &seekp(streamoff offset, seek_dir direction);
   streampos tellp();
};
```

8.2 Function Descriptions—ostream

All functions described next require the inclusion either of iostream.h or of some header file which itself includes iostream.h. The ostream class is derived from class ios, so all functions listed for class ios can also be called for an ostream object.

Prefix and suffix functions

```
int ostream::opfx();
void ostream::osfx();
```

These two functions are responsible for error checking and propagation and are provided to simplify the coding of inserter functions. The first one, the prefix function, does any flushing required by the associated ios tie; the second one, the suffix function, does any flushing required if either ios::unitbuf or ios::stdio are set.

The prefix function returns a nonzero value if translation can proceed, that is, if none of the bits in the error state are set; otherwise it returns 0. The suffix function has no return value. Routine use of the prefix function ensures that insertion operations can't affect an ostream that has its error state set.

The latest ANSI discussion documents indicate that both may also perform other system-dependent actions. A typical such action is locking and unlocking a thread in a multi-threaded environment. The prefix function locks the thread and the suffix function subsequently unlocks it, thus ensuring that the unit output operation isn't interrupted. However, no assumptions can be made about such unspecified extra actions. It follows that the prefix and suffix functions should be used when coding an inserter for a user-defined type, even if they appear to be redundant. For example, consider the following trivial class Pair:

```
struct Pair {
   int a, b;
};
```

```
ostream &operator<<(ostream &s, const Pair &p)
{
  if (s.opfx()) {
    s << '(' << p.a << ':' << p.b << ')';
    s.osfx();
  }
  return s;
}
```

The specification of the `opfx` and `osfx` functions isn't entirely satisfactory. As we hinted, if there are no system-dependent actions, the `Pair` inserter code contains redundant function calls. The insertion of '(' will cause the prefix function to be called, and the suffix function will be called as part of the insertion of ')'.

On the other hand, such unspecified actions can be very useful for modifying the behavior of an `ostream`. For example, you can make the suffix function insert a space between output items, thus allowing

```
double i,j,k;
cout << i << j << k << endl;
```

rather than

```
cout << i << ' ' << j << ' ' << ' ' << k << endl;
```

Another example relates to the width setting for the stream. The field width is normally set back to 0 by an insertion operation. This can be done conveniently by the suffix function. In some applications, such as displaying tables, it might also be convenient to latch the width setting. Such latching is easily implemented in a suffix function that is responsible for resetting the field width.

As it is, implementors of IOStreams have two options if such extra facilities are to be provided. They can use the prefix and suffix functions and tell the user that `opfx` and `osfx` must always be called in an inserter for a user-defined type. Alternatively, they can write the extra operations into the built-in inserters. The first requires less of the user and generally should be the preferred method. In the latter case, the user must be cautioned to include the same extra operations in any user-defined inserter, if they are required. Either way the implementation is likely to be nonstandard. Alternatively, you might assume, they can derive a new `ostream` type class with the required behavior. The snag here is that since class `ostream` has no virtual functions except for its destructor, variants can't be derived that differ only in their prefix and suffix behavior.

It might be that the prefix and suffix functions should be virtual. Then it would be possible to provide a base version of IOStreams in which the prefix and suffix functions performed no unspecified operations. Derived versions could provide extra or system-dependent facilities using alternative versions of the prefix and suffix functions. However, these functions would still need to be called routinely in all inserters.

Inserters shown as examples in this book will make the conservative assumption and call the prefix and suffix functions even if they don't appear to be necessary.

In an implementation that supports exceptions, the prefix function will throw an exception if it is called when any bit in the error state corresponds to a bit in the exception mask. Since at that point it's not possible to determine what caused the error, the exception thrown should be of type ios::failure.

Insertion operations–operator<<

The following inserter functions are supplied as part of the IOStreams library:

```
ostream &operator<<(const char*);
ostream &operator<<(const signed char*);
ostream &operator<<(const unsigned char*);

ostream &operator<<(char c);

ostream &operator<<(signed char);
ostream &operator<<(short);
ostream &operator<<(int);
ostream &operator<<(long);

ostream &operator<<(unsigned char);
ostream &operator<<(unsigned short);
ostream &operator<<(unsigned int);
ostream &operator<<(unsigned long);

ostream &operator<<(float);
ostream &operator<<(double);

ostream &operator<<(void *);

ostream &operator<<(streambuf *);

ostream &operator<<(ostream &(*)(ostream &));
ostream &operator<<(ios &(*)(ios &));  // manipulator inserter
```

All the built-in inserters except the manipulator inserter first call the inserter prefix function opfx. If that function returns 0—signifying some error has occurred—

then the inserter returns immediately. Otherwise the function inserts a character sequence representing the argument object into the associated `streambuf`. If the operation fails, the error flags will be set. This should only occur because of an `EOF` condition returned by the associated `streambuf`. In an implementation that supports exceptions, if the error bits set include one that is set in the exception mask, the inserter will rethrow the `streambuf` exception it caught.

The conversion process is controlled by the format flags and state variables of the parent `ios` part of the `ostream` object. For the built-in types, the process happens as follows. First, if `ios::right` (right justification) is set or if no flag bit in `ios::adjustfield` is set and the set width for the `ostream` is not 0, then an appropriate number of the currently set fill characters are inserted. Then the type object is inserted. The actions for specific types are set out in the following paragraphs.

After the translation of the type value, if `ios::left` (left justification) is set and the set width for the `ostream` is nonzero, an appropriate number of the currently set fill characters are inserted. After the width setting has been used to determine how many fill characters are required, the width format parameter for the stream is reset to 0.

Finally, except in the case of output from a `streambuf`, the `ostream` suffix function `osfx` is called. User-defined inserters should generally follow the spirit of these conversion rules and, in particular, should call `opfx` and `osfx` in the same way. The inserter functions for the built-in types return a reference to the `ostream` into which the insertion was made. User-defined inserters should do the same. The syntax is by now familiar, as follows:

```
int i;
double d;
char *string;

cout << i << d << string;
```

In this example, the first use of the `<<` operator, `cout << i`, evaluates to a reference to the `ostream cout`, so the next use of the `<<` operator is `cout << d`, and so on. The sequence of outputs therefore resolves to

```
(((cout.operator<<(i)).operator<<(d)).operator<<(string);
```

If a user-defined inserter doesn't return an ostream reference, it won't be able to participate as an item to the left of the `<<` operator in output sequences like the one in the example.

The built-in types and the results of their translation and insertion are as follows:

```
char
signed char
unsigned char
```

No translation is performed; the character is inserted in the `streambuf` as is.

```
char *
unsigned char *
signed char *
```

The character sequence the pointer addresses, up to but not including the terminating `'\0'` character, is transferred as is with each element treated as type `char`.

```
short
int
long
unsigned short
unsigned
unsigned long
```

If either `ios::oct` or `ios::hex` is set and format flag `ios::showbase` is also set, octal values are prefixed with a `'0'` character and hex values are prefixed either with `"0x"` or with `"0X"` (if format flag `ios::uppercase` is set). Otherwise, if the argument is negative, a minus sign is generated; if the argument is positive and the `ios::showpos` flag is set, a plus sign is generated. If `ios::internal` is set and the set width for the `ostream` is nonzero, then an appropriate number of the currently set fill characters are inserted.

Translation of the integer is to a string of digits consisting of the following:

- `'0'`–`'7'` if format flag `ios::oct` is set
- `'0'`–`'9'` and `'a'`-`'f'` or `'A'`-`'F'` if `ios::hex` is set
- `'0'`–`'9'` otherwise

If `ios::oct` or `ios::hex` is set, the representation is of the argument as an unsigned value.

Note that the distinct types `signed char` and `unsigned char` are treated as if they are plain `char`. We think this is inappropriate. In practice such variables are mostly used as byte-wide integers, that is, values in the ranges −128 to 127 and 0 to 255 respectively. They could well be treated this way on output, since single characters are adequately represented by the type `char`.

```
void *
```

This inserter provides for the display of the value of pointer variables. The actual representation of pointers is implementation dependent. In IOStreams implementations for MS-DOS or the 16-bit versions of OS/2, when some of their memory models are used, the pointer value can be displayed as a segment-offset pair, usually represented as hex digits (hhhh:hhhh). In the case of small model (single-segment) programs, the segment part is usually omitted and a plain hexadecimal offset value (hhhh) displayed. In the case of systems with a large linear address space, the pointer representation can be either the same as that of an unsigned `long` with `ios::showbase` set (0xhhhhhhhh) or a plain hex number.

```
float
double
long double
```

Negative numbers are always preceded by a minus sign. Positive numbers are preceded by a plus sign only if `ios::showpos` is set. If `ios::internal` is set and the set width for the `ostream` is nonzero, then an appropriate number of the currently set fill characters are inserted. If the `ios::scientific` format flag is set, the floating-point inserters produce a representation with one digit before the decimal point and a number of digits after the decimal point equal to the return value of `precision()`. The exponent is introduced by the character `'e'` or if `ios::uppercase` is set, by `'E'`. The exponent part is always explicitly signed. Extraneous trailing 0's and the decimal point, if there are no nonzero digits after it, are stripped, unless `ios::showpoint` is set. In the latter case, the decimal point and any trailing 0's necessary to pad out to the required precision are retained.

If the `ios::fixed` format flag is set, then the floating-point inserters use `precision()` to determine the number of digits after the decimal point. As with `ios::scientific` trailing 0's and the decimal point are stripped unless `ios::showpoint` is set.

Finally, if neither `iso::scientific` nor `ios::fixed` is set, numbers with exponents smaller than −4 or greater than `precision()` are printed, just as if `ios:scientific` were set. Other numbers will be printed using 0's as required to explicitly show the decimal point.

Note, the radix flags, `ios::dec`, `ios::oct`, and `ios::hex` do not affect floating-point output.

```
streambuf*
```

All characters that can be extracted from the `streambuf` are sent without padding or translation to the `ostream`. The process stops only when the source `streambuf` signals an `EOF` condition.

```
ostream &(*)(ostream &)
ios &(*)(ios &)
```
Pointers to functions of these particular forms[†] are treated specially. They act as parameterless manipulators. That is, the `operator<<` function doesn't necessarily translate them into characters in the output stream; rather it has some effect on

the `ostream` object involved. By the same token, no padding is applied to these insertions. The following manipulators of this sort are provided in the standard implementation of IOStreams:

```
os << dec;          // os.setf(ios::dec, ios::basefield);
os << oct;          // sets ios::oct similarly
os << hex;          // sets ios::hex similarly
os << flush;        // Flushes the streambuf
```

Some manipulators of this type, as follows, do produce output and might or might not also have side effects, such as flushing the stream:

```
os << ends;         // Null terminates a string
os << endl;         // Adds a newline and flushes
```

This selection seems somewhat arbitrary. Gratuitous pollution of the global name-space should be avoided, but if that were the primary consideration it seems unlikely that this set of manipulators would be provided. Convenience is also a consideration.

Manipulators could well be provided for all of the changes that can be made by appropriate setting of format state flags, specifically those listed below:

```
os << leftjust;     // os.setf(ios::left, ios::adjustfield);
os << rightjust;    // os.setf(ios::right, ios::adjustfield);

os << showbase;     // os.setf(ios::showbase);
os << showpoint;    // os.setf(ios::showpoint);
os << uppercase;    // os.setf(ios::uppercase);

os << fixed;        // os.setf(ios::fixed, ios::floatfield);
os << scientific;   // os.setf(ios::scientific,
                    //            ios::floatfield);
os << floating;     // os.unsetf(ios::floatfield |
                    // ios::showpoint | ios::showpos);
                    // - floating-point defaults
```

These extra manipulators can easily be added to the standard IOStreams system by users. They are implemented by providing functions like the following:

```
// built-in manipulator
ios &dec(ios &s)
{
  s.setf(ios::dec, ios::basefield);
```

---

†Pointer to function taking `ostream` reference argument, and returning `ostream` reference, and pointer to function taking `ios` reference argument, and returning `ios` reference.

```
    return s;
}

// user supplied manipulator
ostream &leftjust(ostream &s)
{
    s.setf(ios::left, ios::adjustfield);
    return s;
}
```

The following useful manipulators should pose no difficulties to IOStreams system designers and could also be provided:

```
os << stickywidth;
                    // don't reset width to zero after each item
os << spacing;      // insert a space after everything but endl,
                    // ends, etc.
os << defaults;     // set stream to its default state
os << page;         // endl + form feed
```

8.3 Unformatted Output Operations

A number of output functions are provided that can be regarded as "raw," or low level. They are, in some cases, also described as binary output functions. These differ from the insertion operators in that they don't call the `osfx` suffix function. This stipulation is made explicitly in the AT&T documentation and in earlier versions of the ANSI discussion document. Later versions of the ANSI document omit it. This discrimination between `opfx` and `osfx` has been taken by some implementors to mean that `opfx` should be called. This has been assumed in the function descriptions which follow.

If these functions are intended only as low-level operations for use in inserter functions, there seems to be no good reason why the prefix or suffix function should be used. This will be done by the surrounding inserter function. Calling the prefix function in the unformatted output functions will result in a needless call to the flush function for any tied `ostream`. Provided the unformatted output functions set the error state on failure, the inserter function is in a position to test their outcome and proceed or quit as appropriate. However, these functions do tend to be used interchangeably with the inserters.

For example, the `Pair` inserter could be rewritten as

```
ostream &operator<<(ostream &s, const Pair &p)
{
```

```
if (opfx()) {
  char buf[80];
  s.put('(');
  itoa(p.a, buf, 10);
  s.write(buf, strlen(buf));
  s.put(',');
  itoa(p.b, buf, 10);
  s.write(buf, strlen(buf));
  s.put(')');
  osfx();
}
  return s;
}
```

The unformatted output functions must set the stream error state if they fail. In an implementation that supports exceptions, error bits set that include one set in the exception mask cause the function to throw an exception. The exception thrown is likely to be one that was thrown by the associated streambuf.

The following put functions first call the prefix function:

```
ostream &ostream::put(char c);
ostream &ostream::put(signed char c);
ostream &ostream::put(unsigned char c);
```

If doing this returns a nonzero value, the argument character is stuffed into the associated streambuf. If the operation fails, the error flags are set. The suffix function is not called. For example,

```
cout.width(3);
cout.put('a');
cout << 'b' << endl;  // output is a  b
                      // width setting applied to 'b'
                      // by inserter
```

Like the previous put functions, the following write functions first call the prefix function:

```
ostream &ostream::write(const char *data,  int size);
ostream &ostream::write(const signed char *data,  int size);
ostream &ostream::write(const unsigned char *data,  int size);
```

If opfx returns a nonzero value, an attempt is made to stuff the size characters, starting at address data, into the associated streambuf. If the operation fails, the error flags are set. The suffix function is not called. For example,

```
Thing x;
```

```
ofstream osf("output.dat", ios::out | ios::binary);
          // a file based ostream
osf.write((char *) &x, sizeof(Thing));
          // copy x as is
```

Like the inserter functions, the unformatted output functions return a reference to the `ostream` object for which they were called.

Since the `write` function is likely to be used in contexts such as the preceding example, it's surprising that the IOStreams definition doesn't more closely mimic the C standard library `fwrite` and provide

```
ostream &ostream::write(const void *data, size_t size);
```

8.4 Flushing an `ostream`

The flush function

```
ostream &ostream::flush();
```

calls the `sync` function of the associated `streambuf` to ensure that all output is up to date, that is, all characters that have been put to the `streambuf` have been sent to their final destination, the external device to which the `streambuf` relates. It is equivalent to `rdbuf()→sync();`

```
cout << "Enter a number between one and ten: ";
cout.flush();   // this is actually extraneous because cin's
                // tie to cout will do the same thing.
int i;
cin >> i;
```

The flush function returns a reference to the `ostream` object for which it was called.

8.5 Seeking on an Output Stream

In the case of the most commonly used output stream, `cout`, which is normally tied to the screen or console output, seeking will probably be an error. However, in the case of `ostream` objects that are tied to a file, it's sometimes desirable to reposition the put pointer of the file. This sort of operation is supported by the `filebuf` class. The following functions that support seeking are provided by the `ostream` class:

```
ostream &ostream::seekp(streampos);
ostream &ostream::seekp(streamoff, seek_dir);
```

These functions position the put pointer of the associated streambuf. In the case of a file-based ostream, the action is similar to that of the stdio fseek function. Positioning is discussed further in Chapter 5 where we described class streambuf and in Chapter 11 dealing with filebuf.

The absolute form (seekp(pos)) is interpreted as seekp(pos, ios::beg), that is, relative to the start of the streambuf (file or sequence). The streampos and streamoff values used as arguments to these functions should be regarded as "magic cookies," that is, not something that is calculated but rather something that was provided by the complementary member function tellp. However, the particular values streampos(0) and streamoff(0) should always be safe.

```
ofstream ofs("output.dat");
ofs.seekp(0);     // position at start of file
ofs.put('\0');    // modify file heads
ofs.seekp(0, ios::end);
                  // back to appending
```

Remember that in some environments (MS-DOS and OS/2 in particular), it's normal to convert newline characters to CR/LF pairs before they are sent to an actual output device and to convert CR/LF pairs to newline characters on input. So in these environments, even if you have kept track of how many characters (n) have been sent to a stream, there is no guarantee that seeking back, os.seekp(-n, ios::cur), will return you to an earlier position.

We don't know of any documentation regarding what happens to the error state if the corresponding streambuf function fails. Typical implementations set the error state to ios::failbit. Failure will occur if the output stream involved doesn't support seeking. In current implementations, the criterion used internally to determine this is usually the UNIX-like function isatty. This function takes an int file descriptor argument and returns nonzero if the device in question is terminal-like. If isatty(file_descriptor) returns 0, an attempt will be made to do the seek.

The seekp functions, which are omitted from the ANSI discussion document, return a reference to the ostream object for which they were called.

```
streampos ostream::tellp();
```

The tellp function returns the current put position in the associated streambuf (see Chapters 4, 11, and 13, which deal with classes streambuf, filebuf, and strstreambuf, respectively). You should treat the return value as a "magic cookie," that is, don't modify it; rather, use it as an argument to seekp to return to the same position later, as shown in the following:

```
ofstream ofs("output.dat");
streampos sp = ofs.tellp();
ofs.seekp(0);        // position at start of file
ofs.put('\0');       // modify status or whatever
ofs.seekp(sp);       // go back to where we were before
```

The return value is of type `streampos`, which is a `long` in many implementations of IOStreams but which is also implementation dependent.

The ANSI discussion documents omit this function.

8.6 Constructor for `ostream`

```
ostream::ostream(streambuf *);
```

The `ostream` constructor takes as its argument a pointer to the `streambuf` object that is to be used as the intermediary between the `ostream` and the actual output device.

8.7 Summary

As we have seen, the sleight of hand involved in

```
cout << "Hello World";
```

no longer seems magical. The comma operator example in Chapter 7 showed us how this output statement works. Remember, however, that IOStreams uses the primitives provided by the `streambuf` class to obtain and dispatch characters where the comma operator example uses the `stdio` facilities. The `ostream`'s capabilities are expanded beyond those of the comma example by overloading the `operator<<` function for more types and by deriving class `ostream` from class `ios` so that its error recording and format specification information can be used. The multiple overloads of `operator<<` are known as **inserters**; they insert character sequences representing data types into the output stream. In the IOStreams system, given

```
class T;    // T is a type, built-in or user-defined
ostream s;
T x;
```

then

```
s << x;
```

is either a compilation error or inserts into the output stream a proper representation of `'x'`. This is possibly converted by the compiler to a type for which there is a matching `operator<<` function. Contrast the behavior with the facilities available in C, where for instance,

```
enum dummy { first, second };
printf("%ld, %ld\n", first, second);
```

will compile but may print garbage if `sizeof(int)` is not equal to `sizeof(long)`.

Class `ostream` provides a set of lower-level functions called unformatted output functions to deal with byte values, that is, single characters, null-terminated strings, and arbitrary-sized blocks of characters. Some functions are provided to access the sequence positioning and synchronization facilities of the associated `streambuf`.

The `ostream` class is derived from class `ios`, so all the functions listed for class `ios` can be called for an `ostream` object also.

9

Input and Bidirectional Translation–Classes istream and iostream

In this chapter, we describe the input-translator base class, istream, and the bidirectional translator class, iostream.

We discuss the public interface of these classes in two ways: first in the form in which it appears in the header file iostream.h—all the functions in the public interface are shown there—and second by describing the functions in more detail and in groups determined by their purpose.

9.1 The Public Interface–Class istream

The istream class is defined in the IOStreams header file iostream.h. The comments describe the groupings that are used in the detailed descriptions of member functions that follow beginning in Section 9.2.

```
class istream : virtual public ios {
public:
// constructor/destructor
    istream(streambuf *);
    virtual ~istream();
```

```
// Prefix function
    int ipfx(int noskipws = 0);

// Extractors
    istream &operator>>(char *);
    istream &operator>>(signed char *s);
    istream &operator>>(unsigned char *s);

    istream &operator>>(char &);

    istream &operator>>(signed char &c);
    istream &operator>>(unsigned char &);

    istream &operator>>(short &);
    istream &operator>>(int &);
    istream &operator>>(long &);

    istream &operator>>(unsigned short &);
    istream &operator>>(unsigned int &);
    istream &operator>>(unsigned long &);

    istream &operator>>(float &);
    istream &operator>>(double &);

    istream &operator>>(streambuf*);

    istream &operator>>(istream &(*)(istream&));
    istream &operator>>(ios &(*)(ios&));

// Unformatted input functions
    istream &get(char *data, int length,
                    char delimiter = '\n');
    istream &get(signed char *data, int length,
                    char delimiter = '\n');
    istream &get(unsigned char *data, int length,
                    char delimiter = '\n');
    istream &get(char &destination);
    istream &get(signed char &destination);
    istream &get(unsigned char &destination);
    istream &get(streambuf &destination,
                    char delimiter = '\n');

    int get();
```

```
    int peek() const;
    istream &read(char *data, int size);
    istream &read(signed char *data, int size);
    istream &read(unsigned char *data, int size);
    istream &getline(char *data, int length,
                     char delimiter = '\n');
    istream &getline(signed char *data, int length,
                     char delimiter = '\n');
    istream &getline(unsigned char *data, int length,
                     char delimiter = '\n');

    int gcount() const;

// Flushing
    int sync();

    istream &ignore(int length, int delimiter = EOF);

    istream &putback(char c);

// Seeking the get pointer
    istream &seekg(streampos);
    istream &seekg(streamoff, seek_dir);
    streampos tellg();
};
```

9.2 Function Descriptions –istream

All functions described next require the inclusion of iostream.h or some header file that itself includes iostream.h.

Input prefix function

```
int istream::ipfx(int noskipws = 0);
```

Provided to simplify coding of extractors, this function is responsible for whitespace skipping and for error checking and propagation. A nonzero error status causes ipfx to turn on ios::failbit and return 0 immediately. If no error is flagged, ipfx flushes any tied ostream. Then if the ios::skipws format flag is set and noskipws is 0, whitespace characters are fetched from the input stream until either an EOF condition is reached, or a nonwhitespace character is detected. If an EOF condition occurs while skipping whitespace, the error state bits ios::failbit | ios::eofbit are set and ipfx returns 0; otherwise it returns nonzero.

Formatted input functions call ipfx with noskipws equal to 0, and unformatted input functions call ipfx with noskipws nonzero.

According to the latest ANSI discussion document, the prefix function may also undertake unspecified system-dependent operations. Note also that the latest discussion document also specifies an input suffix function as follows:

```
void istream::isfx();
```

It's not clear at this time what this will do. Its purpose is presumably to provide a placeholder for the undoing of the unspecified system-dependent operations allowed by ipfx.

Because the input prefix and suffix functions can undertake unspecified operations, they, or at least in current versions the prefix function, should be included routinely in extractors for all user-defined types, as shown in the following. (We discuss this type of requirement in Section 8.3, where we cover the ostream prefix and suffix functions.)

```
struct Pair {
  int a, b;
};
istream &operator>>(istream &s, Pair &p)
{
  if (ipfx(0)) {
    // whatever is required
    // isfx();
    // in the future
    ...
  }
  return s;
}
```

Because ipfx() sets the flags on failure, it's equally acceptable to use

```
istream &operator>>(istream &s, Pair &p)
{
  if (!ipfx()) return s;

  // whatever
  return s;
}
```

In an implementation that supports exceptions, the prefix function may throw an exception. This will happen if it detects an error state and sets ios::failbit and then one of the error state bits set corresponds to a bit in the exception mask. The exception thrown will be of type ios::failure since no other information will be available.

Extraction operations - operator>>

The following extractors are supplied as part of the IOStreams library:

```
istream &operator>>(char *);
istream &operator>>(signed char *s);
istream &operator>>(unsigned char *s);

istream &operator>>(char &);

istream &operator>>(signed char &c);
istream &operator>>(short &);
istream &operator>>(int &);
istream &operator>>(long &);

istream &operator>>(unsigned char &);
istream &operator>>(unsigned short &);
istream &operator>>(unsigned int &);
istream &operator>>(unsigned long &);

istream &operator>>(float &);
istream &operator>>(double &);
istream &operator>>(long double&);

istream &operator>>(streambuf*);

istream &operator>>(istream &(*)(istream&));
istream &operator>>(ios &(*)(ios&));
```

These extractors first call the extractor prefix function ipfx with its default argument value of 0. If ipfx returns 0, that is, some error has occurred, then the inserter does nothing; otherwise it parses the incoming character sequence in an attempt to form a value of the required type.

If the operation fails, the error flags will be set. The ios::failbit flag is set if input of the required type is detectably incomplete, and either an unexpected character or EOF condition is detected. In the latter case, ios::eofbit is also set. The `ios::failbit` flag should also be set if the input is such as to cause overflow of the specified type. For example, scanning the stream

```
abcdefg
```

for an integer will result in `failbit`'s being set because no suitable characters were found though none will be lost.

On the other hand, scanning the stream

```
1.2e-a1
```

for a double will cause `failbit` to be set. In some implementations, it might cause `badbit` to be set, since characters will probably have been lost in determining that the input is not a proper representation of a floating-point number. Note, the ANSI discussion document calls only for setting of `failbit`.

For the shorter stream

```
1.2e-
```

`failbit`, `eofbit`, and possibly `badbit` will be set, since the input was not complete, characters were taken, and there is an `EOF` condition.

In an implementation that supports exceptions, the extractor will throw an exception if at this point one of the error state bits that are set matches a bit in the exception mask. The exception thrown may be one that was thrown by the associated `streambuf` and caught by the extractor.

The conversion process is controlled by the format flags and state variables of the `ios` part of the `istream` object.

Conversion of the Built-in Types.   Built-in type objects are converted as follows

```
char&
signed char&
unsigned char&
```

A single character is taken from the input stream and stored in the referenced character variable. Remember that whitespace will be skipped unless skipping has been explicitly disabled. If what you need is the next character value, regardless of what it is, use `istream::get`, or disable whitespace skipping.

```
char*
signed char*
unsigned char*
```

Characters are extracted and stored in the indicated array until a whitespace character is encountered, or if `width()` is nonzero until `width()-1` characters have been extracted, or until an `EOF` condition is encountered. If termination is by a whitespace character, that character is not extracted. A terminating null character is then stored in the array, and if EOF was encountered storing of a null may be the only result. The field width is reset to 0.

```
short&
int&
long&
unsigned short&
unsigned&
unsigned long&
```

Conversion is controlled by the basefield format flags. The first character may be a sign, either '+' or '-'. Digits are then accepted until a nondigit is encountered. If ios::oct is set, the acceptable digits are '0' through '7'; if ios::dec is set, '0' through '9'; and if ios::hex is set, '0' through '9' and 'a' through 'f' (either uppercase or lowercase). If no basefield format flag is set, then the character stream is interpreted according to C++ language conventions. That is, if the number starts with a '0', then scanning proceeds as if ios::oct were set. If the sequence begins with "0x" or "0X", then scanning proceeds as if ios::hex was set; otherwise scanning looks for a decimal integer.

As in the ostream case, the signed and unsigned char variants get lumped in with plain char, when they might well be treated as byte-wide integers.

```
float&
double&
long double&
```

Conversion is according to the C++ syntax for constants of these types, excluding any suffix character. That is,

```
1.2e-01f  // float constant - 'f' not scanned
1.2e-01L  // long double const, but 'L' not scanned
```

```
streambuf*
```

All the characters that can be extracted from the input source are transferred as is to the referenced streambuf. Extraction stops only when an EOF condition occurs on the istream or the streambuf. If no characters are extracted from the istream (because of an immediate EOF), the error state bits ios::failbit | ios::eofbit are turned on. If the transfer stops because of an EOF on the istream, then ios::eofbit is turned on. However, if the transfer stops because a put to the target streambuf failed, the character remains available on the istream and the error state is unchanged.

```
istream &(*)(istream &)
ios &(*)(ios &)
```

Pointers to functions of this particular form[†] are treated specially. They act as parameterless manipulators, that is, the `operator>>` function doesn't necessarily cause characters to be taken from the input stream and translated to give a value; rather it has some effect on the `istream` object involved. Manipulators of this sort are provided as follows:

```
is >> dec;        // is.setf(ios::dec, ios::basefield);
is >> oct;        // sets ios::oct similarly
is >> hex;        // etc

is >> ws          // strips characters from the input stream
                  // for as long as they are whitespace
```

Following is an example of several type objects being extracted in sequence:

```
int i;
double d;
char buffer[10];

cin.width(10);
cin >> buffer >> i >> d;
```

In the example, the first use of the `>>` operator, `cin >> buffer`, evaluates to a reference to the `istream cin`, so the next use of `operator>>` is `cin >> i`, and so on. Therefore the sequence of inputs resolves to

```
((cin.operator>>(buffer)).operator>>(i)).operator>>(d);
```

The extractor functions all return a reference to the `istream` for which they were called.

Unformatted input operations

Several input functions are provided that can be regarded as "raw," or low level. They differ from the extraction operators in that they call the `ipfx` prefix function with a nonzero argument value. The result is that `ipfx` disables them if the error state is set. Otherwise these functions will flush any tied `ostream` but will **not** strip whitespace characters. The following unformatted input functions are therefore suitable as low-level operations for use in extractor functions:

```
int istream::get();
int istream::peek() const;
```

[†]Pointer to function taking `istream` reference argument and returning `istream` reference, and pointer to function taking `ios` reference argument and returning `ios` reference.

These functions return the value of the next character in the input stream or an EOF if no further character is available. The prefix function (ipfx(1)) is called, but the error state is not affected.

get advances the associated streambuf get pointer, while peek leaves it as it was, as follows:

```
// Input stream  "abcdefg"
int c = cin.peek()
if (c != EOF)
  cout << char(c);  // output is 'a'
c = cin.get();
if (c != EOF)
  cout << char(c);  // output is 'a'
c = cin.get();
if (c != EOF)
  cout << char(c);  // output is 'b'
```

Both functions return a positive int representing the character peeked or gotten, or EOF if no character was available.

The following unformatted-input get functions call the istream prefix function with a nonzero argument value, which means that no whitespace stripping takes place.

```
istream &istream::get(char &destination);
istream &istream::get(signed char &destination);
istream &istream::get(unsigned char &destination);
istream &istream::get(char *data, int length,
                                  char delimiter = '\n');
istream &istream::get(signed char *data, int length,
                                  char delimiter = '\n');
istream &istream::get(unsigned char *data, int length,
                                  char delimiter = '\n');
istream &istream::get(streambuf &sb, char delim = '\n');
```

The first three extract a single character and place it in the referenced variable. Those dealing with the various flavors of char* store characters in the indicated array, data, until one of the following occurs:

- The character nominated as delimiter is encountered (the delimiter is defaulted to the newline character)
- length-1 characters have been extracted
- An EOF condition is encountered

The delimiting character is not extracted. A null terminating character is then stored in the array, even if no characters were extracted.

The last one extracts characters and places them in the specified `streambuf` until one of the following occurs:

- The delimiter character is extracted
- `length-1` characters have been extracted
- An EOF condition is encountered on the destination `streambuf` or on the `istream`

The delimiter character is **not** transferred to the `streambuf`.

In all cases, if no characters could be got before the EOF on the `istream` the `failbit` as well as the `eofbit` flags are set. If the error bits set include one that is set in the exception mask, the function will throw an exception. The exception thrown is probably one that was thrown by the associated `streambuf`. The number of characters transferred in each case can be determined by immediately calling `gcount`.

```
// Input stream contains
// "The quick brown fox! - jumped or not?"

char buffer[80];
cin.get(buffer,80, '!');
// gets "The quick brown fox" into buffer
char c;
cin.get(c);
// gets '!' in c
cin.get(); cin.get(); cin.get();
char buf[6];
cin.get(buf,6);        // gets "jumped" into buf
int n = cin.gcount(); // n gets 6
```

```
istream &istream::getline(char *dest, int length, char delim = '\n');
```

This function acts in the same way as `get(char*, int, char)`, except that the delimiting character is extracted from the stream and thrown away. The number of characters transferred can be determined by immediately calling `gcount()`.

```
// Input stream contains
// "The quick brown fox! - jumped or not?"

char buffer[80];
cin.getline(buffer,80, '!');
// gets "The quick brown fox" into buffer
cin.get(c);
// gets a space in c - the delimiter is junked
```

The get/getline functions return a reference to the istream object for which they are called.

```
istream &istream::read(char *dest,  int n);
istream &istream::read(signed char *dest,  int n);
istream &istream::read(unsigned char *dest,  int n);
```

The read functions attempt to extract n bytes from the input stream and to place them at the specified address, dest. If fewer than n characters are transferred because of an EOF condition, the error state is set to ios::failbit | ios::eofbit. The number of characters transferred can be determined by immediately calling gcount(), as follows:

```
Thing x;
ifstream ifs("things.dat");
ifs.read(&x, sizeof(Thing));
if (ifs.gcount() != sizeof(Thing))
  ..;     // end of file before enough characters read
```

If there is no error, it's not necessary to check gcount because the requested number of characters will have been transferred. The read function also returns a reference to the istream object for which it was called.

```
int istream::gcount() const;
```

This function may be called after calling any of the unformatted input functions (get, getline, or read) to determine how many characters were transferred. gcount should be called immediately after the unformatted input function, since formatted input functions can use the unformatted functions and thus modify the value that will be returned. Examples of the use of this function is shown under the discussion of istream::read and on page 128.

```
istream &istream::ignore(int n, int delim = EOF);
```

This function causes characters to be taken from the input and ignored until one of the following occurs:

- n characters have been disposed of
- A character matching delim is extracted
- An EOF condition is encountered

If the default value for delim (EOF) is used, ignore stops only when n characters have been wasted or an EOF condition is reached.

```
// Input stream "abcdefghijk\n"
char buffer[80];
if (cin.ignore(80,'h').eof())
  ...;
```

```
} else {
  cin >> buffer;
  cout << buffer;  // output is "ijk"
}
```

This function also returns a reference to the istream object for which it was called.

Returning a character to the istream

```
istream &istream::putback(char c);
```

This function attempts to put the streambuf associated with the istream back into the condition it was in before the last character was extracted. The argument character should be the one that was just extracted from the stream; if it isn't, the behavior of the putback function is undefined (putback(c) is in fact rdbuf()->sputbackc(c)). If putback fails, the error state is set. The istream prefix function isn't called. However, if the error state was set when putback was called, putback does nothing. This function also returns a reference to the istream object for which it was called.

Synchronizing an istream

```
int istream::sync();
```

The sync function attempts to make the external source of characters (that which feeds the associated streambuf) consistent with the characters that have been extracted. Note that this might return characters that had been buffered to their original source.

This function is implemented as rdbuf()->sync(); it simply calls the sync function for the associated streambuf. As such its action is similar to the flush function of an ostream.

```
istream is(...);
// Ultimate source  "abcdefghijklmnopqrstuvwxyz"
// bold characters not yet read
// streambuf contents  "opqr"
// last character read was 'n'
is.sync();
// Ultimate source  "abcdefghijklmnopqrstuvwxyz"
// bold characters not yet read
// streambuf empty
// last character read was 'n'
```

As you can see, the source is effectively wound back by the four characters that remained available in the buffer.

The sync function returns EOF if an error occurs; otherwise it returns some other integer value. If there are characters in the buffer, the synchronization will involve seeking on the source. If the source doesn't support seeking, this action should cause an error return. The standard input is one such case. Usually it's not possible to seek on cin. So if there are characters in the buffer, cin.sync() should return EOF. What happens to the contents of the buffer under such circumstances is implementation dependent. They might well be thrown away. Consequently you might see code that uses the sync function as an alternative to the ignore function when the rest of an input line is to be ignored, as follows

```
cin.sync();        // should return EOF if characters waiting
                   // but may empty the buffer as a side effect
cin.ignore(INT_MAX,'\n');
                   // explicitly dumps characters up to and
                   // including the newline.
```

If portability is an issue, use ignore.

Seeking on an input stream

As just noted, seeking will probably be an error in the case of the standard input, which is normally tied to the keyboard or console input. However, in the case of istream objects that are tied to a file, it's often desirable to reposition the file's get pointer. This sort of operation is supported by the filebuf class. The following functions to support seeking are provided by the istream class:

```
istream &istream::seekg(streampos);
istream &istream::seekg(streamoff, seek_dir);
```

These functions position the get pointer of the associated streambuf. In the case of a file-based istream, the action is similar to that of the stdio fseek function. Positioning is discussed further in Chapters 5, 11, and 13, where we describe classes streambuf, filebuf, and strstreambuf.

The absolute form (seekg(pos)) is interpreted as seekg(pos, ios::beg), that is, relative to the start of the streambuf (file). The value used as the first argument to seekg should be regarded as a "magic cookie," that is, not something that is calculated, but rather something that was provided by the complementary member function tellg. The particular values streampos(0) and streamoff(0) are safe, however.

In the case of relative seeks (for example, seekg(0, end)) the seekoff value 0 is safe; other values, however, should be treated with caution. Remember that under DOS, for instance, it is normal to convert newline characters to CR/LF pairs before they are sent to an actual output device and to convert CR/LF pairs to newline characters on input.

```
ifstream ifs("input.dat");
...;
ifs.seekg(0);              // position at start of file
int status = ifs.get();    // read data from file header
```

We know of no documentation of what happens to the error state if the corresponding `streambuf` function fails. Typical implementations will set the error state to `ios::failbit`.

Both of these functions return a reference to the `istream` object for which they were called. Note that the ANSI discussion document omits these functions.

```
streampos istream::tellg();
```

This function returns the current "position" in the associated `streambuf` (see Chapters 5, 11, and 13, where we discuss classes `streambuf`, `filebuf`, and `strstreambuf`). You should treat the return value of `tellg` as a "magic cookie," that is, don't modify it; rather just use it as an argument to `seekg` to return to the same position later.

```
ifstream ifs("input.dat");
...;
streampos sp = ifs.tellg();
ifs.seekg(0);    // position at start of file
...;
ifs.seekg(sp);
             // go back to whatever
```

The return value is of type `streampos`, `long` in many implementations of IOStreams but may be a class type. You should make no assumptions. Note that the ANSI discussion document omits this function.

Constructor–`istream`

```
istream::istream(streambuf *);
```

The `istream` constructor requires as its argument a pointer to the `streambuf` object that is to be used as the intermediary between the `istream` and the actual input device.

9.3 Bidirectional IO–Class iostream

Class iostream provides both the input operations of class istream and the output operations of class ostream. The current version of the ANSI discussion document doesn't include this class because the same effect should be available by instantiating an istream and an ostream to use the same streambuf.

Like the constructors for istream and ostream, the constructor takes as its argument a pointer to an appropriate streambuf.

9.4 The Public Interface–Class iostream

The public interface of class iostream is the union of the interfaces of classes ios, ostream, and istream, and it differs only in the constructor and destructor.

```
class iostream : public istream, public ostream {
public:
    iostream(streambuf*);
    ~iostream();

    // No extra public functions beyond those provided by
    // ios
    // istream
    // ostream
};
```

9.5 Summary

Class istream provides input operations that mirror the output operations of class ostream. The right shift operator is overloaded to provide a similar convenient notation for input operations. These overloads deal with input of the user-defined types. Class istream is designed to make implementation of input for built-in types simple and type-safe. The multiple overloads of the operator>> function are known as extractors, that is, they extract typed values from character sequences in the input stream. In the IOStreams system, given

```
class T;  // T is a type, built-in or user-defined
istream s;
T x;
```

then

```
s >> x;
```

either is a compilation error or causes the input to be parsed to translate it into a value of type T. If the character stream is inconsistent with the type, the error state will be set appropriately.

A set of lower-level functions called unformatted output functions are provided to deal with byte values, that is, single characters, character sequences with a specified terminator character, and arbitrary-sized blocks of characters. Functions are provided to access the character putback, sequence positioning, and synchronization facilities of the associated `streambuf`.

The `istream` class is derived from class `ios`, so all the functions listed for class `ios` can be called for an `istream` object also. Class `iostream` combines the facilities of an `istream` and an `ostream`.

10

Streams with Assignment

The streams already discussed have had copying operations explicitly excluded by giving class ios a private copy constructor and private operator=. This is done because it's not clear what constitutes appropriate assignment behavior for streams. It has been the practice, however, to write code of the following general form:

```
main(int argc, char *argv[])
{
    if (argc > 1) {
            // file name supplied as source of input,
            // so attempt to open it and use instead of cin
            ifstream *ifp = new ifstream(argv[1]);
            if (ifp->good())
                cin = *ifp;
    }
    cin << ...;
    ...;
}
```

This means that if a filename is provided as a source of input, an istream is to be constructed using the file, and this istream assigned to cin. The rest of the program simply assumes that input comes from the standard input.

Classes that support assignment are defined to support code that uses this technique. The C++ standard streams `cin`, `cout`, `cerr`, and, where applicable, `clog` are instances of stream classes of this sort.

10.1 Derivation of the Streams with Assignment

The with-assignment classes are derived as follows:

```
class istream_withassign : public istream { ... };
class ostream_withassign : public ostream { ... };
class iostream_withassign : public iostream { ... };
```

The ANSI discussion document suggests that support for assignment should be the norm for all stream classes.

10.2 The Public Interfaces

The additional public interfaces provided by these classes are as follows:

```
class istream_withassign : public istream {
public:
    istream_withassign();
    istream_withassign(streambuf *);
    ~istream_withassign();
    istream_withassign &operator=(istream &);
    istream_withassign &operator=(streambuf *);
};

class ostream_withassign : public ostream {
public:
    ostream_withassign();
    ostream_withassign(streambuf *);
    ~ostream_withassign();
    ostream_withassign &operator=(ostream &);
    ostream_withassign &operator=(streambuf *);
};

class iostream_withassign : public iostream {
public:
    iostream_withassign();
    iostream_withassign(streambuf *);
```

```
    ~iostream_withassign();
    iostream_withassign &operator=(ios &);
    iostream_withassign &operator=(streambuf *);
};
```

10.3 Default Constructors

```
istream_withassign::istream_withassign();
ostream_withassign::ostream_withassign();
iostream_withassign::iostream_withassign();
```

These constructors create a stream-with-assignment object that isn't functional but which supports assignment. The error state of the created stream is set to `ios::badbit`. A subsequent assignment to it sets the state to some suitable value. For example,

```
istream_withassign cin2;
cin2 = cin;
int i;
cin2 >> i;       // same as input from cin

ostream_withassign cout2;
cout2 = cout;
int i;
cout2 << i;      // same as output to cout
```

10.4 Assignment Operators

```
istream_withassign &operator=(istream &);
istream_withassign &operator=(streambuf *);
ostream_withassign &operator=(ostream &);
ostream_withassign &operator=(streambuf *);
iostream_withassign &operator=(iostream &);
iostream_withassign &operator=(streambuf *);
```

A stream-with-assignment object can have either another corresponding type object (`istream`, `ostream`, or `iostream`) or a `streambuf` pointer assigned to it. When assignment is from a translator object, the state variables of the translator from which they are assigned are inherited unchanged. When assignment is from a `streambuf`, the state of the stream-with-assign object is the default state for an `ios`.

```
istream_withassign cin2;
cin2 = cin;
int i;
cin2 >> i;       // same as input from cin
istream_withassign cin3;
cin3 = cin.rdbuf();
cin3 >> i;       // same as input from cin
```

The assignment operator functions return a reference to the object for which they were called.

10.5 Summary

Derived versions of the translator classes are provided that support assignment from another object of similar type or from a `streambuf*`, that is,

Target type	Types that can be assigned
istream_with_assign	istream or a derived class, streambuf*
ostream_with_assign	ostream or a derived class, streambuf*
iostream_with_assign	iostream o r a derived class, streambuf*

Assignment from a similar type is taken to mean that the `streambuf` in use by the object assigned *from* is to be used by the object assigned to. The state of the object assigned *from* is also copied to the object assigned *to*. Assignment from a `streambuf*` is taken to mean that the object assigned to uses the indicated `streambuf`. The state of the object assigned to is set to the default state of class `ios`.

11

A streambuf Specialized for Files–filebuf

The filebuf class is derived from streambuf and uses a file as its ultimate source and/or destination for input or output. Characters are obtained from the file, in the case of underflow, by reading; they are disposed of, in the case of overflow, by writing.

The get and put pointers of a filebuf should be thought of as tied together because we usually think of a file as having a single currency, or file pointer. The file pointer is the point in the file from which the next character is read or at which point the next character is written.

The term file has been used vaguely during the development of the IOStreams system and only in the most recent ANSI discussion document has it been defined other than by inference. Unfortunately that definition doesn't correspond to the idea of a file prevalent in current implementations of the IOStreams library. For this reason, there is a greater need to establish the context in which the class, in this case filebuf, is used than there was with previous class descriptions. This is the focus of the first section of this chapter.

11.1 Relation between Files and `filebuf`

Defining a file

Throughout the development of IOStreams, the term file has been used to mean a UNIX-style disk file or file-like device. This definition has always posed problems for implementors of the IOStreams library in other operating environments. These difficulties have been progressively recognized in succeeding versions of the ANSI discussion document. The latest version finally ties down the concept. A file is to have the same meaning as it does in the standard C header file `stdio.h`. This definition links the concept of a file to the ANSI C standard rather than to its meaning in a particular operating system. However, note that most existing versions of IOStreams were not designed using this definition.

Files and current implementations

The `filebuf` class can be implemented using file handling facilities available at the operating system level. This is potentially good for efficiency and can eliminate the coupling between C++ and the C standard libraries. When current IOStreams implementations were designed, such decoupling was considered to be a good thing; it wasn't clear then whether C++ was to depend on the C standard library or stand alone with a library of its own. This design approach led to implementations that use relatively low-level facilities. Accordingly it's generally not possible to mix the IO facilities provided by IOStreams with those provided by the standard C `stdio` system. The order of appearance of output from the two separate systems depends on when their respective buffers are flushed. As a result, the output might be intermixed and garbled. However, IOStreams provides facilities that allow the two systems to be intermixed reliably, although at the expense of efficiency. We describe these in Chapter 16.

Tying the get and put pointers

The underlying `streambuf` abstraction makes no provision for tying the get and put pointers, therefore this behavior in `filebuf` must be enforced by the implementation. `filebuf` must synchronize the get and put pointers with the file whenever operations change from getting to putting, or vice versa. The required tying effect is then assured because at any point in time we care only about the position of one of the pointers. A consequence of this requirement, however, is that it might be inefficient to run a `filebuf` operation in a way that constantly alternates between getting and putting.

Similar considerations apply in the C `stdio` system. There, if a file is opened for reading and writing, only one of these operations can be performed at a time. To switch from one to the other requires an intervening call to the `fseek` function.

There is an exception to this tied pointer behavior. It's possible to specify that a `filebuf` always append any overflowed characters (characters disposed of from the put area to the final destination) to the end of the file. In this case, for the system to be of much use, the get and put pointers must be decoupled.

`filebuf` **seeking capabilities**

If the file supports seeking, then `filebuf`'s, `seekpos` and `seekoff` functions support seek operations that are somewhat analogous to the capabilities provided by the `fseek` function from the C standard library. However, a `filebuf` must also work with nonseeking file-like devices such as terminals; in these cases, seek attempts are treated as errors.

Character putback in a `filebuf`

Four characters of putback are supported by the AT&T implementation of `filebuf`. Although this seems an arbitrary figure, it's supported in other implementations. You should assume in these cases that the four-character limit applies to the worst case scenario; that is, it's possible to put back four characters when no characters have actually been gotten. Note, however, that the current ANSI discussion document has dropped this requirement and now asks no more of a `filebuf` than is specified for the abstract base type `streambuf`, that is, one character of putback.

Text and binary files

The primary purpose of the IOStreams system is the input and output of text. As noted at the beginning of this section, implementations have taken files as being UNIX-like. UNIX text files or file-like devices use a single newline character to delimit "lines" of text. Terminal or console drivers, or the hardware, are charged with either expanding such newline characters into whatever sequence of bytes is necessary to position the output device at the start of a new line, or filtering out any extraneous bytes generated by pressing the `Enter` key.

Implementations of the C and C++ standard libraries for DOS and OS/2 have always had to cope with a different practice, whereby line ends in files are coded explicitly as CR/LF (carriage return/line feed) pairs. The directions sent to the screen driver are then specific, and no translation is required. Input from the keyboard via the operating system also contains equivalent CR/LF pairs. Customarily this has been dealt with by assuming all programs in C or C++ are written according to the UNIX conventions and by having the library functions do whatever translation of newline characters is required. In the IOStreams system this capability might need to be localized in the implementation of the `streambuf` class, where it can be incorporated as part of the working of the `overflow` and `underflow` functions. This must be done when low-level file operations are used in environments where such file operations are purely binary.

If IOStreams is to serve as the principal IO mechanism in C++, as `stdio` does in ANSI C, then using text file conventions won't always be what is required. Many files must be treated as raw binary data. The distinction in ANSI C is illustrated by the following:

```
#include <stdio.h>
FILE *fp1 = fopen("text.dat","r");
        // open file for reading in text mode
FILE *fp2 = fopen("binary.dat","rb");
        // open for reading in binary mode
```

If the `filebuf` implementation uses low-level file operations and such operations don't distinguish between text and binary modes, some state information must be held in the `filebuf` object. This state information will allow the `filebuf` to note whether a text or binary operation is required.

Appending to a file

State information might also be required in a `filebuf` object to determine whether written data is to be appended to the file, for example, in an environment that doesn't have system facilities to do this automatically. A state variable consisting of flag bits also can be used to ensure that a `filebuf` is not employed for purposes for which it was not set up, for example, writing when it was only intended for reading, or vice versa.

State information and the `filebuf` class interface

The requirement that `filebuf` contain state information relating to IO mode is not explicit nor implicit in either the AT&T design or the ANSI discussion document. To provide for it requires either extra arguments to the functions that are specified in these descriptions or extra functions in the public interface. Defaulted extra arguments provide the best level of code portability; they must be provided in the constructor functions and in other functions that set up a `filebuf` prior to its use.

Buffering

Buffering is another significant issue in the design and behavior of classes such as `filebuf`, that derive from `streambuf`. In some cases, each character fetched must be got directly from the file and each character stored must be sent directly to the file. That is, file operations must be unbuffered. At the same time, we would want the translator classes to be able to use exactly the same interface.

This requirement is recognized in AT&T's base class design, `streambuf`, and in the earlier ANSI discussion document. In these, either a constructor or the `setbuf` function can specify that operations are to be unbuffered. However, the extent to which such operations can be implemented by a derived `filebuf` class is questionable. Should `sputbackc(c)` adjust the contents of the file? Should `sgetc` take a character from the file, note its value, and then reset the file pointer back one place so that a subsequent use of `sgetc` will produce the same character, or is a one-character buffer acceptable? How are these considerations to be applied when the file is a device incapable of seeking? These questions aren't explicitly answered by any IOStreams descriptions we have seen.

The ANSI discussion document neatly eliminates such problems by having `streambuf` be a pure abstraction of a character sequence that doesn't deal with buffering at all. Instead handling details like buffering is left to particular derived classes. The proposed `filebuf` class also omits stipulations about unbuffered operation. This will no doubt be for the best in the long run because unbuffered operation is not a common requirement. In many cases, setting the `ios::unitbuf` format state flag of an `ostream`, which causes flushing after each type representation has been converted to a character sequence, will achieve the results that were to be ensured by unbuffered operation. In all but the most extreme cases (formatted output of single characters), this setup will also be more efficient. If genuinely unbuffered operation is required, a special-ized `streambuf` type can be derived that would deal only with devices that can genuinely support this model.

Despite all these considerations, we next describe `filebuf` as it's usually implemented at present, that is, with optional "unbuffered" operation.

11.2 The Additional Public Interface

The extra public interface introduced by the derivation of class `filebuf` from class `streambuf` follows. The functions are described in detail in Section 11.3.

As noted we added defaulted arguments not present in the AT&T implemen-tation or the ANSI discussion document. We included them to allow for an implementation that is compatible with both UNIX and MS-DOS conventions and with typical MS-DOS C library facilities. The latest ANSI discussion document dispenses with the member functions that have file descriptor arguments and adds a constructor that takes filename and open mode arguments.

```
class filebuf : public streambuf {
public:
    enum { openprot = 0644 };

// Constructors
    filebuf();
    filebuf(int file_descriptor,          // extra argument
                int io_mode = ios::in | ios::out);
    filebuf(int file_descriptor, char *memory, int length,
                                           // extra argument
                int io_mode = ios::in | ios::out);
    ~filebuf();

// Attach a file to an existing filebuf
    filebuf *attach(int file_descriptor,
                                           // extra argument
                int io_mode = ios::in | ios::out);

// Open a file and attach it to an existing filebuf
    filebuf *open(const char *name, int io_mode,
                int protection = openprot);
// Close the file associated with the filebuf
    filebuf *close();

// Information functions
    int fd() const;
    int is_open() const;

// Seek functions (virtual)
    streampos seekpos(streampos, int which_pointers);
    streampos seekoff(streamoff offset,  ios::seek_dir
                                int which_pointers);

// Offer a buffer area for use (virtual)
    streambuf *setbuf(char *memory, int length);

// Synchronize the file with the filebuf (virtual)
    int sync();
};
```

11.3 Function Descriptions

The following functions require the inclusion of file `fstream.h`, which automatically includes file `iostream.h`. Once again we emphasize that some of these functions show defaulted arguments that are not present in all implementations.

Constructors

```
filebuf::filebuf();
filebuf::filebuf(int file_descriptor,  int io_mode = ios::in|ios::out);
filebuf::filebuf(int file_descriptor, char *memory,  int length,
          int io_mode = ios::in|ios::out);
```

The default constructor creates a `filebuf` with dynamic get and put area allocation, and with its associated file descriptor set to `EOF`, to signify that it is unattached.

The second constructor also creates a dynamic allocating `filebuf` but associates it with the specified file. The defaulted `io_mode` argument isn't present in either the AT&T implementation or the ANSI discussion document.

The third one creates a `filebuf` using user-specified memory for its get and put areas. Choosing a buffer size appropriate to the operating system will probably improve efficiency, particularly in binary mode. This constructor also has the extra defaulted `io_mode` argument. If this constructor is used with a 0 memory argument and/or a length argument that is less than or equal to 0, then operation of the `filebuf` will be unbuffered and each character transaction will be directly to or from the associated file. Examples of the use of each are as follows:

```
filebuf fb1;          // unattached filebuf - unusable
filebuf fb2(1);       // similar to cout's buffer
char buffer[1024];
int fd = open(...);   // get a file descriptor
filebuf fb3(fd, buffer, 1024);
filebuf fb4(fd, ios::out | ios::bin); // binary output
filebuf fb5(2,0,0);                   // unbuffered
```

Some environments don't have file-descriptors represented by an `int`, in which cases the default constructor must be used, followed by `filebuf::open` as described below.

Functions to associate a file with a `filebuf`

```
filebuf *filebuf::attach(int file_descriptor,
                        int io_mode = ios::in | ios::out);
```

This function attaches the specified file to an existing `filebuf`. If a file is already attached, `filebuf::close` should be called first. An extra defaulted `io_mode` argument is included here that is not in the AT&T implementation or the ANSI discussion document.

```
filebuf fb;          // unattached filebuf - unusable
int fd = open(...);
if (fb.attach(fd)) {
    ...;             // useable now
} else {
    ...;             // possibly already attached
                     // - use fb.close() first
}
```

The `attach` function returns a pointer to the object for which it was called; on failure, it returns 0. Using `attach` also depends on the existence of file descriptors represented by an `int`, which might not be the case in all environments. Where applicable, use `close` followed by `open`.

```
filebuf *filebuf::open(const char *name,  int io_mode,
                                 int protection = openprot);
```

This function attempts to open the file specified by the `name` argument, in mode `io_mode`, with protection defaulted to `filebuf::openprot`, and then to attach that file to the `filebuf`. The `io_mode` argument should be a bit-mask containing one or more of the following values from the enumeration `ios::open_mode`:

`ios::in`	The file is opened for reading.
`ios::out`	The file is opened for writing.
`ios::ate`	Set the file currency to end-of-file.
`ios::app`	Open the file in append mode.
`ios::trunc`	Truncate the file on open.
`ios::nocreate`	Do not attempt to create the file if it doesn't exist.
`ios::noreplace`	Cause the open to fail if the file exists.
`ios::binary`	Possibly `ios::bin`. Open file in binary mode.

This function will fail if the `filebuf` is already attached, in which case, use `filebuf::close` first, as follows:

```
filebuf fb;          // unattached filebuf - unusable
if (fb.open("thing.dat", ios::out|ios::app)) {
    ...;             // usable now
} else
    ...;             // possibly a file was already attached
                     // - use fb.close() first
```

The open function returns a pointer to the filebuf object for which it was called; on failure, it returns 0. The filebuf destructor will close a file opened in this way.

Detaching a file from a filebuf

```
filebuf *filebuf::close();
```

This function finishes any output held in the filebuf put area to the file. The file is then closed and the filebuf marked as unattached (the file descriptor is set equal to EOF). If an error occurs, close returns 0. The associated file gets closed whether an error occurs during flushing or not.

```
filebuf fb;
int fd = open(...);
fb.attach(fd);
...;
if (!fb.close()) {
    ...;                // error during flush or close
} else{
    fd = open(...);
    fb.attach(fd);    // ok to attach fb to another file
}
```

The close function returns a pointer to the filebuf object for which it was called; on an error, it returns 0.

In environments without int file descriptors, the sequence to initialize a filebuf is

```
filebuf fb;
fb.open("thing.dat", ios::out);
if (!fb.close()) {
    ...;    // something wrong
} else
    fb.open("another.dat",ios::out);
```

Status reporting functions

```
int filebuf::fd() const;
```

This function returns the descriptor for the file to which the filebuf is attached; it returns EOF if it is unattached.

```
int filebuf::is_open() const;
```

This function returns nonzero if the `filebuf` is attached to a file; it returns 0 otherwise.

```
filebuf *fbp1, *fbp2;
int fd = open(...);
if (!fbp1->is_open() {
    fbp1->attach(fd);        // check if this is already in use
else
    fbp2 = new filebuf(fd);// if so use alternate
```

File pointer positioning

```
streampos filebuf::seekpos(streampos,
                                int mode = ios::in|ios::out);
```

This function moves the file currency (file pointer) and adjusts the contents of the get and put areas so that any subsequent get or put will effectively be to or from the specified position in the file. Remember, in a `filebuf` the get and put pointers are normally tied, that is, they are nominally the same. For this reason, the mode argument is ignored. If the `filebuf` was created or attached to a file or opened a file in append mode (using `ios::app`), the effect is to change the get position; the put position is always at the end of the file.

The `streampos` type is implementation dependent and must be able to represent any possible pointer position in a file. It's often implemented as a `long`.

Values of type `streampos` should be regarded as "magic cookies," that is, a value provided by the `seekpos` and `seekoff` functions that can subsequently be used as an argument to the `seekpos` function and that shouldn't be modified. However, `streampos(0)` and `streampos(EOF)` are special cases: The value 0 may safely be used as an argument to `seekpos`, while if an error occurs, `seekpos` returns an `EOF`, for example:

```
filebuf fb;
fb.open(...);
...;
streampos newpos = fb.seekpos(0);// position at start of file
if (newpos == EOF)..;
```

The `seekpos` function returns a value of type `streampos` that encodes the current file pointer position in some implementation-dependent way.

It will do nothing but return an error value (`streampos(EOF)`) if the associated file does not support seeking.

```
streampos filebuf::seekoff(streamoff, ios::seek_dir
                           int mode = ios::in|ios::out);
```

This function resembles `seekpos` except that the position specification is relative to either the beginning, the end, or the current get/put position. The `streamoff` type is implementation dependent and must be able to represent any offset in a file. It's often implemented as a `long`.

The enumeration name `seek_dir` is misleading because the seek direction is controlled by the effective sign of the `streamoff` argument, which may be positive or negative. The `seek_dir` argument determines whether the offset is to be relative to the beginning of the file, the current file position in the file, or the end of the file.

The `seekoff` function moves the file currency (file pointer) and adjusts the contents of the get and put areas so that any subsequent get or put will be at the specified position in the file. Remember, in a `filebuf` the get and put pointers are normally tied; that is, they are nominally the same. For this reason, the `mode` argument is ignored. It's there only for compatibility with other classes derived from `streambuf` in which it might have significance.

The `seekoff` function does nothing except return an error value (`stream-pos(EOF)`) if the file doesn't support seeking.

```
filebuf fb;
fb.open(...);
...;
streampos pos = fb.seekoff(0,cur);
fb.seekpos(0);      // do something at start of file
fb.seekoff(0,end);  // do something at end
fb.seekpos(pos);    // back to where we were
```

The return value from `seekoff` is a value of type `streampos` that indicates the absolute current file pointer position.

Nominating a buffer area–controlling buffering

```
streambuf *filebuf::setbuf(char *memory, int length);
```

This function offers a buffer area for use by the `filebuf`. Implementations may ignore the offer unless either the memory argument is 0 and/or the length argument is less than or equal to 0. In the latter case, unbuffered operation is initiated.

```
filebuf fb(fd);
...;            // buffered operations
fb.setbuf(0,0);
...;            // unbuffered operations
```

The setbuf function returns a pointer to the streambuf for which it was called if the operation succeeded, that is, if the offer of an area of memory was accepted or if unbuffered operation was initiated or was requested and was already in force. Otherwise it returns 0.

Synchronizing the filebuf with the file

```
virtual int filebuf::sync();
```

This function moves back the file pointer by the number of characters that are available to be gotten from the get area (streambuf::in_avail(() and throws away the contents of the get area. If there are characters in the get area and the file doesn't support seeking, sync must return EOF. The contents of the put area are then written after the current file pointer position and the file's currency is advanced by the number of characters written.

```
// Used by ostream flush() for example, which calls
rdbuf()->sync();
```

The sync function returns EOF on failure and some other int value otherwise.

11.4 Summary

The filebuf class is a specialization of a streambuf that deals with files. In this context the term file hasn't been well defined; in most current IOStreams implementations, it corresponds to the sort of file or device represented by a UNIX-style integer file descriptor.

In addition to the functions in the public interface of class streambuf, class filebuf provides functions to associate the filebuf object with a specific file and IO mode. Versions of filebuf in future implementations will likely equate the term file with the FILE* type of ANSI C. The files dealt with can be text or binary. The nature of a text file will vary among environments; a binary file consists of a sequence of undifferentiated bytes.

Finally, objects of type filebuf can be created that deal with the file on a character-by-character basis, a mode known as unbuffered operation. Future support for unbuffered operation in class filebuf will probably disappear.

12

Translators Specialized on Files

In this chapter, we describe classes derived from `istream`, `ostream`, and `iostream` that use a file either as the source or destination of characters or simultaneously as both. A similar effect can be achieved by instantiating a `filebuf` object and using its address to initialize an `istream`, an `ostream`, or an `iostream`. However, we'll see how classes `ifstream`, `ofstream`, and `fstream` shortcut this process by providing constructors that take a filename or file descriptor argument directly. Default constructors and functions to associate the resulting objects with particular files are included.

12.1 Files and IOStreams

As mentioned in Chapter 11, the AT&T versions of IOStreams and the early ANSI discussion document didn't address specifically what is meant by the term file. Historically a file in the IOStreams context was taken to be a UNIX-style file with an `int` file-descriptor. The latest version of the ANSI discussion document, however, requires a file to be the type referenced by the `FILE*` type of the standard C `stdio` system.

This chapter deals with IOStreams systems as users are likely to find them at the time this book is completed, warts and all. Features that are likely to change or cause particular difficulties are noted.

12.2 Common Features of File–specialized Translators

The input, output, and bidirectional variants of the file-specialized translators all have member functions or basic functionality in common. It is convenient, both from the point of view of implementation and of presentation, to group these common features in an intermediate class. The file-oriented translators can then inherit these properties from this intermediary. The class used for this purpose here is called `fstream_common`. Particular implementations may use a similar intermediate class with another name, for example, `fstreambase` or `fstream_base`. The ANSI discussion document doesn't require the file-specialized translators be implemented in this way. If they aren't, however, each must provide the extra functions supplied here by the `fstream_common` class.

Class `fstream_common` objects must set the stream error state if some error occurs, therefore they need access to the associated `ios` object. This can be accomplished by making class `ios` a virtual base class.

```
class fstream_common : virtual public ios {
public:
  void close();
  void setbuf(char *memory, int length);
  filebuf *rdbuf() const;
protected:
  ...;          // constructors and common capabilities
private:
  ...;
  filebuf fb; // all the derived objects use
              // this embedded filebuf
};
```

12.3 Function Descriptions–Class `fstream_common`

Detaching an `fstream_common` **type from a file**

```
void fstream_common::close();
```

With this function, the file associated with the embedded filebuf is closed and the filebuf is put into an unattached state. The error state should be set to ios::badbit to signify the stream is unusable, although this isn't required by the ANSI discussion document. The ios::failbit flag should also be set if there is some error in flushing the associated filebuf or if the file close failed.

```
ifstream ifs;
ifs.open("input.dat");
ifs.close();
if (ifs.rdstate() & ios:failbit) {
    ...; something went wrong
}
```

filebuf **buffer manipulation**

```
void fstream_common::setbuf(char *memory, int length);
```

The rdbuf function returns a pointer to the associated filebuf. Note that it's typed differently than the rdbuf function in the istream, ostream, and iostream classes that return a pointer to a streambuf (see Chapters 8 and 9).

Access to the filebuf

```
filebuf *fstream_common::rdbuf();
```

The rdbuf function returns a pointer to the associated filebuf. Note that it's typed differently than the rdbuf function in the istream, ostream, and iostream classes that return a pointer to a streambuf (see Sections 8 and 9).

12.4 **File-based Input Streams–Class** ifstream

Class ifstream provides input streams specialized on files. Objects of type ifstream have the public interface of classes ios, istream, and fstream_common, and their own public interface as detailed in this section.

The following class definition includes some member functions with defaulted arguments that aren't present in the AT&T version and some member functions that have been dropped from the current ANSI discussion document. The defaulted arguments allow the corresponding functions to be called in the same way as the AT&T implementation (or the earlier ANSI papers) did. These extra arguments

control the discrimination between text and binary files, as described for class
`filebuf` in Chapter 11.

```
class ifstream : public fstream_common, public istream {
public:
  ifstream();
  ifstream(const char *name,
        int io_mode = ios::in,
        int protection = filebuf::openprot);

// Following constructors not in ANSI discussion document,
// io_mode argument not in AT&T implementation.
  ifstream(int file_descriptor, int io_mode = ios::in);
  ifstream(int file_descriptor, char *memory,
          int length, int io_mode = ios::in);
  ~ifstream();
// attach not in ANSI discussion document,
// io_mode argument not in AT&T implementation.
  void attach(int file_descriptor, int io_mode = ios::in);
  void open(const char *name,
        int io_mode = ios::in,
        int protection = filebuf::openprot);
};
```

12.5 Function Descriptions–Class `ifstream`

The following functions require the inclusion of file `fstream.h`.

Constructors

```
ifstream::ifstream();
ifstream(const char *name, int io_mode = ios::in,
        int protection = filebuf::openprot);
ifstream(int file_descriptor, int io_mode = ios::in);
ifstream(int file_descriptor, char *memory,
        int length, int io_mode = ios::in);
```

Four constructor options are provided. The default constructor sets up an
`ifstream` with a `filebuf` that dynamically allocates its buffer area and can
later be associated with a file using the `attach` or `open` functions. The second
one attempts to open the named file. The default open mode can be overridden, for

instance to read a file without newline translation, as can the file protection. The third sets up an ifstream using the file descriptor of an already opened file, while the fourth does the same but allows the user to specify a buffer area. Unbuffered operation can be forced by a 0 memory argument or a length argument <=0.

The constructors should probably set the error state to ios::badbit if they don't establish a connection with a file, since the stream will be unusable. Note that this error setting isn't required by the ANSI discussion document.

```
ifstream ifs1;          // dynamic, unattached and unusable
ifstream ifs2("input.dat");
                        // dynamic, attached and ready to go
                        // if no errors
int fd = open(...);
ifstream ifs3(fd);      // dynamic, attached and ready to go
                        // if no errors
ifstream ifs4(fd,0,0);
                        // unbuffered, attached and ready to
                        // go if no errors
```

The defaulted io_mode argument is an implementation subterfuge. It allows the use of low-level file access in an environment in which the low-level file operations are binary but newline translation is required in text mode. The AT&T implementation assumes that mode information is implicit in the file descriptor; in this case, no mode argument is required. The MS-DOS environment in particular doesn't have this discrimination; rather an indication of the requirement may have to be passed to the filebuf so the distinction can be handled there.

For binary operations the argument must be used explicitly. For example,

```
ifstream ifs(fd, ios::in | ios::binary);
```

Functions to associate a file with an ifstream

```
void ifstream::attach(int file_descriptor,
                  int io_mode = ios::in);
```

This function attaches the specified file to an existing ifstream. The state flags are adjusted to reflect the result of this action. If the stream is already attached to a file, ios::failbit is set; in this case, ifstream::close should have been called first.

```
ifstream ifs;         // unattached stream - unusable
int fd = open(...);
ifs.attach(fd);
if (ifs) {
```

```
    ...;            // useable now
} else {
    ...;            // was perhaps already attached
}                   // use ifs.close() first
```

This is another case where in order to force binary operations, some implementations will require the mode argument to be used explicitly, as in

```
ifs.attach(fd, ios::in | ios::binary);
```

```
void ifstream::open(const char *name,  int io_mode = ios::in,
                    int protection = openprot);
```

This function attempts to open the file specified by the name argument—in mode io_mode with protection defaulted to filebuf::openprot—and to attach it to the ifstream. The io_mode argument should be a bit-mask containing one or more of the values from class ios enum open_mode, as follows:

ios::in	Open for reading.
ios::out	Open for writing.
ios::ate	Position to the end-of-file initially.
ios::app	Position to end-of-file for all writes.
ios::trunc	Truncate the file on open.
ios::nocreate	Don't attempt to create the file if it doesn't exist.
ios::noreplace	Cause the open to fail if the file exists.
ios::binary	Perform no newline translation or whatever.

If the stream is already attached, the ifstream::open function will fail. In this case, use ifstream::close first.

```
ifstream ifs;        // unattached stream - unusable
ifs.open("thing.dat", ios::out|ios::app);
if(ifs) {
    ...;             // usable now
} else{
    ...;             // was perhaps already attached
}                    // use ifs.close() first
```

12.6 File-Based Output Streams–Class ofstream

Output streams specialized on files are provided for by class ofstream. Objects of type ofstream have the public interface of classes ios, ostream, and `fstream_common`. Their own public interface is as follows:

```
class ofstream : public fstream_common, public ostream {
public:
    ofstream();
    ofstream(const char *name, int io_mode = ios::out,
                    int protection = filebuf::openprot);
    ofstream(int file_descriptor, int io_mode = ios::out);
    ofstream(int file_descriptor, char *memory, int length,
                    int io_mode = ios::out);
    ~ofstream();
    void attach(int file_descriptor,
                    int io_mode = ios::out);
    void open(const char *name,
                    int io_mode = ios::out,
                    int protection = filebuf::openprot);
};
```

No detailed function descriptions are presented because they closely match the `ifstream` functions given in Section 12.5, which can be used for reference for `ofstream`.

12.7 File-based Bidirectional Streams–Class `fstream`

Class `fstream` provides the capability to use both the `istream` and `ostream` paradigms on the same file. Objects of type `fstream` have the public interface of classes `ios`, `istream`, `ostream`, and `fstream_common`. Their own public interface is as follows:

```
class fstream : public fstream_common, public iostream {
public:
    fstream();
    fstream(const char *name,
                int io_mode = ios::in|ios::out,
                int protection = filebuf::openprot);
    fstream(int file_descriptor,
                int io_mode = ios::in|ios::out);
    fstream(int file_descriptor, char *memory, int length,
                int io_mode = ios::in|ios::out);
    ~fstream();
    void attach(int file_descriptor,
                int io_mode = ios::in|ios::out);
    void open(const char *name,
```

```
                int io_mode = ios::in|ios::out,
                int protection = filebuf::openprot);
};
```

As with `ofstream` function descriptions, we don't include detailed function description of `fstream` because of their close match with the `ifstream` functions given in Section 12.5.

12.8 Summary

The file-oriented translators provide the same IO operations as the base class translators `istream`, `ostream`, and `iostream`. The extra functionality they add enables them to be associated with a file. That association can also be broken. In this context, files may be described by name or by an `int` file descriptor, and the required open-mode or usage-mode of the file may be specified. They also support the seek and synchronization operations provided by the associated `filebuf` through the facilities provided in the base translator classes.

13

A streambuf for In-memory Operations

The `strstreambuf` class is a derivation of `streambuf` that uses an area of memory, either user nominated or dynamically allocated, as the ultimate source and/or destination of characters. Stream classes using a `streambuf` of this sort typically use formatted IOStream input to process a string already present in memory; for example, to parse an environment string to which a pointer had been obtained or a line of input when it's probable that backtracking will be required. They can also be used to assemble formatted output to a memory buffer for use in some other output processes, or as a function argument.

13.1 The Public Interface

A `strstreambuf` object inherits the public interface of a `streambuf`. The extra features added are as follows:

```
class strstreambuf : public streambuf {
public:
    strstreambuf();
    strstreambuf(char *memory, int length, char *put_area);
```

```
  strstreambuf(void *(*allocator)(size_t),
       void (*deallocator)(void *));

  void freeze(int n = 1);
  char *str();
// Redefined virtual functions
  streampos seekoff(streamoff, ios::seek_dir,
            int which = ios::in | ios::out);
  streambuf *setbuf(char *memory, int length);
};
```

13.2 Function Descriptions

The following functions require the inclusion of file `strstream.h`. In MS-DOS or similar systems, the required file might be named `strstrea.h` because DOS restricts the number of characters in a filename to eight. However, using `#include <strstream.h>` in your code will work in this case, and will make the code portable.

Constructors

```
strstreambuf();
strstreambuf(char *memory, int length = 0, char *put_area = 0);
strstreambuf(void *(*allocator)(size_t),  void (*deallocator)(void *));
```

The first constructor creates an empty `strstreambuf` in dynamic allocation mode, which means memory will be allocated as required. The get and put areas of such a `streambuf` are contiguous; it's not possible to get characters until some have been put.

The second one creates a `strstreambuf` to use a user-nominated area of memory; in this case, there is no dynamic reallocation. If `length` is positive, then the `length` bytes starting at `memory` are used. If `length` is 0, then `memory` is assumed to point at a null terminated string and `strlen(memory)` bytes will be used. If `length` is negative, the memory region is assumed to be of indefinite length. The `put_area` argument is used to divide up the `strstreambuf` into get and put areas. If `put_area` is greater than `memory`, then the area between `memory` and `put_area` is the get area and the area pointed at by `put_area` is the put area. If `put_area` equals `memory`, initially there is no get area. However, once characters have been put, the get area should be regarded as extending over the put characters.

The third constructor resembles the first except that the allocator and deallocator functions required to manage the dynamic allocation can be specified. If the first argument is 0, the `new` operator is used to allocate the memory. If the second argument is 0, `delete` is used for deallocation. The allocator and deallocator should be compatible (e.g., `malloc/free` or `useralloc/userfree`) not mixed as in `malloc/userfree`.

```
strstreambuf ssb1;      // dynamic
char buffer[1024];
...;
strstreambuf ssb2(buffer,1024,buffer+512);
                    // half get, half put
strstreambuf ssb3(buffer,1024,buffer);
                    // no initial get area
strstreambuf ssb4(0, -1);
                    // arbitrary get source
strstreambuf ssb5("abcdefghijklmnopqrstuvwxyz")
                    // get only, length is strlen(), i.e. 26
strstreambuf ssb6(malloc, free);    // ok
strstreambuf ssb7(operator new, operator delete);  // ok
strstreambuf ssb8(malloc,0);        // may be disaster
```

Functions to preserve, access, and control a `strstreambuf` memory area

```
void strstreambuf::freeze(int = 1);
```

A nonzero argument to `freeze` inhibits any further dynamic allocation by the `strstreambuf` and the ultimate deletion of the allocated memory by the `strstreambuf` destructor. Put operations to a frozen `strstreambuf` are, in principle, an error, although in current implementations the effect is not defined. Most likely they will succeed until any remaining put area has been used up; after that, put operations will return EOF. The latest ANSI discussion document doesn't say the effect is undefined, so the presumption must be that in an ANSI conforming implementation a subsequent put operation will be declined and return either EOF or zero characters moved.

Putting to a frozen `strstreambuf` can be resumed if `freeze` is called again with a 0 argument, thus thawing it.

```
strstreambuf d;
d.sputn("some arbitrary text");
d.freeze();
```

```
d.sputn("xxxxxxxxxxxxxxxxxxxxxxxxxxxx", 32);
        // will not cause further allocation, d may end up with
        // just "some arbitrary textxxxxxxxxxxxx" (assuming a
        // 32 byte initial allocation)
d.freeze(0);
d.sputc('.');
        // "some arbitrary textxxxxxxxxxxxx."
```

The `freeze` function has no return value.

```
char *strstreambuf::str();
```

This function freezes the `strstreambuf` and returns a pointer to the start of the memory area. Unless the user has specifically added a terminating null byte to the stream (using `<< ends`), there's no guarantee the string pointed at is null terminated.

A dynamic `strstreambuf` may return a null pointer in response to the `str` function if no characters have been put. Once the `str` function has been called, it's the caller's responsibility to delete the memory pointed at by the return value. If the constructor that specifies the allocation functions has been used, this deletion should be with the deallocation function that corresponds to the allocator.

```
char *get_some_string()
{
    strstreambuf d;
    d.sputn("Speed the plough");
                // dynamically allocated
    return d.str();
                // allocation not deleted when d destructor called
}

void foo()

{
    char *p = get_some_string();
    ...;
    delete[] p;    // caller's responsibility to delete
}
```

It might be an error to delete the pointer returned by the `str` function of a stream that was not created using one of the dynamic constructors. Whether this happens depends on the nature of the buffer area provided by the constructor. This danger could be avoided by having `str` return a null pointer in cases where the `strstreambuf` had not allocated the buffer itself. In such cases, the user would already know its location.

```
streambuf *setbuf(char *memory, int length);
```

This function ignores the memory argument. In class `strstreambuf`, it controls subsequent dynamic allocation. In this case, it uses the `length` argument to determine the size of the next allocation. If no characters have been put into the `strstreambuf`, the next allocation will be the first one.

```
strstreambuf d;
d.setbuf(0,1024);
for (int i = 1024; i--;)
    d.sputc(' '); // only one allocation
```

The `setbuf` function in this case can't fail. The allocation doesn't happen until it's actually required as a result of some put operation, so `strstreambuf::setbuf` always returns a pointer to the object for which it was called.

Seeking the `strstreambuf` pointers

```
streampos seekoff(streamoff offset, ios::seek_dir relative,
                  int which =ios::in|ios::out);
```

The purpose of the virtual `seekoff` function was described in Chapter 5.

The implementation of `seekoff` in `strstreambuf` should be capable of moving either the get or put pointer, or both, without restriction, within the currently specified or allocated area of memory. One problem arises, however. If both pointers are specified (`ios::in | ios::out`) with a relative value of `ios::cur`, to which current pointer should the search be relative? In the examples given in Chapter 21, we assume the resulting offset will be relative to the previous get position, probably a useful assumption since it permits a get/modify/put sequence. We should also note that seeking relative to the end of a dynamically allocating `strstreambuf` leads to unpredictable behavior in that there is no guarantee any characters were written to such a position, so that any meaningful characters are there to be read.

13.3 Summary

The `strstreambuf` class maps the sequence abstraction of class `streambuf` to an area of memory. A `strstreambuf` object by default dynamically allocates memory; alternatively, it can use an area of memory nominated by the user. Functions are provided to give user access to the buffer area.

14

Translators for In-memory Formatting

Classes istrstream, ostrstream, and strstream provide input, output, and bidirectional stream facilities to memory using a strstreambuf. However, the bidirectional class has been dropped in the latest ANSI discussion document on the grounds that it's redundant; the same results can be obtained by instantiating an istrstream and an ostrstream to use the same area of memory.

14.1 The Public Interface

Objects of these types share the public interface of classes ios, and istream, or ostream, or iostream. Their own public interface is as follows:

```
class istrstream : public istream {
public:
    istrstream(char *string);
    istrstream(char *memory, int length);

    strstreambuf *rdbuf() const;
};
```

```
class ostrstream : public ostream {
public:
    ostrstream();
    ostrstream(char *memory, int length, int mode = ios::out);

    char *str();
    int pcount() const;

    strstreambuf *rdbuf() const;
};
class strstream : public iostream {
public:
    strstream();
    strstream(char *memory, int length, int mode);

    char *str();
    strstreambuf *rdbuf() const;
};
```

14.2 Function Descriptions–strstream Classes

The following functions require the inclusion of file strstream.h. In MS-DOS or similar systems, the required file might be named strstrea.h, because DOS restricts the number of characters in a filename. However, using #include <strstream.h> in your code will work in that case and will be portable.

Constructors

```
istrstream::istrstream(char *string);
istrstream::istrstream(char *memory, int length);
```

The first constructor allows the creation of an istrstream from a null-terminated string. The second allows the same but from an arbitrary area of memory of specified length.

```
char *s = "a string that is to serve as source";
istrstream iss(s);
char buffer[20];
iss >> buffer >> buffer;
```

```
cout << buffer;    // output is "string"
```

```
ostrstream::ostrstream();
ostrstream::ostrstream(char *memory, int length, int mode = ios::out);
```

The first of these creates a dynamically allocating ostrstream. The second uses an arbitrary area of memory of specified length. If the mode argument has either or both of ios::ate or ios::app set, the memory specified is assumed to start with a null-terminated string, and storage of inserted items starts at the null character.

```
ostrstream dynamic;
for (;;) {
    dynamic << "Some useless rubbish ";
    if (!dynamic)
            cerr << "Memory filled with rubbish\n";
            break;
    }
}
char work[512] = "Zoom in on this!";
ostrstream oss(work, 512, ios::out | ios::ate);
oss << " Wow!!" << ends;
// work contains "Zoom in on this! Wow!!"
```

```
strstream::strstream();
strstream::strstream(char *memory, int length, int mode);
```

The first one creates a dynamically allocating strstream. The second uses an arbitrary area of memory of specified length. If the mode argument has either or both of ios::ate or ios::app set, the memory specified is assumed to start with a null-terminated string, and storage of inserted items starts at the null character.

In either case, the get area starts at the beginning of the area pointed at by memory. In the dynamic case, nothing will be available to be got until something has been put, and the behavior will then be queue-like, with the get pointer of the associated strstreambuf following the put pointer. In the static case, if a get area has been reserved (using ios::app or ios::ate) those characters will be immediately available, followed by any characters that are subsequently added to the put area.

```
strstream ss1;  // dynamic
char buffer[80];
ss1 << "Figaro";
ss1 >> buffer;
strstream ss2(buffer, 80, ios::app);
```

```
ss2 << " here!";
char buf2[80];
ss2.get(buf2,80, '!');    // leaves buf2 with "Figaro here"
```

Functions to access the associated memory

```
char *ostrstream::str();
char *strstream::str();
```

Each of these functions returns a pointer to the memory being used by the associated `strstreambuf`. See also the discussion on `strstream-buf::freeze` and `strstreambuf::str` in Chapter 13.

```
ostrstream oss;
oss << "Whatever we wrote in there." << ends;
cout << oss.str();    // output is
                      // "Whatever we wrote in there."
```

Status reporting functions

```
int ostrstream::pcount() const;
```

This function returns the number of characters written into the put area. The result is valid only if no seeks have been performed.

```
strstreambuf *istrstream::rdbuf() const;
strstreambuf *ostrstream::rdbuf() const;
strstreambuf *strstream::rdbuf() const;
```

These functions resemble `istream::rdbuf`, which returns a pointer to the `streambuf` object associated with the translator. With these functions, however, the pointer returned is of type `strstreambuf*`.

```
strstream ss;
strstreambuf *sbp = ss.rdbuf();
```

14.3 Summary

The memory-oriented translators provide the same IO operations as do the base class translators `istream`, `ostream`, and `iostream`. The extra functionality they add allows them to be associated with an area of memory.

15

Manipulators and Applicators

We encountered manipulators when we discussed the inserter and extractor functions of the base `ostream` and `istream` classes in Chapters 8 and 9. In those classes, special inserters and extractors are defined to deal with pointers to functions of some particular types, specifically

```
ios &(*)(ios &);
  // pointer to function taking ios reference argument and
  // returning ios reference
istream &(*)(istream &);
  // pointer to function taking istream reference argument
  // and returning istream reference
ostream &(*)(ostream &);
  // pointer to function taking ostream reference argument
  // and returning ostream reference
```

These extractors and inserters, in combination with a set of functions that match these pointer-to-function types, provide what are usually referred to as parameterless manipulators. The parameterless manipulators enable usage such as

```
cout << hex;
```

Insertion of the manipulator `hex` into `cout` switches the standard output stream into a state where it displays all integer output in hexadecimal notation.

To set the floating-point precision for `cout`, using the facilities we presented in previous chapters, you must call a member function explicitly, as follows

```
cout.precision(8);
```

However, IOStreams provides an extension to allow manipulators with parameters. This gives rise to the following alternative notation for setting the precision:

```
cout << setprecision(8) << 1.0/3;
// output to be 0.33333333
```

Facilities used in IOStreams to implement manipulators like `setprecision` can be used by users to define their own manipulators. Such manipulators may take multiple parameters. Manipulator operations can also be implemented by classes specifically designed for that purpose.

15.1 Manipulators without Parameters

The following parameterless manipulators are usually supplied by IOStreams:

Manipulator	Type of stream	Effect
oct	istream or ostream	Force octal integer conversion.
dec	istream or ostream	Force decimal integer conversion.
hex	istream or ostream	Force hexadecimal integer conversion.
ws	istream	Extract whitespace characters.
endl	ostream	Insert newline and flush the buffer.
ends	ostream	Add a terminating null character.
flush	ostream	Flush the buffer.

Suppose we wanted integer output to be explicitly hexadecimal with the leading base indication "0x." Given only the manipulators supplied as standard by IOStreams, this would require

```
cout << hex;
cout.setf(ios::showbase);
```

The hex manipulator is implemented by a global function, as follows:

```
ios &hex(ios &s)
{
  s.setf(ios::hex,ios::basefield);
  return s;
}
```

Additional manipulators can be provided if the pollution of the global namespace is tolerable. For example, a showbase manipulator could take the form

```
ios &showbase(ios &s)
{
  s.setf(ios::showbase);
  return s;
}
```

This then would allow the following rather more convenient expression:

```
cout << hex << showbase;
```

Using showbase as a global function name doesn't conflict with the enumerator ios::showbase, which is in the scope of class ios.

15.2 Manipulators with Parameters

IOStreams also provides the following parameterized manipulators, which can be applied to either an istream or an ostream:

Manipulator	Effect
setfill(char)	Set fill character.
setw(int)	Set field width.
setprecision(int)	Set floating-point precision.
setiosflags(long)	Set specified format flags.
resetiosflags(long)	Reset specified format flags.

A manipulator with a parameter, such as setprecision, must be an object we can insert into a stream, as in

```
cout << setprecision(8);
```

The effect of this insertion needs to be equivalent to

```
cout.precision(8);
```

The parameters involved in this operation are an ios object (in this case, cout), a member function of class ios, and an integer. The value on the left-hand side of the insertion operation provides the ios object. It follows then that the object inserted must specify the member function and the integer. The type to be inserted could specify the required inserter function as a friend and have a constructor and data members, as follows:

```
class Manipulator_for_ints {
friend ostream &operator<<(ostream &,
                    const Manipulator_for_ints &);
public:
  Manipulator_for_ints(int (ios::*)(int), int);
  ...
private:
  int (ios::*memberfunc)(int);
  int value;
};
```

The first data member here is a pointer to a member function of class `ios` that takes an `int` argument and returns an `int`. The second data member is the required integer parameter. The inserter can then take the following form:

```
ostream &operator<<(ostream &s, const Manipulator_for_ints &m)
{
  (s.*m.memberfunc)(m.value);
  return s;
}
```

The only element required to complete a system of this sort is a function taking an `int` argument that generates a `Manipulator_for_ints` value, as follows:

```
Manipulator_for_ints setprecision(int n)
{
  return Manipulator_for_ints(&ios::precision, n);
}
```

In effect the manipulator is a specification for a class `ios` member function call with some particular argument value. The actual function call is made by the inserter function for the manipulator type.

A system like this would be suitable for all the format parameters defined by class `ios`. These each have a setup member function of the form

```
T ios::setup_function(T);  // e.g. int ios::width(int);
                           //      long ios::unsetf(long);
```

The method could be generalized using the following template class:

```
template<class T> class manipulator {
friend ostream &operator<<(ostream&, const manipulator<T>&);
public:
  manipulator(T (ios::*f)(T), T v): func(f), value(v) {}
private:
```

```
   T (ios::*func)(T);
   T value;
};
```

A corresponding template function, as follows, would generate the inserters:

```
template<classT> ostream &operator<<(ostream &s,
                            const manipulator<T> &m)
{
   (s.*m.func)(m.value);
   return s;
}
```

Then all that remains is to provide some way of generating manipulator objects that embody the required member function and parameter value. This can be done using a global function `setprecision(int)` as was done in the example of `Manipulator_for_ints`. Alternatively it can be done using an applicator class, as in

```
template<class T> class applicator {
public:
   applicator(T (ios::*f)(T)) : func(f) {}
   manipulator<T> operator() (T param)
      { return manipulator<T>(func,param); }
private:
   T (ios::*func)(T);
};
```

An applicator object of this form is initialized to the address of a class `ios` member function. It provides an `operator()` function taking a `T` argument, which returns a `manipulator<T>` object. The following applicator objects would then provide the IOStreams standard parameterized manipulators:

```
applicator<char> setfill(&ios::fill);
applicator<int> setw(&ios::width);
applicator<int> setprecision(&ios::precision);
applicator<long> setiosflags(&ios::setf);
applicator<long> resetiosflags(&ios::unsetf);
```

This is an elegant way to implement manipulators that have a corresponding stream member function with a single argument matching its return type. However, the concept of manipulators can easily be generalized so that this restriction is removed. All that's required is to store a more generalized function pointer in the manipulator object. This is done as follows in the template class `SMANIP` and its related classes as they are specified in the IOStreams header file `iomanip.h`:

```
template <class T> class SMANIP {
```

```
  friend istream &operator>>(istream &, const SMANIP<T> &);
  friend ostream &operator<<(ostream &, const SMANIP<T> &);
public:
  SMANIP(ios &(*f)(ios &, T), T v) : func(f), val(v) {}
private:
  ios &(*func)(ios &, T);
  T val;
};
```

```
istream &operator>>(istream &s, const SMANIP<T> &m)
{ m.func(s,val); return s; }
ostream &operator<<(ostream &s, const SMANIP<T> &m)
{ m.func(s,val); return s; }
```

The stored function pointer in this template class is a pointer to a function that returns an ios reference and that takes an ios reference and the parameter type as arguments. The corresponding applicator template class is

```
template <class T> class SAPP {
public:
  SAPP(ios &(*f)(ios &, T)) : func(f) {}
  SMANIP<T> operator()(T val) { return SMANIP<T>(func,val); }
private:
  ios &(*func)(ios &, T);
};
```

The greater generality costs an extra function call in those cases in which a suitable class ios member function already exists. For example, setprecision must now be implemented as follows:

```
// iomanip source file - APPLICATOR version

static ios &precision_set_function(ios &s, int p)
{
  s.precision(p);
  return s;
}
```

```
SAPP<int> setprecision(&precision_set_function);
```

The header file iomanip.h can then contain the template definitions for SMANIP and SAPP and declarations of applicator classes. Following are the applicator class declarations for the standard manipulators with parameters:

```
extern SAPP<char> setfill;
extern SAPP<int> setw;
```

```
extern SAPP<int> setprecision;
extern SAPP<long> setiosflags;
extern SAPP<long> resetiosflags;
```

Using the `setprecision` manipulator resolves to a call to `SAPP<int>::operator()` with the required integer value as an argument. This function returns an `SMANIP<int>`, and it's the insertion of this value that modifies the state of the stream, as shown in the following:

```
cout << setprecision(8);
     // resolves to
cout << SAPP<int>::operator()(8);
     // which generates
cout << SMANIP<int>(&precision_set_function, 8);
     // the insertion then does
cout.precision(8);
```

The same capabilities can alternatively be provided by functions that return manipulator types, as in

```
// iomanip source file - function version

static ios &precision_set_function(ios &s, int p)
{
  s.precision(p);
  return s;
}

SMANIP<int> setprecision(int p)
{
   return SMANIP<int>(&precision_set_function, p);
}
```

In this case, a set of functions that returns `SMANIP` objects would be declared in `iomanip.h`:

```
SMANIP<int> setfill(int);
SMANIP<int> setw(int);
SMANIP<int> setprecision(int);
SMANIP<long> setiosflags(long);
SMANIP<long> resetiosflags(long);
```

and the operations resolve as follows:

```
cout << setprecision(8);
    // generates
cout << SMANIP<int>(&precision_set_function,8);
```

```
    // the insertion then does
cout.precision(8);
```

15.3 Manipulators for the Translator Classes

The following manipulator and applicator template classes and functions are also
defined in iomanip.h. These are intended for use in manipulators that apply only
to an istream or only to an ostream respectively, but not to an IOS.

```
template<class T> class IMANIP {
  friend istream &operator>>(istream &, const IMANIP<T> &);
public:
  IMANIP(istream &(*f)(istream &, T), T) : func(f), val(v) {}
private:
  istream &(*func)(istream &, T);
  T val;
};

template<class T> class IAPP {
public:
  IAPP(istream &(*f)(istream &, T));
  IMANIP<T> operator()(T v) { return IMANIP<T>(func, v); }
private:
  istream &(*func)(istream &, T);
};

template<class T> istream &operator>>(istream &s,
                const IMANIP<T> &m)
{ (*m.func)(s, m.val); }

template<class T> class OMANIP {
  friend ostream &operator<<(ostream &, const OMANIP<T> &);
public:
  OMANIP(ostream &(*f)(ostream &, T), T ) : func(f), val(v) {}
private:
  ostream &(*func)(ostream &, T);
  T val;
};

template<class T> class OAPP {
public:
  OAPP(ostream &(*f)(ostream &, T));
```

```
   OMANIP<T> operator()(T v) { return OMANIP<T>(func, v); }
private:
   ostream &(*func)(ostream &, T);
};


template<class T> ostream &operator<<(ostream &s,
               const OMANIP<T> &m)
{ (*m.func)(s, m.val); }
```

15.4 Manipulators Using Macros

Most compilers now implement templates; no doubt all will follow. If the facility is not available, you can fake it using macros, including the predefined macros in the file `generic.h`. The same system as was described above using templates can be done with macros as follows:

```
#include <generic.h>

#define SMANIP(T) name2(SMANIP,T)

#define SMANIPdeclare(T) class SMANIP(T) {\
friend istream &operator>>(istream &, const SMANIP(T) &);\
friend ostream &operator<<(ostream&, const SMANIP(T) &);\
public:\
   SMANIP(T)(ios &(*f)(ios &, T), T v) : func(f), val(v) {}\
private:\
   ios &(*func)(ios &, T);\
   T val;\
};\
class SAPP(T) {\
public:\
   SAPP(T)(ios &(*f)(ios &,T)) : func(f) {}\
   SMANIP(T) operator()(T val) { return SMANIP(T)(func, val); }\
private:\
   ios &(*func)(ios &, T);\
};\
istream &operator>>(istream &s, const SMANIP(T) &m)\
{   (*m.func)(s, m.val); }\
ostream &operator<<(ostream &s, const SMANIP(T) &m)\
{   (*m.func)(s, m.val); }
```

```
declare(SMANIP,int);
SAPP(int) setprecision(&precision_set_function);
```

15.5 Using Parameterized Manipulators

One of the methods of implementing parameterized manipulators described in Sections 15.3 and 15.4 should work with all compilers. In either case the appropriate definitions are in file iomanip.h. Either method will allow the following usage:

```
cout << setfill('0');          // pad with zeroes not spaces
cout << setprecision(8);       // e.g. 0.33333333
cout << setw(10);              // make next item 10 cols wide

cout << setiosflags(ios::showpoint);
                               // show decimal point and
                               // trailing zeroes on
                               // floating-point output
cout << resetiosflags(ios::showpoint);
                               // back to default behavior
```

Example of a multiple parameter manipulator

Let's suppose we need a manipulator with multiple parameters; for example, we want to write

```
char *p;
cout << grid(7, 19, p, '1', '0');
```

and we want output in the following form:

```
1000000000000000000
1111000000000000000
1111111000000000000
1111111111000000000
1111111111111000000
1111111111111111000
1111111111111111111
```

which is determined by the bit pattern found in the array of characters pointed at by p.

It's useful to have a class that represents such a grid, as follows:

```
#include <iomanip.h>

class Grid {
public:
  Grid(int r, int c, char *list, char yes, char no);
  int bit(int i);
  int rows() const { return _rows; }
  int cols() const { return _cols; }
  char rep(int n) const { return n? on: off; }
                // character standing for 0 or 1

  static ostream &grid(ostream &, Grid);
private:
  int _rows, _cols;
  char on, off, *source;
  int cc, cb;
};
```

This `Grid` class constructor sets up two private variables to select the 0 bit of the first character, as follows:

`Grid::bit()` returns 1 or 0 depending on the setting of the next bit in the stream, and is as follows:

```
{
  cc = *source++;
  cb = 0;
}
```

`Grid::bit()` bit function returns 1 or 0 depending on the setting of the next bit in the stream, and is as follows:

```
int Grid::bit(int i)
{
  if (cb >= 8) {
    cc = *source++;
    cb = 0;
  }
  int rv = cc & 1;
  cc >>= 1;
  ++cb;
  return rv;
}
```

`Grid::grid()` is the function to which the manipulator stores a pointer and that actually outputs the pattern. Because it actually does the work of an inserter, it calls the prefix and suffix functions:

```
ostream &Grid::grid(ostream &o, Grid g)
{
  if (o.ppfx()) {
    int i = 0;
    for (int r = g.rows(); r--;) {
      for (int c = g.cols(); c--;) {
        int point = g.bit(i++);
        o << g.rep(point);
      }
      o << '\n';
    }
    o.osfx();
  }
  return o;
}
```

Finally, the following is the global manipulator function that creates a `Grid` object and from that, a manipulator object storing a pointer to the static `Grid::grid` function and a copy of the `Grid` object, as follows:

```
OMANIP<Grid> grid(int a, int b, char *list, char on, char off)
{
  Grid g(a,b,list,on,off);
  return OMANIP<Grid>(Grid::grid, g);
}

char *s = "The quick brown fox jumped";

void main()
{
  cout << s << "\nlooks like\n\n" << grid(7,19, s, '.', ' ');
}
```

15.6 An Example of an Applicator

We noted in Section 15.3 that applicator type classes can be used to achieve effects similar to those produced by manipulators. Recall that an applicator is a class that stores a pointer to a function that takes an `ios` reference argument (or a reference to one of the derived translators) and an argument of the type for which the applicator is parameterized. The applicator classes have the function-call operator overloaded so as to simulate a function call with an argument of the parameter type.

We illustrate the use of applicators in the following simple example for an `ostream` applicator parameterized for type `int`. First, we show the function to which the applicator stores a pointer. This function is essentially an inserter, so it calls the prefix and suffix functions, as follows:

```
static ostream &_paren(ostream &s, int n)
{
  if (s.opfx()) {
    for (int i = n; i--;) s << '(';
    s << n;
    for (i = n; i--;) s << ')';
    s.osfx();
  }
  return s;
}
```

Next, a global applicator for type `int` can be initialized with the address of the `_paren` function:

```
OAPP<int> paren(_paren);
```

All that's required to test this is the following:

```
main()
{
    cout << paren(5);
}
```

which results in the output

```
(((((5)))))
```

If the applicator facility was provided by the macro technique, the appropriate declarations would be

```
#include <generic.h>
#include <iomanip.h>
declare(OAPP,int);
OAPP(int) paren(_paren);
```

15.7 Manipulator Classes

We can obtain the actions of manipulators with parameters in an alternative way. This is done by defining a class whose name will be the name of the manipulator and then providing an appropriate inserter or extractor function for that class. We illustrate this approach by referring to the manipulator Setw and to the grid example which we discussed in Section 15.5.

The alternative implementation of setw, using a different name, is as follows:

```
class Setw {
friend ostream &operator<<(ostream&, const Setw&);
friend istream &operator>>(istream&, const Setw&);
public:
  Setw(int w) : width(w) {}
private:
  int width;
};

inline ostream &operator<<(ostream &s, const Setw &sw)
{
  s.width(sw.width);
  return s;
}

inline istream &operator>>(istream &s, const Setw &sw)
{
  s.width(sw.width);
  return s;
}

cout << Setw(10);
```

The alternative for grid is:

```
class Grid {
friend ostream &operator<<(ostream&, Grid&);
public:
    Grid(int r, int c, char *list, char yes, char no);
    int bit(int i);
    int rows() const { return _rows; }
    int cols() const { return _cols; }
    char rep(int n) const { return n? on: off; }
            // character standing for 0 or 1
private:
    int _rows, _cols;
    char on, off, *source;
    int cc, cb;
};
```

```
Grid::Grid(int r, int c, char *list, char yes, char no)
 : _rows(r), _cols(c), source(list), on(yes), off(no)
{
    cc = *source++;
    cb = 0;
}

ostream &operator<<(ostream &o, Grid &g)
{
    int i = 0;
    for (int r = g.rows(); r--;) {
        for (int c = g.cols(); c--;) {
            int point = g.bit(i++);
            o << g.rep(point);
        }
        o << '\n';
    }
    return o;
}

cout << Grid(7,19, s, '.', ' ');
```

These implementations are easy to understand and economical in terms of the
quantity of code involved.

You can usually provide manipulators like `setw` more efficiently, in terms of
code quantity, using the generalized manipulator route. This is because `setw` takes
an `int` parameter and can share parts of the template-style implementation with
other manipulators such as `setprecision` and `setfill`, which also take an
int parameter. However, because they have a higher function-call overhead, they
are also likely to execute more slowly. The `grid` example, on the other hand,
favors the manipulator class approach. Probably no other output operations will
need to be parameterized by the `Grid` type, and in the case where there is no code
sharing benefit, the code generated will usually be smaller and will execute more
quickly if the technique shown in this section is adopted.

15.8 An Antidote for `printf`

Even given the flexibility provided by manipulators and applicators, it's possible that
a C programmer will continue to suffer from "`printf` deprivation." In our final
example in this chapter, we show how you can simulate the `printf` facility using the
IOStreams system without involving the `stdio` facilities. We don't recommend you
do this, however; the `printf` simulation will certainly cause problems if you use the

header file `stdio.h` or any header file that includes it. We recommend instead that you use IOStreams. Regardless, the simulation provides an interesting example of the use of classes as stream manipulators, so we include it here.

Given the conclusions reached in Section 15.7 about the economy of manipulator implementation, we provide this facility by defining the following `format` class. Note that this class acts only as a shell around the C library function `vsprintf`.

```
int vsprintf(char *, const char *, va_list);
```

This function acts similarly to the `sprintf` function. The values to be output are determined at run time by decoding the string addressed by the second argument. They then are assumed to be present in the memory pointed at by the third argument. The type `va_list` is usually a pseudonym for `char *`. The result of the operation, which places the formatted string in the memory indicated by the first pointer argument, can be of any length and can write beyond the memory that should properly be accessed. As noted in Chapter 3, the C facilities are not at all type safe.

The `format` class has only a constructor, with arguments that match those to the `printf` function, and a destructor, since the constructor allocates memory to hold the formatted representation. So that it can deal effectively with `printf`-deprivation symptoms it defines `printf` as a macro. It is this feature that would cause trouble if `stdio.h` were included.

```
// format.h
#include <stdarg.h>
#include <iostream.h>

#define printf cout<<format
const int PRINTF_BUF_LEN = 1024;

extern "C" int vsprintf(char *, const char *, va_list);

class format {
friend ostream &operator<<(ostream&, const format&);
public:
    format(const char *, ...);
    ~format();
private:
    char *buf;
    int len, alloc;
};
```

The implementation is as follows. The inserter that simulates `printf`-style output calls the prefix and suffix functions as usual and uses the low-level `ostream::write` function to transfer the already-formatted character string:

```
#include <assert.h>
#include <iostream.h>
#include "form.h"

ostream &operator<<(ostream &s, const format &f)
{
  if (s.opfx()) {
  s.write(f.buf,f.len);
  s.osfx();
  {
  return s;
}
```

The `format` class constructor attempts to allocate a substantial chunk of memory. If it fails, the instance is set up to produce an error message. Otherwise, the facilities in `stddef.h` are used to obtain a pointer to the variable part of the argument list. The `vsprintf` variant of the `printf` family is then used as follows to set up the required formatted string:

```
format::format(const char *fs, ...)
  : alloc(1)
{
    buf = new char[PRINTF_BUF_LEN];
  if (!buf) {
    buf = "Printf simulator - Not enough memory";
    len = 36;
    alloc = 0;
    return;
  }
  va_list va;
  va_start(va,fs);
  len = vsprintf(buf,fs,va);

// If too many characters written, crash as
// gracefully as possible
  assert(len < PRINTF_BUF_LEN);
  if (!len)
    buf[0] = '\0';
}
```

The destructor simply deletes any memory that was allocated, as shown in the following. Because the `format` class is used only to create a temporary variable, the memory usage should be of very short duration.

```
format::~format()
{
  if (alloc)
    delete[] buf;
}
```

You'll notice that the following test program for the format class looks familiar:

```
#include "form.h"

void main()
{
    printf("Conventional %d style %d output %d\n", 12, 13, 14);
}
```

Note that this program doesn't include stdout and that using printf statements of this sort doesn't involve mixing stdio and IOStreams output. Again, we don't recommend this method; we merely offer it to illustrate the flexibility of the IOStreams system.

15.9 Summary

IOStreams provides manipulators that can change the state of, or perform composite IO operation on, both input and output streams. If appropriate, such manipulators can use parameters. They can also provide a very convenient and succinct notation for complex IO operations.

A set of template classes is defined that provides most of the code needed to implement manipulators with parameters. User-defined parameterized manipulators can take advantage of these template classes, usage of which is particularly economical if the user-defined manipulator takes an int or a long parameter. Such cases can share code with the built-in manipulators. Manipulator facilities can also be provided using user-defined types designed specifically for that purpose. This approach can be more efficient in terms of code size and processing speed if some complex output operation with multiple parameters is required.

16

Using IOStreams and `stdio` Facilities Simultaneously

The older Streams library specified that input and output through the standard C++ streams `cin`, `cout`, and `cerr` could be mixed without restriction with C-style IO using `stdin`, `stdout`, and `stderr`. This introduced substantial inefficiency into the C++ IO facilities, since it required in practice that each character be dispatched or obtained by a call to the C `stdio` functions `fgetc`/ `fputc`. This threw away the speed advantage of the inline functions used for most of the operations on a `streambuf`'s get and put areas.

Current versions of the IOStreams library don't support this behavior. The two systems (IOStreams and `stdio`) have separate buffering. If the two are mixed, the order of actual IO will probably be garbled, since it will depend on the order in which the independent buffers are flushed rather than on the order of IO of individual items. For cases in which mixing the two IO systems is unavoidable, the IOStreams library provides another buffer class derived from `streambuf`. This class, `stdiobuf`, ensures that the C++ and `stdio` facilities coexist without mutual interference, although at the expense of efficiency.

A static member function of class `ios`, `sync_with_stdio`, initiates operation of the standard streams with a `streambuf` of this sort. Under these circumstances, the format state of the associated `ios` object is adjusted so that the `ios::unitbuf` and `ios::stdio` flags are set. These flags cause the associated `streambuf` and the corresponding `stdio` stream to be flushed by the `ostream` suffix function.

16.1 The Public Interface–Class `stdiobuf`

The public interface of `stdiobuf` differs from that of `streambuf` as follows:

```
#include <stdio.h>
#include <iostream.h>

class stdiobuf : public streambuf {
public:
    stdiobuf(FILE *);
    FILE *stdiofile();
};
```

16.2 Function Descriptions–Class `stdiobuf`

Users of this class need to include `stdiostream.h`.

Constructor

```
stdiobuf::stdiobuf(FILE *);
```

   The single constructor takes as an argument a `FILE` pointer as defined in `stdio.h`:

```
FILE *fp = fopen(...);
stdiobuf stdb(fp);
```

Status reporting

```
FILE *stdiobuf::stdiofile() const;
```

   This function returns the file pointer associated with the `stdiobuf`.

16.3 Using Streams with `stdiobuf`

This facility impairs efficiency, therefore you should use it only when mixing code using `stdio` facilities and IOStreams facilities is unavoidable.

The following is the simplest of programs to demonstrate the properties of stdiobuf:

```
#include <iostream.h>

void main()
{
    ios::sync_with_stdio();
// This call to the static member function of class ios
// fixes up the standard streams to use an stdiobuf, and
// adjusts their format flags

    for (;;) {
            cout << "The quick brown fox jumped\n";
            puts("over the lazy dog\'s back.");
    }
}
```

This program should result in the two strings being printed out properly interleaved, as follows:

The quick brown fox jumped
over the lazy dog's back.
The quick brown fox jumped
over the lazy dog's back.
The quick brown fox jumped
over the lazy dog's back.
...

Without the call to sync_with_stdio, the output would appear in separate blocks, arbitrarily mixed up, something like:

The quick brown fox jumped
The quick brown fox jumped
The quick brown fox jumped
The quiover the lazy dog's back.
over the lazy dog's back.
over the lazy dog's back.
over the lazy dog's ck brown fox jumped
The quick brown fox jumped
The quick brown fox jumped
The quick brown fox jumped
...

16.4 Trends in IOStreams

The current ANSI discussion document proposes a return to behavior when mixing IOStreams with `stdio` similar to that of the old Streams library, as if `ios::sync_with_stdio` had been called in the current version of IOStreams. Presumably `ios::sync_with_stdio` will be retained as a do-nothing function to maintain compatibility with existing IOStreams versions.

16.5 Summary

If you need to mix `stdio` and IOStreams IO on the standard streams, first call the class `ios` static member function `ios::sync_with_stdio`. Doing this will cause their output to be properly interleaved. It will, however, result in a sacrifice of some efficiency with current versions of IOStreams; but it should be entirely compatible with future versions.

17

Deriving Buffer Classes
from `streambuf`

IOStreams is intended to be extendable. The most significant mechanism for extension is the derivation of `streambuf` types specialized for some particular IO context. The contexts covered by IOStreams as standard are file IO and IO to or from memory. Examples of other contexts where derived `streambuf` types might be required are memory mapped video output, raw keyboard input, and IO to or from a window in a GUI.

In this chapter, we present an implementation of the IOStreams `filebuf` class, which is the specialization of `streambuf` for file IO. We chose the `filebuf` class because its implementation is arguably the most demanding in the set of IOStreams classes derived from `streambuf`. To complicate matters further, this implementation incorporates translation of newline characters. The decomposition of operations used in this example should provide a good indication of how the problems of implementing other `streambuf` types can be broken down.

The `filebuf` design targets a file that approximates an MS-DOS text file. The target model consists of an arbitrary sequence of characters, except that the sequence `'\r\n'` represents the newline character, which makes the file not quite an MS-DOS text file, since MS-DOS also uses character `'\x1a'` as an end-of-file marker. However, the model incorporates the most awkward feature—the newline—and the representations it deals with are acceptable to MS-DOS.

The example implementation can also treat the file as an arbitrary sequence of characters, that is, it provides a binary mode. It's assumed there is no system-provided capability either to translate newline characters or to append all output to the end of a file. Also assumed is the availability of UNIX-like open, close, read, write, lseek, and isatty functions; although not ANSI C library functions, these functions are widely available. Descriptions of these functions are contained in Appendix 2.

Before we discuss this implementation, we first need to describe the protected interface of class streambuf.

17.1 The Protected Interface–Class streambuf

Elements of the streambuf definition intended for use in the implementation of derived classes are as follows. Note, users of this class must include iostream.h.

```
class streambuf {

protected:

// Functions to provide information about the buffer
// area, and to set it up
  char *base() const;
  char *ebuf() const;
  int blen() const;
  void setb(char *buf, char *endbuf, int allocated = 0);

// Functions for the get area
  char *eback() const;
  char *gptr() const;
  char *egptr() const;
  void gbump(int);
  void setg(char *start, char *get, char *limit);

// Functions for the put area
  char *pbase() const;
  char *pptr() const;
  char *epptr() const;
  void pbump(int);
  void setp(char *start, char *limit);

// Functions to set and examine the buffering state
  void unbuffered(int);
```

```
  int unbuffered() const;
// Buffer allocation
  int allocate();
  virtual int doallocate();

// Special cases
  virtual int pbackfail(int c);
};
```

17.2 Functions for the Buffer Area

```
char *base() const;
char *ebuf() const;
```

The base function returns a pointer to the area of memory being used to accommodate the get and put areas. The ebuf (end-of-buffer) function returns a pointer to the character position one beyond the buffer area. (Note, some discussions call the buffer area the reserve area.) Both may return 0 when the streambuf is one intended to allocate its buffer dynamically, and when no operation has yet been requested.

```
int blen() const;
```

This function, which is equivalent to (ebuf()-base()), returns the length in characters of the combined area available for the get and put areas.

```
void setb(char *buf, char *endbuf, int allocated = 0);
```

This function sets up the streambuf internal pointers to its buffer area. The first argument must point to the start of the nominated area and the second to the character one after the last available character position. The final argument indicates whether the streambuf destructor is responsible for deleting the buffer; the default value doesn't require this, while a nonzero value does. If a previous call to setb indicated that the buffer would require deletion, setb must delete it.

17.3 Functions for the Get Area

```
char *eback() const;
char *gptr() const;
char *egptr() const;
```

These functions return pointers to the start of, respectively, the current get area, the current get position (that is, a pointer to the next position from which a character is to be fetched), and the character position one beyond the end of the current get area. The `eback` function is so named because it's the end of the range of positions to which a character may be put back without any special action.

These functions all return either 0 or pointers into (or past the end of) the get area as described. Note that they can return 0 regardless of whether the buffer area has been set up. If the buffer area has been set up, a zero return value indicates getting is not allowed.

```
void gbump(int n);
```

This function moves the get pointer `n` characters. The argument may be positive or negative, and no checking is done on its value.

```
gbump(n);
```

is equivalent to

```
get_pointer += n;
```

```
void setg(char *start, char *get, char *limit);
```

This function sets up the `streambuf` internal pointers for the get area. The first argument must point to the required start position; the second to the position from which the next character is to be got, often the same as the start, and the last to the character position one after the end of the get area.

17.4 Functions for the Put Area

```
char *pbase() const;
char *pptr() const;
char *epptr() const;
```

These functions return pointers to, respectively, the start of the current put area, the current put position (that is, a pointer to the position at which the next character is to be put), and the character position one beyond the end of the current put area.

The functions all return either 0 or pointers to the put area as described. Note that they can return 0 regardless of whether the buffer area has been set up. If the buffer area has been set up, a 0 return value indicates putting is not allowed.

```
void pbump(int);
```

This function arbitrarily moves the put pointer. The argument may be positive or negative, and no checking is done on its value.

```
pbump(n);
```

is equivalent to

```
put_pointer += n;
```

```
void setp(char *start, char *limit);
```

This function sets up the `streambuf` internal pointers to the put area. The first argument must point to the required start position and the last to the character one after the end of the put area. The actual put pointer is set to the start of the put area.

17.5 Buffering State Functions

```
void unbuffered(int);
int unbuffered() const;
```

The first of these functions marks the `streambuf` as being intended to operate with no buffering, with characters being read from or written to the ultimate source/destination as they are required. It sets a flag and is not intended to switch between states. The `setbuf` function might be able to do that although derived classes can ignore `setbuf` requests. A nonzero argument to the `unbuffered` function indicates unbuffered operation is in force, while a 0 argument indicates buffering.

The second function simply reports the state of the flag, returning a nonzero value if the `streambuf` is set up for unbuffered operation.

17.6 Buffer Allocation Functions

```
int allocate();
virtual int doallocate();
```

The `allocate` function determines whether it's necessary to dynamically allocate a buffer area. Allocation is required if an operation is to be buffered and the `base` function returns 0. If allocation is not required, `allocate` returns 0.

When allocation is required, `allocate` calls virtual function `doallocate` to attempt to get some space. If `doallocate` returns `EOF`, so does `allocate`;

otherwise `allocate` returns 1 to signal that a buffer area was allocated and the pointers to it were set up. Return values from `doallocate` are as follows:

Return value	Meaning
0	No allocation was required (unbuffered, or buffer user specified)
1	Allocation ok and buffer pointers set up
EOF	Error

`doallocate` is responsible for actually allocating memory. If it fails, it returns `EOF`. Otherwise it calls `setb` to set up the buffer pointers, with a nonzero third argument to indicate that deletion is required by the destructor. In implementations in which `streambuf` is not an abstract base class, the `doallocate` function should have an implementation in the base class that attempts to get some memory using the `new` operator.

17.7 Putback Failure

```
virtual int pbackfail(int c);
```

This function is called when an attempt is made to put back a character (back up the get pointer) when the get pointer is already at the start of the get area (the position corresponding to the `eback` function). It has an implementation in the base class, where it simply returns `EOF`. Derived classes should provide their own implementation if they can deal with this situation in some way. If so, `pbackfail` should return the argument value on success and `EOF` on failure. An argument value of `EOF` should produce a return value of `EOF`.

17.8 A Derivation from `streambuf`– Class `filebuf`

We presented a specification for class `filebuf` in Chapter 11. A complete class definition might be as follows. Note that the definition is presented in terms of the worst-case requirement, with differentiation between text and binary mode for "difficult" environments.

```
const int filebuf_buffer_size = SYSTEM_BUFFER_SIZE;
// SYSTEM_BUFFER_SIZE is a dummy - use whatever buffer size
// will be most efficient for the environment

class filebuf : public streambuf {
public:
```

```
  enum { openprot = 0644 };

// Constructors
  filebuf(int io_mode = ios::in | ios::out);
  filebuf(int file_descriptor,
          int io_mode = ios::in|ios::out);
  filebuf(int file_descriptor, char *memory, int length,
          int io_mode = ios::in|ios::out);
  virtual ~filebuf();

// Attach a file to an existing filebuf
  filebuf *attach(int file_descriptor,
          int io_mode = ios::in|ios::out);

// Close the file associated with the filebuf
  filebuf *close();

// Open a file and attach it to an existing filebuf
  filebuf *open(const char *name,
          int io_mode, int protection = openprot);

// Information functions
  int fd() const;
  int is_open() const;

// Seek functions
  virtual streampos seekpos(streampos, int which_pointers);
  virtual streampos seekoff(streamoff offset, ios::seek_dir,
                                  int which_pointers);

// Offer a buffer area for use
  virtual streambuf *setbuf(char *memory, int length);

// Synchronize the file with the filebuf
  virtual int sync();

protected:
  virtual int underflow();
  virtual int overflow(int = EOF);

  virtual int pbackfail(int);

private:
```

```
int file;
    // File descriptor for the associated file.
short mode;
    // IO mode
short reserve;
    // remaining putback reserve
char unbuf[2];
    // two character buffer for "unbuffered" operation
char do_not_seek;
    // Set if the file (device) does not support seeks.
char own_file_descriptor;
    // Set if the file descriptor is from open, and
    // the file should be closed by the destructor.

// Private member functions - see implementation below
int syncin();
int syncout();
int flushbuf();
int fillbuf();
};
```

Some implementations of class `filebuf` might provide an extra member function to control the distinction between text and binary mode rather than controlling this behavior with constructor arguments; for example,

```
class filebuf : public streambuf {
public:
  ...
  int setmode(int = 0);
      // default text mode, use fb.setmode(ios::binary)
      // to switch to binary mode
  ...
};
```

17.9 Underflow/Overflow

Implementation of the `underflow/overflow` virtual functions is the most important feature of the derivation of a new `streambuf` type; therefore we deal with them first.

Whether the `filebuf` is using user-nominated memory or is to dynamically allocate a buffer, get or put operations eventually will determine that either the get or put area is exhausted and consequently make a call to one of these two virtual functions. The functions that get and put characters in the underlying streambuf are unable to tie the get and put pointers in a way appropriate for a single file acting as both source and sink. Rather this tying must be simulated by insisting that the filebuf does one thing at a time, that is, if getting is active, all the put area pointers are zeroed, and vice versa. The underflow and overflow functions of the derived filebuf class make this context switch and use the components of the sync function to enforce the notional tying. The constructors and setup functions for filebuf must ensure that both the get and put areas are initially disabled (setg(0,0,0), setp(0,0)).

This implementation of the filebuf class supports the concept of IO modes. These modes are enforced at the underflow and overflow function level. If the mode doesn't allow putting, overflow immediately returns EOF. If it doesn't allow getting, underflow returns EOF.

underflow is called to fill the get area, and is implemented as follows:

```
int filebuf::underflow()
{
  if (!(mode & ios::in))
    return EOF;
```

If fetching is allowed, first check to see whether there is a buffer. If not, an attempt must be made to allocate one, as follows:

```
  if (!base()) {
    if ((allocate()) == EOF) return EOF;
    setp(0,0);  // No puts without overflow
  } else {
```

If characters are available, return the value at the get pointer, as follows:

```
    if (in_avail())
      return (unsigned char) *gptr();
          // avoid sign extension
```

otherwise the file pointer needs to be adjusted to allow for any characters waiting in the put buffer. This action is a subset of what the sync function does and is implemented by a private member function:

```
    if (out_waiting()) {
      if (syncout() == EOF)
        return EOF;
    }
  }
```

After this an attempt can be made to refill the get area from the file. In this implementation a private member function, `fillbuf`, is used to isolate the details of the refill operation:

```
int result = fillbuf();
if ( result == EOF) {
  setg(0,0,0);      // disable the get area
  return EOF;
}
return (unsigned char) *gptr();
}
```

The `overflow` function first checks to see if storing is permitted:

```
int filebuf::overflow(int c)
{
  if (!(mode & ios::out))
    return EOF;
```

If there isn't a buffer, it tries to allocate one, as follows:

```
if (!base()) {
  if (allocate() == EOF) return EOF;
  setg(0,0,0);      // No gets without underflow
} else {
```

Otherwise, synchronization of the get and put pointers must be forced. This is done as follows by calling the components of `sync` to adjust the file pointer for any characters that are waiting in the get area and then to dispose of the characters in the put area.

```
  if (in_avail()) {
    if (syncin() == EOF)
      return EOF;
  }
  if (out_waiting()) {
    if (syncout() == EOF)
        return EOF;
  }
}
```

If unbuffered operation has not been specified, as much buffer area as possible is set up as a put area. Notice that when newline characters must be translated, only half the buffer is made available. If it were filled entirely with newline characters, the other half would be required to accommodate the translation.

```
if (!unbuffered()) {
```

```
    int bl = blen();
    setp(base(),
        base()+((mode & ios::binary)? bl: bl/2));
}
```

If the character is not EOF and there is a put area, that is, if operation is buffered, the overflow character can simply be entered into the first position. In the unbuffered case, it must be written directly to the file, with newline translation if required.

```
if ( c != EOF ) {
  if ( pptr() < epptr() ) {
    *pptr() = c;
    pbump(1);
  } else {
    char b = c;
    long cp, rv;
```

The next branch of the function deals with the unbuffered case. If ios::app is specified, everything must be written at the end of the file. This can be guaranteed only by doing a brute force seek, as follows. Then the character can be written, with or without translation.

```
    if (mode & ios::app) {
      cp = lseek(file, 0L, 1);
            // note the current position
      if (cp == -1L)
        return EOF;
      rv = lseek(file, 0L, 2);
            // seek to end
      if (rv == -1L)
        return EOF;
    }
    if (!(mode & ios::binary) && c == '\n') {
      if(write(file,"\r\n",2) != 2)
        return EOF;
    } else {
      if (write(file, &b, 1) != 1)
        return EOF;
    }
```

In the ios::app case, the user has every right to expect the get context to be unchanged, so the file currency must then be put back where it was,

```
    if (mode & ios::app)
      if (lseek(file, cp, 0) == -1)
        return EOF;
```

```
    }
  }
  return 0;
}
```

Synchronizing the file currency

Both `overflow` and `underflow` must synchronize the file currency (file pointer) with the current state of the get and put areas. Synchronizing a `filebuf` requires one of the following two actions. If characters are available in the get area, the file pointer needs to be wound back by that number of characters, as if they had never been read. If characters are waiting in the put area, they need to be written to the file and the file pointer advanced accordingly. Usually the file pointer is advanced in exactly the required way when the file is written to. Only one of these actions should be needed, since the `filebuf` pointer tying mechanism is single minded. The `sync` function presented here is implemented by two private member functions that separate the get and put synchronization requirements.

The first deals with the get area. Significant action is required only if the file or device supports seeking; this will have been determined by the `filebuf` constructor.

```
int filebuf::syncin()
{
  if (!do_not_seek) {
```

If seeking is supported, we must determine how many characters remain in the get area. Note, each newline character is counted twice.

```
    long offset = in_avail();
    if (!(mode & binary)) {
      char *p = gptr();
      for (int n = 0; p < egptr(); ++p)
        if (*p == '\n') ++n;
      offset += n;
    }
    setg(0,0,0);
```

This counting of newline characters is a weak point. At this stage, we have no choice but to assume that in translated mode, all newline characters in the read buffer were derived from CR/LF pairs in the file. This of course might not be the case for there might have been isolated newline characters in the file. This possibility is one of the penalties of mimicking UNIX in the DOS environment.

When the number of characters in the get area has been estimated, seek back so it appears they were never read, as follows:

```
    if ( offset > 0 ) {
      if (lseek(file, -offset, 1) == -1L)
        return EOF;
    }
  } else {
```

If seeking is not permitted, it's less obvious what is required of the synchronization function. If the overriding requirement is that the next character got be the next character in the file sequence, then the get area can simply be wasted. However, if the overriding requirement is to signal that seeking on the file is an error, `syncin()` must return `EOF`, as follows:

```
    if (in_avail())  // error on non-seeking devices
        return EOF;
  }
  return 0;
}
```

The second of the two synchronization functions deals with the put area. If `ios::app` is specified, the file is first positioned so that any characters written are appended, as follows:

```
int filebuf::syncout()
{
  long cp, rv;
  if (mode & ios::app) {
    cp = lseek(file, 0L, 1);
    if (cp == -1L)
      return EOF;
    if (lseek(file, 0L, 2) == -1L)
      return EOF;
  }
```

The private `flushbuf` function translates any newlines and writes the contents of the put area to the file. In the `ios::app` case the file context must then be put back as it was, as follows:

```
  if (flushbuf() == EOF) return EOF;

  if (mode & ios::app) {
    if (lseek(file, cp, 0) == -1L)
      return EOF;
```

```
    }
    setp(0,0);
    return 0;
}
```

The actual `sync` function combines `syncin` and `syncout`, as in the following. If the `filebuf` is not attached to a file, it returns `EOF`.

```
int filebuf::sync()
{
    if ( file == EOF )
        return EOF;

    if (in_avail())
        if (syncin() == EOF) return EOF;
    if (out_waiting())
        return syncout();
    return 0;
}
```

Filling and emptying the buffer

The `underflow` and `syncout` functions use private member functions to deal with some of their low-level operations, specifically extraction of characters from the file into the get area and output of characters in the put area to the file. This allows most of the considerations related to newline translation to be isolated. Only the character-by-character writes required under unbuffered operation are dealt with elsewhere (in the `overflow` function).

In this implementation, the put buffer is placed at the beginning of the buffer area. During translation, the contents of the put area get copied to the other end, with newline characters inserted as required.

The `flushbuf` function is called only by `syncout`, and `syncout` is called only if there are characters waiting in the put area.

```
int filebuf::flushbuf()
{
    int n;
    char *q;

    if (mode & ios::binary) {
        q = pbase();
        n = pptr() - q;
    } else {
```

```
    char *p = pptr()-1;
    q = ebuf();
    for (; p >= pbase();) {
      *--q = *p--;
      if (*q == '\n')
        *--q = '\r';
    }
    n = ebuf()-q;
  }

  if (write(file,q,n) < n) return EOF;
  return 0;
}
```

The inverse function, fillbuf, attempts to fill the buffer from the file. In the text file case, this requires reading a bufferfull, then stripping out CR/LF pairs and substituting newlines. It's possible of course that reading a bufferfull of characters from the file will leave a return character that is part of a \r\n pair in the last position in the buffer. This is dealt with by reading a nominal bufferfull of characters, checking for the return character, and then if it's found, reading an extra character. At this point, anything but another return character is acceptable. A second return character merely perpetuates the uncertainty, so it is ignored and the file is stepped back. With typical input, however, this will happen infrequently. The constructors and other setup functions have to allow for the extra character space required.

This sounds clumsy. Why not simply read a bufferfull and if the last character is a return character, ignore it and step the file back 1. The problem is the file involved might not support seeking. It could for example be the standard input. The method described still steps the file back if a second return character is read, but in the case of streams like the standard input, this usually won't happen because the accompanying line feed character will be there. If input is redirected, characters could be missed. We have here another penalty of mimicking UNIX in another environment.

A similar glitch exists in the unbuffered case when, in the worst case (an isolated return character and no seeking), two characters are read from the file at the same time.

```
int filebuf::fillbuf()
{
  int trans = (mode & ios::binary)? 0: 1;
  int required;
  char *p, *q;

  if (unbuffered()) {
```

```
      p = base();
      if (::read(file,p,1) != 1)
        return EOF;        // no more characters
      if (trans && *p == '\r') {
        p[1] = '\0';
        if (read(file,p+1,1) == 1) {
          if (p[1] == '\n')
            *p = '\n';
          else {
```

If there is an isolated `'\r'` character and seeking is not allowed, the extra character must be retained in the buffer. The file can't be stepped back.

```
            if (do_not_seek) {
              setg(base(),base(),base()+2);
              return 2;
            }
            lseek(file,-1L,1);
          }
        }
      }
      setg(base(),base(),base()+1);
      return 1;
    }
```

The putback mechanism in the buffered case requires space for four characters to be reserved before the start of the get area. When newline characters are represented by a `'\r\n'` pair, it might also be necessary to read an extra character. A total of five characters of the total buffer area must then be withheld.

```
    reserve = 4;
    p = base()+4;
    required = blen()-(trans? 5: 4);
    int t = read(file,p,required);
    if (t <= 0) return EOF;    // no more characters
    if (trans) {
      q = p+(t-1);
      if (*q++ =='\r') {
```

If there is an isolated `'\r'` character, determine if it's part of a pair. If the next character is another `'\r'`, then step the file back. Isolated `'\r'` characters should happen only infrequently. Usually the next character will be part of a CR/LF pair or some other character.

```
        if (read(file,q,1) == 1) {
```

```
      if (*q == '\r') {
        lseek(file,-1L,1);
          // will fail if seeking not allowed
      } else
        ++t;
    }
  }
```

Finally, do the newline translation, as follows:

```
  q = p;
  for (; t--;) {
    if (t > 0 && *p == '\r' && *(p+1) == '\n') {
      ++p;  // skip the '\r'
      --t;
    }
    *q++ = *p++;
  }
  t = q-base()-4;  // the translated length
}

setg(base()+4,base()+4,base()+t+4);
return t;
}
```

17.10 Seeking the File Pointer

We noted in the discussion of class `streambuf` that the `seekpos` function can be implemented in terms of the `seekoff` function. In this case, only an implementation of `filebuf::seekoff` must be provided. In some environments, the absolute seek can be implemented more efficiently than can the relative seek, in which case it's appropriate to override both of these virtual functions.

At some point in this function, we need translations of the enumerators `ios::beg`, `ios::cur`, and `ios::end` to the corresponding values adopted by the UNIX-like `lseek` function. These can be picked up from an appropriate C header file and the values used to initialize a private static data member of class `filebuf`. The usual values are hard-coded in the example below.

Note that the final argument to `seekoff` is ignored in the case of class `filebuf`, as shown in the following. There is only one file pointer to adjust.

```
const int filebuf::lseek_consts[3] =
```

```
    { 0, 1, 2 };
streampos filebuf::seekoff(streamoff offset,
                           ios::seek_dir from, int)
{
// Seeking on a device that does not support it is an error.
  if ( do_not_seek )
    return streampos(EOF);
// Eliminate the effects of buffering.
  sync();
```

This implementation deals only with files in which positions can be represented by a long, as in

```
long result;
if ((result = lseek(file, long(offset), lseek_consts[from]))
                              >= 0)
    return streampos(result);
  else
    return streampos(EOF);
}
```

17.11 Nominating a Buffer Area

The base class, streambuf, has a virtual function setbuf, which is to some extent left over from the earlier Streams library and is only partly supported in IOStreams. It offers an area of memory for streambuf to use as a buffer, although derived classes are not obliged to take up this offer. The function does have another property, however, that is sometimes useful: if it's called with a 0 memory pointer argument and/or a length argument <= 0, it switches the streambuf to unbuffered operation.

In this implementation of class filebuf, the offer of memory is accepted only if the filebuf doesn't already have a buffer or is not already set up to work unbuffered.

```
streambuf *filebuf::setbuf(char *memory, int length)
{
  if (unbuffered() || base())
      // already satisfactorily set up
    return 0;
```

Some suggestions for a buffer might be unacceptable. For example, in the present case the absolute minimum is six bytes: four for the reserve, one for a possible extra character in `fillbuf`, and one in which to read a character.

```
if (length > 0 && length < 6)
  return 0;
if (!memory || length <= 0) {
```

When unbuffered operation is requested, any provision made for this in the base class is overridden to allow for text mode translation requirements, as follows:

```
  if (mode & ios::binary)
    setb(unbuf,unbuf+1,0);
  else
    setb(unbuf,unbuf+2,0);
} else {
  if (!streambuf::setbuf(memory,length))
    return 0;
}
```

To enforce the notational tying of the get and put pointers, both the get and put areas need to be initially disabled.

```
  setp(0,0);
  setg(0,0,0);
  return this;
}
```

The minimal one or two character buffer in the "unbuffered" state supports the `sgetc` function, which is normally implemented inline, something like

```
inline int streambuf::sgetc()
{
  return _gptr < _egptr? *_gptr: underflow();
}
```

In unbuffered operation, the get area usually is a one-character buffer area, with the get pointer pointing at the position after the area. A call to `sgetc` resolves to a call to `underflow` that, if successful, will read one character into the get area, return its value, and leave the get pointer pointing at the character. Subsequent calls to `sgetc` return that character without a further file read. Any other get function call that advances the get pointer forces a return to direct fetches from the file.

`sgetc` often gets called as part of a conditional `sbumpc` with `stossc`, for example,

```
while ((c = sgetc()) != EOF) && isspace(c))
  stossc();
```

This is a close approximation to unbuffered operation, with such a loop dominated by the single character read operation that occurs as part of `underflow`.

17.12 Allocation

In this implementation of `filebuf`, `doallocate` doubles up on the buffer if text mode translation is required. If allocation is successful, it calls `setb` to set up the buffer pointers, with a nonzero third argument to indicate that deletion is required by the destructor, and then returns 0,

```
int filebuf::doallocate()
{
  int bs = filebuf_buffer_size;
  if (!(mode & ios::binary)) {
    bs *= 2;
    bs += 5;      // putback reserve plus one extra char
  } else
    bs += 4;      // putback reserve
  char *p = new char[bs];
  if (!p) return EOF;
  setb(p, p+bs,1);
  return 0;
}
```

Note that it's possible to write this function so that it defaults to unbuffered operation if the allocation fails. If such behavior is required, it's probably better to derive a further specialized version of `filebuf`. Only the `doallocate` function need be different.

17.13 Constructors and Destructor

Three constructors are provided for class `filebuf`:

1. A default constructor that sets up a `filebuf` with no buffer area and no associated file.

2. One that sets up a `filebuf` with no buffer area but that is associated with a specified file.

3. One that allows specification of the associated file and of the buffer area. As is customary for a `streambuf`, if the buffer area is specified by a 0 pointer or with length <= 0, then operation is unbuffered.

   Instances of `filebuf` set up with the first two constructors will dynamically allocate a buffer when required, unless the `setbuf` function is used to specify a buffer or to request unbuffered operation before the object is used.

The explicit constructors have a defaulted final argument that can be used to force binary operation in environments in which binary mode is distinct from text mode. Where there is no distinction between these two modes, these arguments can be omitted.

The first constructor sets the file data member to EOF to indicate that the filebuf object is not attached to a file, as follows:

```
filebuf::filebuf()
  : file(EOF),
    mode(0),
    do_not_seek(1),
    own_file_descriptor(0),
    reserve(0)
{}
```

The second sets up a filebuf to use a file that is specified by an int file descriptor, as follows:

```
filebuf::filebuf(int descriptor, int io_mode)
  : file(descriptor),
    mode(io_mode),
    do_not_seek(isatty(descriptor) ||
         lseek(descriptor, 0L, 0) == -1L),
    own_file_descriptor(0),
    reserve(0)
{
```

This constructor must assume that the file may not have been opened in a mode that positioned the file currency at the end of the file.

```
  if (mode & ios::ate)
    lseek(file, 0L, 2);
}
```

The third constructor takes a file descriptor argument plus arguments that specify the required buffer, as follows:

```
filebuf::filebuf(int descriptor, char *memory, int length,
                     int io_mode)
  : streambuf(memory, length),
    file(descriptor),
    mode(io_mode),
    do_not_seek(isatty(descriptor) ||
         lseek(descriptor, 0L, 0) == -1L),
    own_file_descriptor(0),
    reserve(0)
```

```
{
  buffer_setup();
// The file may not have been opened with O_APPEND
  if (mode & ios::ate)
    lseek(file, OL, 2);
}
```

The destructor calls the `sync` function to flush any outstanding characters in the put area to the file. Then if the file was attached to the `filebuf` using `filebuf::open`, it closes the associated file, as follows:

```
filebuf::~filebuf()
{
  sync();
  if (own_file_descriptor)
    close();
}
```

17.14 Attaching and Detaching a File

When a `filebuf` has been created using the default constructor, it can be associated with a file in one of two ways: either using the `attach` function, which uses an already opened file, or the `open` function, which opens a specified file and attaches it to the `filebuf`. Both of these functions also accept mode information. The possible modes are specified in the enumeration `open_mode` in class `ios` and are as follows:

`ios::in`	Open for reading.
`ios::out`	Open for writing.
`ios::ate`	Position to the end-of-file initially.
`ios::app`	Position to the end-of-file before each write (`ios::app` implies `ios::out`).
`ios::trunc`	Truncate the file on open.
`ios::nocreate`	Do not attempt to create the file if it doesn't exist.
`ios::noreplace`	Cause the open to fail if the file exists.
`ios::binary`	Is not a text file.

The `open_mode` enumerators represent bits that can be orred together to form compound mode specifications.

```
filebuf *filebuf::attach(int file_descriptor, int io_mode)
{
// If the filebuf is already attached, this is an error
```

```
    if (file != EOF)
        return 0;

    file = file_descriptor;
    mode = io_mode;

// Check if seeking is supported
    if (isatty(file) || lseek(file, 0L, 1) == -1L)
        do_not_seek = 1;
    else {
// The file may not have been opened in a mode which
// positioned the currency at end-of-file
        if (mode & ios::ate)
            lseek(file, 0L, 2);
    }
    return this;
}
```

The open function takes a file name, mode information, and a file protection argument, as shown in the following. The latter is defaulted to whatever is appropriate for the environment.

```
filebuf *filebuf::open(const char *name, int io_mode,
                              int protection)
{
// If the filebuf is already attached, this is an error
  if (file != EOF)
    return 0;

  int open_mode = 0;
  mode = io_mode;

// First figure out which of reading or writing or both
// are permitted
  if (mode & (ios::out|ios::app)) {
    if (mode & ios::in)
      open_mode |= O_RDWR;
    else
      open_mode |= O_WRONLY;
  } else if (mode & ios::in)
    open_mode |= O_RDONLY;
  else
// Must have one or both of ios::in and ios::out set
    return 0;
```

```
// If specifically ios::trunc, or logically necessary then
// specify truncation
  if (mode & ios::trunc
         || (mode & ios::out &&
           !(mode & (ios::in|ios::ate|ios::app)))))
    open_mode |= O_TRUNC;

// Allow creation if it is not prohibited by ios::nocreate
  if (!(mode & ios::nocreate))
    open_mode |= O_CREAT;

// Enforce exclusivity
  if (mode & ios::noreplace)
    open_mode |= O_EXCL;

  if ((file = ::open(name, open_mode, protection)) == EOF)
    return 0;

  own_file_descriptor = 1;  // Make the destructor call close

  if (isatty(file) || lseek(file, 0L, 1) < 0)
    do_not_seek = 1;
  else if (mode & ios::ate) {
    if (lseek(file,0L,2) == -1L)
      return 0;
  }
  return this;
}
```

The `close` function flushes any outstanding characters in the put area, closes the file, and marks the `filebuf` as unattached. It returns 0 if there was any failure along the way; otherwise, it returns a pointer to the `filebuf` object.

```
filebuf *filebuf::close()
{
  int result = sync();

  int rv = ::close(file);  // The C standard library close
  file = EOF;

  if ( result == EOF || rv)
    return 0;
  else
```

```
    return this;
}
```

17.15 Summary

filebuf is probably one of the more difficult derivations from the IOStreams base class streambuf. The filebuf example in this chapter is a guide to the way that other similar derivations might be structured and to points that must be given special attention when this is done.

Derived streambuf types for specific purposes will provide implementations of some or all of the streambuf base class virtual functions. The following tabulation shows what the versions in the base class should do, the circumstances under which they need to be overridden in the derived class, and the subcomponents described in the previous sections that might be useful examples in doing this.

Virtual function	Base class action	Derived class	Suggested subcomponents
underflow	Returns EOF or may be pure virtual.	Overrides if the derived type is a character source; otherwise returns EOF.	fillbuf syncout
overflow	Returns EOF or may be pure virtual.	Overrides if the derived type is a character sink; otherwise returns EOF.	syncin syncout
doallocate	Attempts to allocate a buffer. Returns EOF on failure.	Overrides if the base class buffer is unsuitable or its behavior is unknown.	
sync	Returns 0 if get and put areas are empty; returns EOF otherwise	Overrides if the device is a character source that supports seeking or is a character sink.	syncin syncout flushbuf
seekoff	Returns EOF.	Overrides if the device supports seeking.	
seekpos	Is implemented using seekoff.	Overrides if absolute positioning is more efficient than relative positioning.	
setbuf	Accepts offered buffer if no buffer is setup.	Overrides if appropriate to the derived type.	

`pbackfail`	Returns EOF.	Overrides to provide character putback if appropriate.

In any particular derivation, it's also necessary to provide the following:

- A default constructor
- Constructors to associate the derived class with its source and/or sink
- Utility functions to associate an object created using the default constructor with a source and/or sink

18

Derivation from the
Translator Classes

Given any particular buffer class derived from `streambuf`, such as `filebuf`, it's possible to derive new translator classes from `istream` or `ostream` that are specialized on the new `streambuf` type. Often, doing this involves little more than encapsulating a `streambuf` of the new kind in the derived translator class and then providing an appropriate set of constructors.

In this chapter, we follow up our `filebuf` derivation by describing the derivation of the translator classes specialized on files. Derivation from the translator classes, in a way that doesn't involve a new `streambuf` type, is subject to some restrictions, which we also discuss in this chapter. Class `ios` provides facilities for extended format parameters, and we show how useful classes can be derived that use such extensions.

We also speculate on the advantages and disadvantages of making the inserter and extractor, and prefix and suffix, functions virtual in the base translator classes.

18.1 Translators Using a `filebuf`

`filebuf`'s capabilities can be utilized by setting up an instance of `filebuf`, then instantiating one of the existing translator classes to use that instance as its `streambuf`, as follows:

```
filebuf fb;
fb.open("thing.dat", ios::out);
```

```
ostream os(&fb);
```

However, because the C++ object-oriented paradigm is all about making programming more convenient and safer for users of classes, it's much better to be able to
use simply

```
ofstream ofs("thing.dat");
```

To do this we need only derive a class from class `ostream` that has an appropriate
set of constructors and member functions equivalent to the `filebuf::attach`,
`filebuf::open`, `filebuf::close`, and `filebuf::setbuf` functions.

18.2 File-oriented Translator Class Definitions

The public interfaces for the file-oriented translators were given in Chapter 13.
These used an intermediate class, `fstream_common`, to encapsulate common
behavior and an instance of class `filebuf`.
    The overall structure for the file-oriented translators is as follows:

```
class fstream_common : virtual public ios {
  ...
private:
  filebuf buffer;
};
```

```
class ifstream : public fstream_common, public istream;
class ofstream : public fstream_common, public ostream;
class fstream : public fstream_common, public iostream;
```

An implementation of such a system follows, starting with class `fstream_common`.

18.3 Implementation of `fstream_common`

The `fstream_common` class has a protected constructor which simply initializes the
base `ios` object. In practice this initialization is ignored, since the virtual base is
initialized by the most-derived object, in this case an actual derived translator class.

```
fstream_common::fstream_common() : ios(fstream_common::rdbuf()) {}
```

The rest of the fstream_common member functions simply set the state flags to reflect the return value of the corresponding filebuf function, as in

```
void fstream_common::attach(int file_descriptor, int io_mode)
{
  if (!buffer.attach(file_descriptor, io_mode))
    clear(ios::failbit | ios::badbit);
  else
    clear();
}

void fstream_common::close()
{
  if (!buffer.close())
    clear(ios::failbit | ios::badbit);
}

void fstream_common::open(const char *name, int io_mode,
          int protection)
{
  if (!buffer.open(name, io_mode, protection))
    clear(ios::failbit | ios::badbit);
  else
    clear();
}
```

18.4 The Derived Translator Classes–ifstream

The ifstream default constructor sets up an object that is not yet associated with a file. It is unusable, and to reflect this its state is set to bad.

Note that class ifstream is part of a multiple inheritance system with a virtual base class, so its constructors must directly initialize the virtual base class ios. When an istream object is instantiated, it's this initializer that is acted on. Any initializations from the intermediate classes fstream_common and istream are ignored.

```
ifstream::ifstream() : ios(fstream_common::rdbuf())
                                    { clear(ios::badbit); }
ifstream::ifstream(int file_descriptor, int io_mode)
  : ios(fstream_common::rdbuf())
{
  fstream_common::attach(file_descriptor, io_mode);
```

```
}

ifstream::ifstream(const char *name, int io_mode,
                    int protection)
  : ios(fstream_common::rdbuf())
{
  fstream_common::open(name, io_mode, protection);
}

ifstream::ifstream(int file_descriptor, char *memory,
                int length, int io_mode)
  : ios(fstream_common::rdbuf())
{
  fstream_common::setbuf(memory, length))
  if (good())
    fstream_common::attach(file_descriptor, io_mode);
}
```

Class ofstream

The ofstream implementation is almost a carbon copy of ifstream, as demonstrated in the following:

```
ofstream::ofstream() : ios(fstream_common::rdbuf())
  { clear(ios::badbit); }

ofstream::ofstream(int file_descriptor, int io_mode)
  : ios(fstream_common::rdbuf())
{
  fstream_common::attach(file_descriptor, io_mode);
}

ofstream::ofstream(const char *name, int io_mode,
                    int protection)
  : ios(fstream_common::rdbuf())
{
  fstream_common::open(name, io_mode, protection);
}

ofstream::ofstream(int file_descriptor, char *memory,
                    int length, int io_mode)
  : ios(fstream_common::rdbuf())
{
  fstream_common::setbuf(memory, length);
```

```
  if (good())
    attach(file_descriptor, io_mode);
}
```

Class fstream

The fstream implementation follows the same pattern as ofstream does:

```
fstream::fstream() : ios(fstream_common::rdbuf())
{ clear(ios::badbit); }

fstream::fstream(int file_descriptor, int io_mode)
  : ios(fstream_common::rdbuf())
{
  fstream_common::attach(file_descriptor, io_mode);
}

fstream::fstream(const char *name, int io_mode, int protection)
  : ios(fstream_common::rdbuf())
{
  fstream_common::open(name, io_mode, protection);
}

fstream::fstream(int file_descriptor, char *memory,
                 int length, int io_mode)
  : ios(fstream_common::rdbuf())
{
  fstream_common::setbuf(memory, length);
  if (good())
    fstream_common::attach(file_descriptor, io_mode);
}
```

18.5 Derivation Restrictions on the Translator Classes

Suppose we need an ostream style class that displays pointer values in some different way. The details are not important. Say the output we need is

->12a4

At first glance this seems simple. All we need is

```
class xostream : public ostream {
```

```
public:
  xostream(streambuf *sb) : ios(sb) {}
  ostream &operator<<(const void *);
};

xostream &xostream::operator<<(const void *p)
{
  if (opfx()) {
    *this << "->" << (unsigned) p;
    osfx();
  }
  return *this;
}
```

However, this code will provoke an error message from the compiler, probably to the effect that unsigned is not an appropriate operand for xostream and the left shift operator. Using more specific, but equivalent, semantics should clarify the situation. We can recast the function as

```
xostream &xostream::operator<<(const void *p)
{
  if (opfx()) {
    this->operator<<("->");
    this->operator<<((unsigned) p);
    osfx();
  }
  return *this;
}
```

The error message now should be close to the following:

```
this->operator<<((unsigned) p);
                  ^
Can't implicitly convert unsigned to void*
```

This looks at first like an argument matching problem. In this member function call, we have an implicit argument of type xostream* (the this pointer) and an explicit argument of type unsigned. These are not a match for the xostream member function of that name:

```
xostream &xostream::operator<<(const void *);
```

Although they look to be a reasonable match for

```
ostream &ostream::operator<<(unsigned);
```

At this point, all that seems to be required is converting the implicit `this` pointer argument from a derived pointer type to a public base pointer type. That is a standard conversion. But this is not what the compiler is protesting. The difficulty here is declaration matching, not argument matching. A choice can be made only between overloaded functions in the same scope. The `ostream` inserter functions, however, are not in the same scope as the `xostream` inserter functions, so they aren't considered as possibilities.

In order to derive `xostream` with different behavior for `operator<<(const void*)`, all inserters must be redefined, as shown in the following. This is simple but tedious.

```
class xostream : public ostream {
public:
  xostream(streambuf *sb) : ios(sb) {}

  xostream &operator<<(char c)
    { return (xostream &) ostream::operator<<(c); }
  xostream &operator<<(int n)
    { return (xostream &) ostream::operator<<(n); }
  xostream &operator<<(double d)
    { return (xostream &) ostream::operator<<(d); }
  // and so on
  ...
};
```

In uncomplicated circumstances, it has the following required effect:

```
xostream os(cout.rdbuf());      // initialize xostream os
                                // from standard output
void *p = (void *) 0xabcd;
int n = 22;
os << p << ' ' << n;            // gives   ->abcd 22
```

However, if some user has previously defined a special pointer class

```
class special_ptr {
friend ostream &operator<<(ostream&, const special_ptr&);
public:
  special_ptr(void *p) : sp(p) {}
  operator void*() const { return sp; }
private:
  void *sp;
};
```

inserting a `special_ptr` object into an `xostream` will not cause the `void*` value to be displayed in the new way:

```
special_ptr spec(p);
os << spec;          // gives  abcd (or however
                     // ostream displays a void*)
```

The `special_ptr` inserter function takes an `ostream` reference argument, so it uses the `ostream` version of `operator<<(const void*)`.

Derivation from the translator classes doesn't behave in an object-oriented way. The reason is clear. The only virtual functions in classes `istream` and `ostream` are the destructors. This appears to severely limit the usefulness of derivation from these classes.

However, if the extractor and inserter functions were virtual, we could define translator classes that changed the behavior of a particular user-defined type. Such classes would require only a minimal implementation, like the first of those given for class `xostream` at the beginning of Section 18.4. Objects of type `xostream` would then work with inserters for a user-defined type defined to take an `ostream` reference argument. If these inserters happened to use the built-in inserter for `void*`, their output would be displayed in the modified form. A typical result would be that the extractor for the user-defined type was unable to translate character sequences produced by its inserter. In effect, redefining the behavior of IOStreams extractors and inserters would modify the behavior of other user types and could break code that depended on that behavior.

There also appears to be justification in terms of efficiency for the way `istream` and `ostream` are designed. Programs using IOStreams are likely to use the inserter and extractor functions often, for example,

```
int a, b, c;
cout << a << ' ' << b << ' ' << c << endl;
```

This has six function calls on a single source line, the price paid for type safety. If the inserters were virtual functions, then six times the virtual function call overhead would be added. Would this be acceptable? We think it would, based on tests we have run; the overhead introduced by virtual functions calls is marginal in the overall timing of insertion and extraction operations.

The most compelling reason to retain the current design would seem to be the one first presented, that is, existing user code could be broken if extractors and inserters for the built-in types were redefined.

18.6 Using the Extended Format Parameters

The designer of the IOStreams system didn't neglect the need for polymorphic behavior in derived translator classes. In object-oriented parlance, we need to be able to pass messages to translator objects. The objects then should make a state change or perform some operation characteristic of their type, which is determined at run time.

We have a mechanism for passing messages to translator objects since manipulators can be inserted or extracted. In addition, class `ios` provides facilities for extended format flags and parameters. So, the required state changes or operations can be implemented in terms of data that's already part of all such types. Derived types that don't implement a particular state change or operation can simply ignore such messages.

Using manipulators in this way doesn't allow overriding the behavior of the standard extractors and inserters. These don't consider the extended format parameters. The derivation possibilities are limited to new capabilities and don't allow modification of existing ones. Because the existing capabilities are not changed, user-defined types that use them aren't affected, and no code is broken.

We can illustrate the techniques by deriving a class to take advantage of ANSI terminal control sequences (escape sequences). For demonstration purposes, we restrict this to modifying the output's color. Note also that the example is complicated by having to allow for a deficiency in current IOStreams specifications. These specifications don't require the values of the extended format parameters to be initialized, although the latest ANSI draft does.

Class `ansios` is a public derivation from `ostream` that adds only two static data members. The first is a static `int`, which is used to note if any objects of type `ansios` have been instantiated. The second holds an integer value obtained from `ios::xalloc`, an index into the extra format parameters provided by class `ios`. The values of these static variables can be read by corresponding static member functions of the `ansios` class. Member functions are provided to read and set the display color, and a constructor is included to initialize an `ansios` object from a regular `ostream`.

```
#include <strstream.h>

const long ansios_id = 0x0fff0000;

class ansios : public ostream {
public:
  enum ansicolors { none, red = 31, green = 32,
                    blue = 34, white = 37 };

  ansios(ostream&);
  ansicolors color() const;
  ansicolors color(ansicolors);

// format parameter index
```

```
  static int fpindex() { return fpi; }
// Any of these objects instantiated?
  static int used() { return init; }
private:
  static int init;
  static int fpi;
};
```

The constructor passes the address of the ostream's streambuf to the parent ios object. It then determines if there are any previous instantiations of ansios. If there aren't, it allocates an extended format parameter and notes its index in the static data member fpi. The default color value is stored in the low word of the format parameter; an identifier for ansios objects is stored in the high word. This complication is required because the extended format parameters might not be initialized; if the parameters were guaranteed to be initialized to 0, it wouldn't be necessary. A nonzero value for the parameter corresponding to ansios::fpindex() would indicate that the translator object was of type ansios.

```
int ansios::init = 0;
int ansios::fpi = 0;

ansios::ansios(ostream &os) : ios(os.rdbuf())
{
  if (!init) {
    fpi = xalloc();
    init = 1;
  }
  iword(fpi) = ansios_id | white;
}
```

The function that reads the display color simply returns the value of the low word of the extended format parameter cast to type ansios::ansicolors, as follows:

```
ansios::ansicolors ansios::color() const
{
  return ansicolors(iword(fpi) & 0xffff);
}
```

The color setting function notes the new color in the extended format parameter and sends the appropriate escape sequence to the terminal:

```
ansios::ansicolors ansios::color(ansicolors c)
{
  char buf[20];
  long &fp = iword(fpi);
```

```
  int t = fp & 0xffff;
  fp = ansios_id | c;
  ostrstream oss(buf,20);
  oss << '\x1b' << '[' << int(c) << 'm' << ends;
  *this << buf;
  return ansicolors(t);
}
```

Manipulators then can be defined to control display color, as shown in the following. The manipulators' type is one for which class ostream already has an inserter. If no ansios objects exist, or the format parameter doesn't identify the object as being of type ansios, these manipulators do nothing.

```
ostream &blue(ostream &s)
{
  if (!ansios::used())
    return s;
  long &fp = s.iword(ansios::fpindex());
  if ((fp & 0xffff0000) != ansios_id)
    return s;
  fp = ansios_id | 34;
  s << "\x1b[34m";
  return s;
}

ostream &red(ostream &s)
{
  ...
}

ostream &green(ostream &s)
{
  ...
}
```

We need to demonstrate that this approach works with a typical inserter for a user-defined type. Class Pair will serve this purpose:

```
class Pair {
friend ostream &operator<<(ostream&, const Pair&);
public:
  Pair(int a, int b) : r(a), c(b) {}
private:
  int r, c;
};
```

```
ostream &operator<<(ostream &os, const Pair &p)
{
  if (os.opfx()) {
    os << '(' << p.r << ',' << p.c << ')';
    os.osfx();
  }
  return os;
}
```

The test program instantiates an `ansios` object, then checks that the color for the object can be read and set. To further establish that `ansios` is general purpose, the instance is then assigned to `cout`. The `color` function can't be called for `cout`, but the output color can be adjusted using the manipulators. This is shown in the following:

```
void main()
{
  Pair p(22,33);
  ansios sos(cout);
  sos << "Color " << int(sos.color()) << endl;
  sos.color(ansios::red);
  sos << "Red output " << p << endl;
  cout = sos;
  cout << blue;
  cout << "Hello World " << p << endl;
  cout << green << "Green" << endl;
}
```

18.7 Operations between Insertions or Extractions

Like the extractor and inserter functions for the built-in types, the `istream` and `ostream` prefix and suffix functions are a part of the behavior of the standard translator classes that can't be affected by extended format parameters. The specified actions of the prefix and suffix functions don't take them into account. The inserter and extractor functions determine how character sequences are to be translated to objects and objects to character sequences. The prefix and suffix functions determine what happens between such operations.

Another style of derivation from the translator classes is inhibited because the prefix and suffix functions aren't virtual. If they were, it would be simple to derive `ostream`-style classes that, for example, space out units of output, latch field widths for the display of tables, and allow indentation. Similar considerations apply to the input prefix function, and in future versions, the input suffix function. A typical input requirement might be the enabling and disabling of the text cursor or caret in a GUI.

Class outs, described next, provides some of these services, given a definition of the base class, ostream, that made the opfx and osfx functions virtual. This is a speculative example, however; *it will not work with a standard implementation of IOStreams.* But it does illustrate once again the use of extended format parameters and manipulators in a derived translator class. In this case, extended format flags have been used. The same effect could be achieved by allocating an extra extended format parameter and using that as an extra flag-bit set. Flags are allocated to indicate that spacing of items is required and that the next output will be at the start of a new line.

```
#include <iostream.h>

class outs : public ostream {
public:
  outs(ostream &os, int step);
  int opfx();    // assumed virtual in ostream  *************
  void osfx();   // assumed virtual in ostream  *************
  void space(int = 1);
  void indentstep(int);
  static unsigned long spaceflag() { return spf; }
  static unsigned long nlflag() { return nlf; }
  static int fpindex() { return fpi[1]; }
  static int isouts(ostream &os);
private:
  static unsigned long spf, nlf;
  static int fpi[2];
  static int init;
};
```

Two extended format parameters are allocated. The first holds a value that identifies the object as being of type outs. The second is used as a pair of short integers to hold an indent step size and the current indentation count.

```
unsigned long outs::spf = 0, outs::nlf = 0;
int outs::fpi[2] = { 0, 0 }, outs::init = 0;

outs::outs(ostream &os, int step)
 : ios(os.rdbuf())
{
  if (!init) {
    spf = bitalloc();
    nlf = bitalloc();
```

```
    fpi[0] = xalloc();
    fpi[1] = xalloc();
    init = 1;
  }
```

The default state of an outs object is set to include spacing between items and place the next output at the start of a line as follows:

```
  setf(spf | nlf);
```

In this example, the object is marked as being of type outs by setting the first of the extended format parameters to the address of a class static data member. The other parameter is set up to the required indentation step size (high word) and an indentation count of 0 (low word).

```
  pword(fpi[0]) = &spf;
  iword(fpi[1]) = long(step) << 16;


}


void outs::space(int s)
{
  if (s)
    flags(flags() | spf);
  else
    flags(flags() & ~spf);
}


void outs::indentstep(int n)
{
  long &fp = iword(fpi[1]);
  short *ip = (int *) &fp;
  *++ip = n;
}
```

Here, the outs::opfx function first calls the ostream::opfx function. If that call returns nonzero, the required number of indentation spaces are inserted into the ostream. The newline flag is then reset.

```
int outs::opfx()
{
  if (ostream::opfx()) {
    if (flags() & nlf) {
      long &fp = iword(fpi[1]);
      short *ip = (short *) &fp;
      int i = ip[0] * ip[1];
```

```
      while (i--)
        put(' ');
      flags(flags() & ~nlf);
    }
    return 1;
  }
  return 0;
}
```

The outs::osfx function checks the spacing flag and outputs a space if required:

```
void outs::osfx()
{
  if (flags() & spf)
    put(' ');
  ostream::osfx();
}
```

A static member function is provided that tests an ostream-style object to establish if it is in fact an outs object:

```
int outs::isouts(ostream &os)
{
  return init && (os.pword(fpi[0]) == &spf);
}
```

The manipulators then use outs::isouts to determine if it's appropriate to modify the corresponding format parameter, as follows. If it isn't, they behave in the same way as the endl manipulator.

```
ostream &newln(ostream &os)
{
  if (outs::isouts(os))
    os.flags(os.flags() | outs::nlflag());
  endl(os);
  return os;
}


ostream &indent(ostream &os)
{
  if (outs::isouts(os)) {
    os.iword(outs::fpindex()) += 1;
    os.flags(os.flags() | outs::nlflag());
  }
  endl(os);
  return os;
```

```
}

ostream &outdent(ostream &os)
{
  if (outs::isouts(os)) {
    if (os.iword(outs::fpindex()) & 0xffff)
      os.iword(outs::fpindex()) -= 1;
    os.flags(os.flags() | outs::nlflag());
  }
  endl(os);
  return os;
}
```

The test program initializes an outs object from cout, setting its indentation step to 4. It then exercises the spacing facility and the indentation manipulators:

```
void main()
{
  outs os(cout,4);
  int i = 1, j = 2, k = 3;

  os << "String" << i << j << k << indent;
  os << i << j << k << newln;
  os << i << j << k << outdent;
  os << "Bye" << endl;
}
```

Bear in mind that to implement this example you need access to the IOStreams source code. The code won't require modification but will need to be recompiled. Only iostream.h requires changes—the functions opfx and osfx would be made virtual.

18.8 Summary

Derivation of new translator types given a new streambuf type will usually be somewhat stereotyped. That from an existing translator already associated with a streambuf requires a different technique. The extended format parameter system provided by class ios is used. The behavior of such derived classes can then be controlled by manipulators of types for which extractors or inserters are already defined.

The flexibility with which derived translator classes could be designed would be increased substantially if some of the functions in the base classes `istream` and `ostream` were virtual. For example, operations between extractions and insertions would benefit if the prefix and suffix functions were virtual. Also, variations in the behavior of particular extractors or inserters would require the extractor and inserter functions to be virtual. However, this latter modification could have unpredictable effects on programs, possibly modifying the behavior of the extractors and inserters for user-defined types.

19

Design of Extractor and Inserter Functions

The benefits of the IOStreams system will accrue in full only if it is used uniformly. For this reason, designers of new types need to ensure that extractor and inserter functions are routinely provided. If the library you are constructing is made suitably granular (that is, there are separate object files for separate functions), your user will lose nothing in executable size if IOStreams IO isn't used. On the other hand, it will be a more predictable development environment if C++ users know that an object of arbitrary type can be inserted into an `ostream`, as in

```
class T t;
cout << t;
```

The character representation of the type should be such that the converse operation

```
cin >> t;
```

can accept the same sequence of characters and properly set the value of `t`.

With many simple user-defined types, inserter and extractor functions can be some of the most complicated operations to provide. They often turn out to be difficult to design and test and might take programmers outside their area of expertise.

235

19.1 Classification of Implementation Techniques

The methods of writing inserters and extractors can be broadly classified. For example, one categorization is by the general approach to translation, whereby the translation method can be one of the following:

- Hand-crafted
- Table-driven

The hand-crafted technique uses functions designed heuristically to have program flow branches that deal with all possible values of the type and all acceptable character sequences. For output, the table-driven technique often will simply comprise output of a predefined string depending on the value of the type object. On the other hand, table lookup techniques with multiple tables could be used to produce quite complex output patterns. Table-driven input can use a fixed pattern-matching function to deal with input of a range of types, using a table lookup technique to determine if each input character is acceptable in its particular context. When it has been determined that a character is acceptable, the character can be stored and the accepted string of characters eventually passed to a conversion function. Alternatively, the characters can be converted cumulatively as they are accepted. We discuss the hand-crafted route first because this method is currently the most often seen. It may also help illustrate why the table-driven approach can be advantageous.

Inserter and extractor implementations can also be classified by level, as follows:

- High-level
- Low-level
- Mixed-level

We can say that an implementation is high-level if it uses only existing type inserters and extractors and low-level if it uses only the character dispatching and fetching functions provided by `streambuf`. Many implementations will mix the two. The high-level technique favors economy of effort. Usually it's easier to write and test inserters and extractors written only in terms of existing ones. Conversely, the low-level technique favors efficiency, since for the most part, the `streambuf` level operations are inlined. This differentiation illustrates a preferred development route: create high-level implementations first when prototyping and follow up with low-level implementations if the performance improvement turns out to be worthwhile.

A further point is worth noting in this context. At the risk of stating the obvious, if dealing with a family of types, provide for input and output as close to the root as you can in the derivation hierarchy so that only minimal differences in the inserters and extractors are dealt with for the individual types.

19.2 The Lowest-level Inserters

Output of a char clearly has to be done the low-level way. No decomposition of this task is possible. The inserter will look something like the following:

```
ostream &ostream::operator<<(char c)
{
  if (!opfx())  // Standard protocol, check ostream state,
                // if not good do nothing
    return *this;

  int err = 0;

// if right justified, or no justification flag is set,
// pad on the left with the current fill char
  if (width() && ((flags() & (ios::right | ios::internal))
                  || !(flags() & ios::adjustfield))) {
    for (int i = width()-1; i > 0; --i) {
      if (rdbuf()->sputc(fill()) == EOF) {
        err = ios::eofbit | ios::failbit;
        break;
      }
    }
  }

// if the stream is still ok, send the character
  if (!err) {
    if (rdbuf()->sputc(c) == EOF)
      err = ios::eofbit | ios::failbit;

// and if it is still ok, and left justification is in force,
// pad on the right
    if (!err && width() && (flags() & ios::left)) {
      for (int i = width()-1; i > 0; --i) {
        if (rdbuf()->sputc(fill()) == EOF) {
          err = ios::eofbit | ios::failbit;
          break;
        }
      }
    }
  }

// If there was an error mark the stream
```

```
    clear(err);
    osfx();                    // Protocol
    return *this;
}
```

It's assumed here that resetting the stream width format state parameter is undertaken by the suffix function.

This function seems remarkably complicated for the output of a single character. However, this is what the AT&T documentation and the ANSI discussion document require as the minimal protocol. It's interesting that the actual AT&T implementation doesn't do this; rather it treats a character insertion as unformatted, ignoring width, padding, and justification. This is probably a mistake. Uniformity of behavior is one of the strengths of the IOstreams approach. Without the protocol for the single character inserter, the code fragment

```
char c = 'c';
int n = 10;
cout << setw(10) << n << endl;
cout << setw(10) << c << endl;
cout << setw(10) << n << endl;
```

would produce the output

```
        10
c
        10
```

which is probably not what the user had in mind.

With the function as presented, if width() is 0, much of the code falls away, and since only inline function calls are used, the function will usually be quite fast. However, you should begin to see why high-level inserter/extractor implementations are attractive.

It's also fairly clear from the character inserter that in an IOStreams implementation where the code size is a consideration, it is useful to have an ostream::pad function to look after justification, similar to the following:

```
int ostream::pad(long position, int n)
{
  if (width()) {
    long fv = flags() & ios::adjustfield;
    if (!fv) fv = ios::right;
    if (position & fv) {
      for (int i = width()-n; i > 0; --i) {
        if (rdbuf()->sputc(fill()) == EOF)
          return ios::eofbit | ios::failbit;
```

```
      }
    }
  }
  return 0;
}
```

The position argument should be one or more of `ios::left`, `ios::right`, or `ios::internal`. The second argument indicates the width of the actual item to be padded out to the `ostream`s set width.

The core of the character inserter then reduces to:

```
int err = pad(ios::right | ios::internal,1);
if (!err) {
  if (rdbuf()->sputc(c) == EOF)
    err = ios::eofbit | ios::failbit;
  if (!err)
    err = pad(ios::left,1);
}
```

It would be useful if the `ostream::pad` function could be exported selectively only to the inserter functions. Of course it can in principle, since such functions can be made friends of class `ostream`. Unfortunately, however, this means that file `iostream.h` would need to be modified each time a new inserter was designed. So in practice we have the choice of either making it public or doing without it. It would do little harm to have `ostream::pad` as a public member function.

19.3 A Low-level Inserter for Integral Types

In one sense, the character case is trivially simple since no translation is involved. In the case of inserters, this simplicity can be maintained to some extent for more complex types by introducing a separate translation function, and with hierarchies or groups of similar types, this is probably the economical way to go.

Consider the case of the inserters for the integral types. Here, we assume the implementation of integers is a conventional two's complement one. We also allow for user definition of extended two's complement integral types. To avoid unnecessary pollution of global name space, we define a class to hide some static functions dealing with two's complement numbers. This can't be used as a base class for the built-in types, since they aren't classes, but the built-in types can be let in on the act if we make class `ostream` a friend of class `_2Comp`. Extended two's complement types can be derived from the two's complement base class, which would, in that case, probably be considerably more complicated than the following version:

```
class _2Comp {
friend class ostream;
  static ostream &insert(ostream&, const void *body,
        int bytes, int issigned);
  static int format(unsigned char *body, char * buf,
        int bytes, int radix, int upper, int negative);
  static short div(unsigned char *body, int divisor,
                    int &remainder);
  static void negate(unsigned char *body, int bytes);
};
```

Assuming that the two's complement member functions are available, the inserters for int and unsigned long, for example, become a simple exercise, as follows:

```
ostream &ostream::operator<<(int n)
{
  return _2Comp::insert(*this, &n, sizeof(int), 1);
}

ostream &ostream::operator<<(unsigned long ul)
{
  return _2Comp::insert(*this, &ul, sizeof(unsigned long), 0);
}
```

The insert function itself isn't too difficult to design, although it still has a number of quirks regarding the overriding of sign by explicit settings of the ios::oct or ios::hex flags. These flags require that the output be as an unsigned integer. Also, internal padding must occur between the base indication and the body of the number. Note, the latest ANSI discussion document doesn't require this for octal representations.

```
ostream &_2Comp::insert(ostream &os, const void *bp,
                    int bytes, int issigned)
{
  if (!os.opfx())
    return os;

  char *s, buf[LONGEST];

  int radix - 10;
  if (os.flags() & ios::hex)
    radix - 16;
```

```
else if (os.flags() & ios::oct)
  radix = 8;
issigned = (radix == 10)? issigned: 0;
```

Determining whether the object is negative is architecture dependent. Just how this line gets written depends on whether the most significant byte is at higher or lower memory. Once we know this, we can use the format function to get a string representation of the integer. Doing this leaves the generated string at the tail end of the buffer.

```
int isneg =
  issigned && (((unsigned char *) bp)[bytes-1] & 0x80);

int length = format((unsigned char*) bp, buf, bytes, radix,
            os.flags() & ios::uppercase, isneg);
s = buf+LONGEST-1-length;
```

Now we must form the actual sign character, if there is one, and determine the total number of characters, as follows:

```
char sign = isneg? '-':
        (issigned && (os.flags() & ios::showpos))? '+': 0);
int fulllength = length+(sign != 0);
if (os.flags() & ios::showbase) {
   if (radix == 16)
     fulllength += 2;
   else if (radix == 8) {
     if (*s != '0') {
```

Octal representations get a leading 0 added only if they are nonzero. Since internal padding is not applied to octal numbers, the leading 0 is added to the digit string in the buffer:

```
        *--s = '0';
        fulllength++;
        length++;
      }
   }
}
```

From here on, the inserter is an expanded version of the character inserter with the pad function, using sputn to move character strings, and checking for the ios::internal case, as follows:

```
int err = os.pad(ios::right,fulllength);
if (!err) {
   if (sign) {
```

```
        if (os.rdbuf()->sputc(sign) == EOF)
          err = ios::failbit | ios::eofbit;
      }
    if (!err) {
      if (os.flags() & ios::showbase && radix == 16) {
        if (os.rdbuf()->sputn((os.flags() & ios::uppercase)?
                        "0X": "0x",2) != 2)
          err = ios::failbit | ios::eofbit;
      }
      if (!err) {
        err = os.pad(ios::internal,fulllength);
        if (!err) {
          if (os.rdbuf()->sputn(s,length) != length)
            err = ios::failbit | ios::eofbit;
          if (!err)
            err = os.pad(ios::left,fulllength);
        }
      }
    }
  }
  os.clear(err);
  os.osfx();
  return os;
}
```

Breaking things up in this way also makes the format function manageable. If a negative representation is required, `format` first calls the `complement` function, as follows:

```
int _2Comp::format(unsigned char *body, char *buf,
            int bytes, int radix, int upper, int negative)
{
  unsigned char local[BIGGEST];
  memmove(local,body,bytes);
        // copy required - it may be modified
  if (negative)
    negate(local,bytes);
        // if it is negative make the corresponding positive
  int q, digits = 0;
  char *p = buf+LONGEST-1;
  *p-- = '\0';
  do {
    q = div(local,radix,bytes); // get successive digits
    int d = (q & 0xff);
```

```
    if (radix == 16) {
      if (d < 10)
        *p-- = '0'+d;
      else if (upper)
        *p-- = 'A'+d-10;
      else
        *p-- = 'a'+d-10;
    } else
      *p-- = '0'+d;
    digits++;
  } while (q & 0xff00);
  return digits;
}
```

The div function here

```
short _2Comp::div(unsigned char *body, int divisor,
                        int bytes);
```

returns a most significant byte value of 0 if the quotient is 0; otherwise it returns with the most significant byte nonzero. The least significant byte of the return value holds the remainder. The quotient is left in the array pointed at by body. This function should almost certainly be coded in assembler, as should the complement function. The complement function negates an n-byte integer by reversing the bit values of the n bytes, then adding 1 to the least significant byte and propagating any carry through all n.

Assuming div and complement are efficient, this implementation is reasonable for the built-in types, and no further work is required if extended two's complement integral or unsigned types are defined. Their inserters can then be defined as follows:

```
class signed_quadword : public _2Comp {
friend ostream &operator<<(ostream &, const signed_quadword&);
  ...
private:
  ...
  char body[8];
};

inline ostream &operator<<(ostream &os,
            const signed_quadword &q)
{
  return q.insert(os, q.body, 8, 1);
}
```

Note that if this generalized approach is not fast enough, the inefficiency will probably be localized in the area of the `_2Comp::format` function. We can dispense with class `_2Comp` and make the format function a private member of class `ostream` written to use the machine's native instructions for the built-in integer types only. This can be done without changing the `insert` function, which in that case would also be made a private member of class `ostream`.

19.4 High-level Inserters

A suitable example of a high-level inserter is the familiar class `complex` as follows:

```
class complex {
friend ostream &operator<<(ostream&, const complex&);
friend istream &operator>>(ostream&, complex&);
public:
  complex(double, double);
  ...
private:
  double re, im;
};
```

However, if the inserter for `class complex` is to be well behaved, it must be somewhat more complicated than the examples often seen, for example,

```
ostream& operator<<(ostream &s, const complex &z)
{
  os << '(' << z.re << ',' << z.im << ')';
  return s;
}
```

This example doesn't use the prefix and suffix functions, which should be included since the latest ANSI discussion document allows them to undertake unspecified system-dependent actions. It also does nothing to implement justification. The example below does. While the way it justifies a complex number might not be aesthetically pleasing, it illustrates the sort of options involved.

```
ostream& operator<<(ostream &os, const complex &z)
{
  if (!os.opfx())     // protocol
    return os;
```

Check the width. If some nonzero value is set, use half of it for the real part and half for the imaginary. The apportionment needs to allow for a pair of parentheses and a comma, as follows:

```
int w = os.width(), rw = 0, imw = 0;
if (w) {
    int aw = w-3 > 0? w-3: 0;
    rw = aw/2;
    imw = aw-rw;
}

os.width(0);   // no width on opening parenthesis
os << '(';

os.width(rw);
os << z.re << ',';
os.width(imw);
os << z.im << ')';

os.osfx();
return os;
}
```

In cases where a failure occurred, a little time could be saved by some additional state testing as in

```
...
if (os) {
    os << z.re << ',';
    if (os) {
        os.width(imw);
        os << z.im << ')';
    }
}
...
```

but we should assume that failure is the least common outcome and opt instead to save on the code size. If a failure does occur, the succeeding operations will be skipped anyway.

Note that this inserter doesn't explicitly reset the width format parameter. However, because it is using built-in inserters, inserting the closing parenthesis will handle that.

19.5 Table-driven Inserters

Table-driven inserters are often appropriate for classes that have no systematic conversion to a character stream format. Also, they are usually fast, although the speed might be obtained at the expense of memory usage if the table required is large. As a trivial example, we can use the following class regular_polygon.

```
#include <iostream.h>

class regular_polygon {
friend ostream &operator<<(ostream &, const regular_polygon&);
public:
  regular_polygon(int n) : sides(n) {}
private:
  static int namelimit;
  static const char *names[...];

  int sides;
};

int  regular_polygon::namelimit = 6;
const char *regular_polygon::names[7] =  {
  "",
  "POINT",
  "LINE",
  "TRIANGLE",
  "SQUARE",
  "PENTAGON",
  "HEXAGON"
};

ostream &operator<<(ostream &os, const regular_polygon &pretty)
{
  if (os.opfx()) {
    os << '[';
    long oldf = os.setf(ios::right,ios::adjustfield);
    if (pretty.sides > pretty.namelimit) {
      os.width(3);
      os << pretty.sides << "_SIDED";
    } else {
      os.width(9);
      os << pretty.names[pretty.sides];
```

```
    }
    os << ']';
    flags(oldf);
    os.osfx();
  }
  return os;
}
```

The table-driven inserter usually needs some safety-net code. In this case, it's the section that constructs a name for a polygon with more than six sides.

The `regular_polygon` inserter formats its output right-justified, nine characters wide in square braces. In this implementation, doing this involves setting the stream flags for right justification. A user of the `regular_polygon` class usually won't expect the inserter to make arbitrary alterations to the stream state, so the state of the flags is saved and restored by the inserter. The code

```
regular_polygon *ap[3];

for (int i = 0; i < 3; ++i) {
  cout.width();
  cout << i << ' ' << *ap[i] << "    ";
}
```

then will produce the output that was presumably intended,

```
1    [    SQUARE]    2    [ 10_SIDED]    3    [ PENTAGON]
```

rather than

```
1    [    SQUARE]        2[ 10_SIDED]        3[ PENTAGON]
```

This point doesn't apply specifically to table-driven inserters. More generally, if your inserter alters format state parameters other than format width, it should save and restore them.

19.6 The Lowest-level Extractors

Once again we can't go any lower than `char`. The character extractor is less intimidating than its inserter, but this state of affairs doesn't extend to other types. Inserters can make assumptions about the value they output; extractors must assume that the input could be, and often is, garbage.

```
istream &istream::operator>>(char &c)
{
```

```
if (!ipfx(0))         // Protocol, check istream state,
   return *this;       // if not good, do nothing
int v;
if ((v = rdbuf()->sbumpc()) == EOF)
   clear(ios::failbit | ios::eofbit);
else
   c = v;              // c unchanged if EOF
                       // no suffix function for extractors
return *this;
}
```

The ipfx function is responsible for whitespace skipping in extractors. This extractor skips whitespace if the ios::skipws flag is set since the argument to ipfx is 0. The character referred to by the extractor function argument is changed only if there is no error. The only thing that can go wrong is an EOF on the input streambuf. This causes ios::failbit and ios::eofbit to be set.

19.7 A Low-level Extractor for Integral Types

For a low-level extractor for integral types, we can adopt an implementation scheme generally parallel to that suggested for integer inserters. In this case, the _2Comp class will need a few extra member functions, as follows:

```
class _2Comp {
   ...
friend class istream;
   istream &extract(istream &is, void *body, int bytes);
   int fromstring(unsigned char *body, int bytes,
                  const char *digitstring,
                  int radix, int negative);
   int mul(unsigned char *body, int bytes, int m);
   int add(unsigned char *body, int bytes, int a);
   ...
};
```

Once again, the actual extractor functions then become very simple.

```
istream &istream::operator>>(int &n)
{
   return _2Comp::extract(*this, &n, sizeof(int));
}
```

The `extract` function must extract characters for as long as they correspond to an integer representation and also determine the intended radix and the sign of the number. We must also take into account the setting of the `basefield` flags. If a flag is set to indicate a specific conversion base—oct, dec, or hex—the input stream will be parsed for corresponding digits only: 0–7 for oct; 0–9 for dec; and 0–9, a–f, or A–F for hex. If no conversion flag is set, the input stream must be converted according to C++ conventions, where a leading 0 implies octal and a leading "0x" or "0X" implies hexadecimal, with decimal assumed otherwise.

The result is an extractor function that is much more complicated than the single character case, as shown in the following:

```
istream &_2Comp::extract(istream &is, void *body, int bytes)
{
  if (!is.ipfx(0))
    return is;
  char buf[20], *p = buf;
  int err = 0, gotsign = 0, negative = 0,
          digits = 0, c, xc, sc;
  int radix, basef = is.flags() & ios::basefield;
```

To determine which characters are acceptable, we first must determine whether any conversion base is mandatory, as follows:

```
  switch (basef) {
  case ios::oct:
    radix = 8;
    break;
  case ios::dec:
    radix = 10;
    break;
  case ios::hex:
    radix = 16;
    break;
  default:        // includes mixed flags
    radix = 0;
  }
```

Now we can look at the first character, which may be a plus or minus sign. If it is either, we note it and then get the next character:

```
  if ((c = sc = is.rdbuf()->sgetc()) == EOF)
    err = ios::eofbit;

  if (!err) {
    if (sc == '-' || sc == '+') {
```

```
    gotsign = 1;
    negative = (sc == '-');
    if ((c = is.rdbuf()->snextc()) == EOF)
      err = ios::eofbit;
}
```

Next we can attempt to read a numeric string. If no specific conversion base is in force, this requires examination of the prefix to see if a radix can be inferred. This process starts by setting the radix to the default, which is decimal:

```
if (!err) {

  if (!radix) {
    radix = 10;
    if( c == '0') {
```

If a leading 0 is found, the sequence is a candidate for an octal or a hexadecimal representation. Either way, we can skip over the 0 character and look at the next one:

```
        is.rdbuf()->stossc();
        if ((xc = is.rdbuf()->sgetc()) != EOF) {
          if (isdigit(xc)) {
```

If this next character is an octal digit, we can assume we are looking for an octal representation. Otherwise we must assume that the input sequence is supposed to contain an isolated 0 and that the character just examined is a part of the next item, as follows:

```
            if (xc < '8') {
              radix = 8;
              c = xc;
            } else {
              *p++ = '0';
              c = 0;
              digits = 1;
            }
          } else if (tolower(xc) == 'x') {
```

If the character is an 'x' or an 'X', we could be looking at a hexadecimal representation. To find out, we must look at another character. If that one is a hex digit, our suspicions are confirmed. Otherwise what we saw was an isolated 0 followed by something starting with 'x', and the upper or lower case 'x' has to be put back on the stream.

```
            if ((c = is.rdbuf()->snextc()) != EOF) {
              if (isxdigit(c))
```

```
            radix = 16;
          else {
            *p++ = '0';  // isolated zero
            c = 0;
            digits = 1;
            is.rdbuf()->sputbackc(xc);
          }
        }
      } else {
```

If the character isn't a digit or an 'x', then we just have an isolated 0.

```
          *p++ = '0';
          c = 0;
          digits = 1;
        }
      } else
        err = ios::eofbit;          // note the eof
    }
  }
```

Once the radix is established, we can read digits until a mismatch with the radix is detected, as follows. At that point, the loop is broken before the `stossc;` therefore the character that broke it stays on the stream.

```
for (; c;) {
  if (!isxdigit(c) || (radix < 16 && !isdigit(c))
        || (radix == 8 && (!isdigit(c) || c > '7'))
    break;
  is.rdbuf()->stossc();
  *p++ = c;
  ++digits;
  if ((c = is.rdbuf()->sgetc()) == EOF) {
    err = ios::eofbit;
    break;
  }
}
```

If there were no digits, then any sign character found can be put back. Also the error log variable must be augmented to indicate failure.

```
if (!digits) {
  if (gotsign)
    is.rdbuf()->sputbackc(sc);
  err |= ios::failbit;  // no digits
}
```

```
    }
  }
  *p = 0;
```

At this point, either we failed or we got a legitimate character string that we must now translate, as follows:

```
if (!(err & (ios::failbit | ios::badbit))) {
  errno = fromstring((unsigned char *) body,
        bytes,buf,radix,negative)?  ERANGE: 0;
  if (errno)
    err |= ios::failbit;
}


// Record the outcome
  is.clear(err);
  return is;
}
```

Because we have this extractor as a context, a word about using the various streambuf character get functions is in order. If what we need is a look at the next character, use sgetc. However, sgetc doesn't advance the streambuf get pointer, so if you like what you see, use either stossc to do the advance or snextc to do the advance and look at the next character. There is an example of this in the _2Comp::extract function when the character sequence starts with a minus sign.

To look at two characters, use sbumpc to get the first character and advance the streambuf get pointer, then use sgetc to look at the second character. Alternatively, use sgetc and snextc to achieve a similar effect. If the two-character combination is unacceptable, a sputbackc will leave things as they were before the two-character lookahead. You can see this work when checking for a hex input when the extract function needs to see the 'x' and a following hex digit. Otherwise, the 'x' gets left on the stream and the number read is just a 0.

The extract function shown will in fact not remove any characters from the stream unless a proper representation of an integer number is encountered. The exception to this is the case in which an isolated minus sign is encountered before EOF. And even that could be put back. Not all extractors can do this well. In fact if they require more than two characters to be examined in order to determine whether the sequence is proper, they might lose characters on failure, since generally only a one-character putback is supported by streambuf types.

Functions of this sort are logically complex and deeply nested. Consequently, it's not easy to demonstrate that they work as intended with all possible input sequences. This is the motivation for the table-driven approach. If further evidence is required, we suggest the reader attempt an extractor to handle floating-point numbers using the same low-level technique.

For an implementation of the integer extractors limited to the built-in types, a suitable translation function from integer to string might already be available in the C standard library. However, the following example can deal with extended two's complement integer types. The worst is over; this is simpler.

```
int _2Comp::fromstring(unsigned char *body, int bytes,
        const char *s, int radix, int negative)
{
  memset(body,0,bytes);
  int overflow = 0;
  for (; *s; ++s) {
    overflow |= mul(body,bytes,radix);
    int a = isalpha(*s)? 10+tolower(*s)-'a': *s - '0';
    overflow |= add(body,bytes,a);
  }
  if (negative)
    complement(body,bytes);
  return overflow;
}
```

You might want to code the `mul` and `add` functions in assembler language in order to get the highest efficiency. These must return nonzero if the operation resulted in a carry beyond the specified number of bytes. The version of the `extract` function presented here notes whether an overflow occurs in the global `errno` variable (defined in `errno.h`) and sets `ios::failbit` in the stream's error state. This is simply an illustration of what might be done. The ANSI IOStreams discussion document doesn't require any specific notification of overflow, just the failure.

19.8 High-level Extractors

We can return to `class complex` for an example of a high-level extractor. Suppose it's acceptable to represent complex numbers as strings like

```
re
(re)
(re,im)
```

where `re` and `im` stand in for character sequences that would be acceptable to the standard extractor for `double` or that could be produced by the standard inserter for `double`.

This implementation is almost a one-to-one translation of an example given in Bjarne Stroustrup's first C++ book (*The C++ Programming Language,* Addison-Wesley, 1986). It has been converted to the IOStreams way of doing things recommended here by adding the input prefix function `istream::ipfx` and some manipulation of the format flags has been added.

```
#include <iostream.h>
#include <complex.h>

istream &operator>>(istream &is, complex &v)
{

  if (!is.ipfx(0))
    return is;

// Put the flags into a known state
  long oldf = is.flags(ios::defaults);

// Set a default value for the imaginary part,
  double a, b = 0;

// and a known value for the scratch character used to
// catch parentheses and comma.
  char c = 0;

// Now go for a character.
  is >> c;
```

If the character is an opening parenthesis, then look for a `double` followed by either a comma or a closing parenthesis, as in

```
  if (c == '(') {
    is.setf(ios::skipws); // honor the parentheses
    is >> a >> c;
```

If a comma is found, look for another `double` and a closing parenthesis. Remember, `c` was preset to 0. If input of the first `double` failed, the stream will be in an error state and these attempted operations will be ignored.

```
    if (c == ',')
      is >> b >> c;
```

Either way `c` should now hold a closing parenthesis, otherwise the input was not a well-formed complex number. If it was not, set the flags to show that the operation failed and, maybe, that characters were lost. The current state needs to be included, since it might be ios::eofbit.

```
if (c != ')')
    is.clear(ios::failbit | is.rdstate());
```

If the first character was not an opening parenthesis, put it back on the stream and try to reparse the input as one double, as follows. (The value of b was preset to 0.)

```
} else {
    is.putback(c);
    is >> a;
}
```

If all is well at this point, we got a good representation of a complex, so the required value can be transferred to v, as follows:

```
if (is.good())
    v = complex(a,b);

// Restore the flags
    is.flags(oldf);
    return is;
}
```

Extractors like this are much less painful than is the low-level example for integers, but they still require careful structuring and testing to ensure they deal properly with all acceptable sequences and reject all incorrect sequences.

Using the high-level approach as outlined means whitespace within character stream representations of complex numbers is acceptable. This means the extractor won't refuse to read such data from a text file simply because it is pretty-printed. Even if whitespace skipping is off, the parentheses have the expected effect.

```
(12.477,  22.69)
(      0,    1.22)
0
```

19.9 Mixed-level Extractors

Sometimes the high-level approach alone is not sufficient, for example, an extractor for a time-of-day class, as follows:

```
class TOD {
```

```
public:
  TOD(int h, int m, int s = 0);
  ...
  friend istream &operator>>(istream &, TOD &);
private:
  int hour, min, sec;
};
```

We might want to mimic the defaulted seconds argument to the constructor in the behavior of the extractor, so that

```
12:30
12:30:35
```

are both acceptable input sequences.

Now if the user of such an extractor written in the high-level way enters 12:30, then presses Enter, the high-level extractor will be skipping whitespace looking for a colon to decide whether the input is going to include seconds. This behavior won't do. The price of the defaulted seconds behavior is a drop into low-level mode to check for the colon. The extractor must contain some lookahead code such as

```
  if (!is)
    return is;
  do {           // OK after minutes
    is.get(c);
    if (c == '\n') {
```

If the user pressed Enter, we should presume that only the hour and minute are being offered and so form the TOD value and return

```
      t.hour = h;
      t.min = m;
      t.sec = 0;
      return is;
    }
  } while (isspace(c));

  if (c != ':') {
```

If the next actual character wasn't a colon, we have lost nothing but whitespace, which is fine. We can then form the TOD value and return

```
    is.putback(c);
    t.hour = h;
    t.min = m;
```

```
    t.sec = 0;
    return is;
}
```

Otherwise we can go for the seconds in the same way used to get the hours and minutes:

```
is >> s;
if (!is)
    return is;
t.hour = h;
t.min = m;
t.sec = s;
return is;
}
```

which allows us a little latitude. Consequently sequences like

```
12:30
12 : 30
12:30:35
12 : 30 : 35
12    :    30    :    35
```

with internal tabs and spaces will be correctly interpreted.

For a fully robust extractor a similar approach could be used to deal with the minutes also, since it's likely to cause confusion if newline characters are acceptable between hour and minute, but not between minute and second, as they would be with the approach just shown.

Mixed-level extractors might also be preferred on grounds of efficiency. As an extreme example, a high-level extractor could use a loop to extract a specified number of single characters, as follows:

```
for (int i = 0; i < max; ++i) {
  is >> buffer[i];
  if (!is) break;
}
```

This would be very inefficient. The extractor function can be prototyped at high level. However, the production version will be more efficient if it uses the unformatted read function and sets the stream flags according to the result, as in

```
is.read(buffer,max)
if (is.gcount() < max) {
  is.clear(ios::failbit | ios::eofbit);
```

19.10 Table-driven Extractors

Table-driven extractors are indicated when the character sequence representing the object can take diverse forms. Also they often are fast, as is commonly the case with table-driven algorithms. However, this speed might be obtained at the expense of memory usage if the required table is large.

The principles can be illustrated by the following extractor for class affirm:

```
class affirm {
  ...
private:
  int yes;
};
```

Suppose that acceptable inputs for a variable of type affirm are

```
y, Y, n, N, yes, YES, no, NO
```

Then it's possible to construct a table of the following form:

```
char     e   n   o   s   y   E   N   O   S   Y

state           transition
0               1*          2*  1*          2*
1                   4*              4*
2           3               3
3                   4*              4*
4
```

This is a transition table for the letters of the alphabet that we are concerned with in the input of affirm objects. The columns of the table can be selected by first consulting an array of 128 integers representing the full range of ASCII characters. If the array entry is -1, the input character is an error. Otherwise the array contains the required column of the transition table. Alternatively, we can check for character acceptability by testing a string and then use the index of the character in the string as a column indicator.

A variable state is maintained, which starts at 0. If an acceptable character is got from the stream, the state changes to that indicated in the row for the current state and the column for the acceptable character. If no state is marked at that point in the table, the character, although part of the acceptable subset of characters, is not appropriate in its particular context and so is an error. If the state at that point in the table is flagged with an asterisk, the implication is that the sequence of characters seen so far is acceptable. We can look at the next character to check that it is not part of an acceptable sequence, then put it back on the input stream. At that point, the value of the affirm variable can be appropriately set.

If the next character is acceptable, we continue to scan characters until we encounter either another asterisk-marked state or an illegal character. In the case of an illegal character, if the previous character was flagged as being an acceptance state, we can put the illegal character back and all is well. Using two-character lookahead, it's possible to do a little better, and so forth.

Transition tables of this type are one way of representing a Deterministic Finite Automaton (DFA). DFA pattern recognition is fast because it is lookup based. The time taken is proportional to the number of characters scanned, regardless of the number of entries in the table. So extractors implemented in this way are able to efficiently chew their way through large quantities of input. The table can be realized for a computer implementation by having the empty places contain 0, with all other state values incremented. (This will allow a table position to contain a legitimate transition to state 0, now represented by a table entry value of 1.) The states with an asterisk then can be made negative to distinguish them as acceptance states. So an extractor could resemble the following:

```
char *ok = "ENOSYenosy";

int tt[5][10] = {
//  E    N    O    S    Y    e    n    o    s    y
    {0, -2,   0,   0,  -3,   0,  -2,   0,   0,  -3},
    {0,   0,  -5,   0,   0,   0,   0,  -5,   0,   0}
    {4,   0,   0,   0,   0,   4,   0,   0,   0,   0},
    {0,   0,   0,  -5,   0,   0,   0,   0,  -5,   0},
    {0,   0,   0,   0,   0,   0,   0,   0,   0,   0}
};

char charset[128];

istream &extract(istream &is, char *p)
{
  if (!is.ipfx(0))
    return is;
  int pc, c = is.rdbuf()->sgetc(), err = 0, state = 0,
    back2 = 0, back1 = 0, last = 0, accept = 0;
  for (;;) {
    if (c == EOF) {
      err = ios::eofbit;
      break;
    }
    int col = charset[c];
```

We assume the array charset[] has been set up to mark the acceptable characters. Unacceptable ones are marked -1.

```
if (col == -1) {
  back2 = back1;      // update acceptance state history
  back1 = last;
  last = 0;
  break;
}
```

If the character is acceptable, the next state can be looked up in the transition table. If the value is negative, we note that it is an acceptance state.

```
state = tt[state][col];
if (state < 0) {
  accept = 1;
  state = -state;
}
state--;  // adjust state to 0 - n
```

Next, the history of encountered acceptance states is updated to include the one we just checked. These, back2, back1, and last, have value either 0 or 1.

```
back2 = back1;
back1 = last;
last = accept;
accept = 0;
```

If the adjusted value of state is negative at this point, the character found, although a legitimate member of the character set, was not acceptable in this context.

```
if (state < 0) break;
```

If the character was acceptable we note its value, so it can be put back if necessary, and then go for the next one:

```
pc = c;
*p++ = c;
c = is.rdbuf()->snextc();
++n;
}
*p = 0;  // terminate the extracted string
```

Now if no acceptance state exists among back2, back1 and last, the extract function can make no sense of the input and must register a failure, as follows:

```
if (!(back2 || back1 || last))
  err |= ios::failbit;
```

Otherwise there is an acceptance state such that any unwanted characters can be left on the stream:

```
else {
  if (last)
    is.rdbuf()->stossc();
  else if (!back1)
    is.rdbuf()->sputbackc(pc);
}

is.clear(err);
return is;
}
```

In summary, in the transition table, the 0's are error entries and negative transitions are acceptance states. Using a combination of sgetc and snextc, the extractor tracks the acceptability of the last character looked at and the two characters before that. When scanning terminates, if any of these are nonzero, the latest of them can be taken as being the end of the input. Subsequent characters are either still on the stream or can be put back.

The following short program sets up the charset array and checks out the extraction behavior:

```
int main()
{
  char buf[80];
  for (int i = 0; i < 128; ++i)
    charset[i] = -1;
  char *p = ok;
  for (i = 0; *p; ++p, ++i)
    charset[*p] = i;
  extract(cin,buf);
  cout << "buf:- " << buf << endl;
  return 0;
}
```

An extractor like this is not tied to a particular type. In fact if each type has a suitable form of transition table, an alphabet (acceptable character set), and a static translate function taking a type pointer and a const char * argument, we need never write another extractor. The table-driven extract function can be generalized and added to class istream.

The transition table can be a simple array of integers. The extract function then will index into it using the column number and the number of characters in the alphabet.

```
class T {
   ...
   friend istream &operator>>(istream &, T &);
private:
   static void translate(T*, const char *);
   static int transitions[...];
   static int alphabet;  // no of acceptable characters
   static int charset[128];
};
```

```
typedef void (*translator_t)(void *, const char *);
istream &istream::extract(void *, int *charset,
             int alphabet, int *tt,
             translator_t f, char *buffer);
```

The istream::extract function will resemble the extract function for class affirm shown previously, except for the following:

```
istream &istream::extract(void *object, int *charset,
             int alphabet, int *tt,
             translator_t transfunc, char *buffer)
{
   char *p = buffer;
   ...
   for (;;) {
     ...
     int col = charset[c];
     ...
// index into one dimensional transition array
     state = tt[state*alphabet+col];
     ...
   }
   *p = 0;
   if (!(back2 || back1 || last)) {
     // fail
   } else {
     // putback as appropriate
     transfunc(object,buffer);
   }
   is.clear(err);
   return is;
}
```

The individual translators, for example, for class T become

```
istream &operator>>(istream &is, T &t)
{
  char buf[BIG_ENOUGH];
  return is.extract(&t, t.charset, t.alphabet,
          t.transitions, T::translate, buf);
}
```

This still begs the question of the actual translation. The translation process is made much easier because it will be presented only with properly formed strings. Also, it's possible that a function like translate will be required to implement one of the constructors for type T (from a string literal representation). Nevertheless it must still be assumed that translation is nontrivial. In fact, in many cases it might be more efficient to use a hand-coded extractor that translates as it goes along, than to use the table-driven approach, which is certainly not a panacea.

We can expand the scheme presented above to give more assistance to the translation process. Suppose the postulated istream::extract function is given two extra arguments, the first of which is of type

```
typedef int (*helper_t)(int, char, void *);
```

that is, a pointer to a function taking an int, a char and a void pointer as arguments. The second extra is a void pointer. The signature of extract becomes

```
istream &istream::extract(void *, int *charset, int alphabet,
        int *tt, translator_t f, char *buffer,
        helper_t hf, void *supplement);
```

Every time a character is checked and put into the buffer for subsequent translation, the helper function in the body of extract is called with the following arguments:

- Number of characters processed
- Current character
- The supplement void *

The translator function gets an extra void * argument, and the supplementary pointer gets passed to that as well. Laying out this whole scheme for type T, we have the following:

```
class T {
  ...
  friend istream &operator>>(istream &, T &);
private:
  static int translator_helper(int, char, void *);
```

```
    static void translator(T*, const char *, void *);
    static int tt[...];
    static int alphabet;
    static int charset[128];
    ...
};

istream &operator>>(istream &is, T &t)
{
  char buf[BIG_ENOUGH];
  struct translation_info {
    ...
  } ti;
  return is.extract(&t, t.charset, t.alphabet,
          t.tt, T::translator, buf,
          T::translator_helper, &ti);
}
```

An example of this approach is shown in Appendix 1, where it's used to implement an extractor for floating-point numbers.

Of course this is only one way of doing it. The supplementary void pointer could be anything, including the address of the object for which the extractor is being called. The helper function could be made to override the table-driven scanning by returning nonzero, which should either terminate the extraction unsuccessfully or return 0 to allow scanning to continue.

Alternatively more information could be built into the transition table. For example, each entry could be a pair of integers. The first would represent the required state transition. The second could represent some action to be taken during translation, or by a helper function as this combination of state and character was encountered. This is the usual way things are done if the UNIX scanner generator Lex is used to build a lexical analyzer. Undoubtedly many other schemes could be devised along these general lines.

A point we have glossed over is the origin of the transition table. A table for a class like affirm can be handwritten but constructing DFA transition tables by hand is not recommended for other than the simplest of cases.

19.11 Regular Expressions and DFAs

DFAs are, among other things, a way of representing regular expressions. It's not appropriate in a book on IOStreams to go into much detail about regular expressions and their conversion to DFAs. However, enough needs to be said to complete the general thread of discussion of table-driven extractors.

Regular expressions are a way of describing patterns. (For comprehensive treatments, see references 2 and 3 in the list at the end of the book.) Simply put, regular expressions comprise the characters of some alphabet (**char**), parentheses, concatenation, and the following two operators:

or alternation (the more familiar '|' will be used later)
*   Kleene closure (0 or more repetitions)

Regular expressions may also contain the empty regular expression consisting of no characters, let's say **null**.

The grammar of regular expressions is

```
<expression> := <term> | <term>or<expression>
<term >:=  <factor> | <factor><term>
<factor> := (<expression>) | char | (<expression>)* | char* | null
```

The following symbols are commonly used to represent frequently used expressions, terms, or factors:

a+   positive closure (one or more repetitions of a), equivalent to aa*
a?   0 or one occurrence of a, equivalent to a **or null**
[abc]   equivalent to a **or** b **or** c
~a   any character but a (b **or** c **or** d **or** e . . .)
a^n n repetitions of a, a^3 equivalent to aaa

Both concatenation (<factor><term>) and alternation (<term> **or** <expression>) are associative, that is,

(a **or** b) **or** c == a **or** (b **or** c) and (ab)c == a(bc)

while alternation is commutative

a **or** b == b **or** a

and concatenation distributes over alternation as follows:

a(b **or** c) == ab **or** ac

Now that these definitions are out of the way, we can drop **or** and use '|' instead. Accordingly, a regular expression representing some acceptable representations of class affirm is as follows:

y|Y|yes|YES|n|N|no|NO

Because concatenation has higher precedence than alternation,

(yes)|(no)

has redundant parentheses, so plain

yes|no

will do. An alternative regular expression for affirm is

y(es)?|Y(ES)?|no?|NO?

The regular expression corresponding to that used in the translation table of the example given previously is more general than these, since it is case insensitive, as follows:

(Y|y)((E|e)(S|s))?|(N|n)(O|o)?

A regular expression for floating-point numbers is

('+'|-)?[0-9]+(.[0-9]*)?((E|e)('+'|-)?[0-9][0-9]?[0-9]?)?

which in words means

optional + or -
digit string representing the whole part
optional decimal point and optional digit string representing the fractional part
optional
    E or e
    optional + or -
    one to three digit exponent

The plus signs in quotes represent the plus sign character; the plus sign not in quotes is a positive closure.

This does not fully describe floating-point constants as defined in C++, but it's sufficiently complicated for the present illustration.

Regular expressions can be represented by Nondeterministic Finite Automata (NFAs) or by DFAs. Finite automata of this sort are characterized by having a number of states and certain permitted transitions from state to state. In a DFA, each transition is associated with a character in the alphabet of the associated regular expression (the set of characters that appear in the regular expression). This is why DFAs are good for the table-driven approach; there is a well-defined action for each state for each character. However, it's easier to go from a regular expression to an NFA than to a DFA, so the sequence of construction usually goes as follows:

regular expression -> NFA -> DFA -> transition table

Both NFAs and DFAs can be represented by state transition diagrams and tables. Figure 19.1 shows a diagram of an NFA for the regular expression we gave for floating-point numbers.

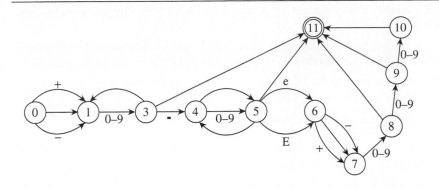

FIGURE 19.1
An NFA for the floating-point regular expression.

The double-circled state 11 is a final state, that is, a state in which a sequence of characters can be accepted. Notice that it's possible to get there from state 0 with only a single character (0,1,3,11) or by a path that represents, say, -99.99e-99 (0,1,3,1,3,4,5,4,5,6,7,8,9,11).

NFAs are characterized by having null transitions (often also known as E (for empty) transitions), represented in the figure by the transition arrows that are not marked with a character or character set. While it's possible to write a pattern-matching function based on a tabular representation of an NFA, such functions are often slow because of the need to search all possible alternative paths introduced by the null transitions.

Making a DFA requires that we derive a similar state transition diagram in which each transition is marked by a character. This is done by using an algorithm called the *Subset Construction,* which uses two sub-algorithms, or operations: *move* and *E-closure.* The move(S, c) operation takes a set of states S and forms the set of all states that can be reached from any state in S by a transition on character c. (So given the set of states [0,1] in the NFA illustrated in Fig. 19.1, move([0,1],'-') gives the set [1].) E-closure(S) takes a set of states S and adds to it all states that can be reached by one or more null (E) transitions. (So given set [0], E-closure produces [0,1].)

The Subset Construction is as follows:

1. Form a set of states initially containing only state 0. Apply E-closure to this set to form the set of all states that can be reached from state 0 by E-transitions. Make this set the first of a numbered list of sets representing the DFA states,

with a marker to say it's not yet handled. At this point, the list contains only DFA state 0.

2. Check the list of DFA states (this is a list of sets of NFA states) to choose a set S that is not yet handled. If there are none, the algorithm terminates.

3. For each character in the alphabet of the DFA, do the following:

   a) Form the set move(S,c). Then apply E-closure to that set to get E-closure(move(S,c)) and add this new set N to the list of sets of DFA states (marked as not dealt with), if it's not already on the list.

   b) Make an entry in the DFA transition table column for character c, opposite the state number of S, noting the number of the new state N and marking the entry as an acceptance state if the set N contains a final state of the NFA.

4. Mark S as dealt with, then go back to step 2.

Applying the Subset Construction to the floating-point example, we find that initially the list of DFA states contains

    0 [0,1]

Next, form move([0,1],'+'), which is just [1] and then E-closure([1]). Note, the latter is still [1] and becomes state 1.

    0 [0,1]
    1 [1]

E-closure(move([0,1],'-') gives rise to the same set, so the list is not further expanded. The transition table at this point is

    + - . 0 1 2 3 4 5 6 7 8 9 E e

    0 1 1

The character set 0–9 must be dealt with next. We call this set **digit**. Move([0,1],digit) is [3] and E-closure([3]]) is [1,3,11], so the state list becomes

    0 [0,1] done
    1 [1]
    2 [1,3,11]

with state 0 marked as done, and the transition table now holding

    + - . 0 1 2 3 4 5 6 7 8 9 E e

    0 1 1   2* 2* 2* 2* 2* 2* 2* 2* 2* 2*

At this point, an acceptance state has been introduced, since [1,3,11] contains the final state of the NFA. Next, state 1 is selected. The only move is on **digit**, which leads to the set of states that is state 2. State 1 is marked as done, and no further states are added. The transition table is then

```
    + - .  0  1  2  3  4  5  6  7  8  9  E  ec


0   1 1     2* 2* 2* 2* 2* 2* 2* 2* 2* 2*
1           2* 2* 2* 2* 2* 2* 2* 2* 2* 2*
```

The moves out of [1,3,11] must now be handled. There are moves on **digit** and the decimal point. Move([1,3,11],digit) is [3], and we have already encountered that path; it leads to state 2. So the transition for a digit is back to state 2. Move([1,3,11],'.') is [4], and E-closure([4]) is [4,5,11], also containing the NFA final state. State 2 is now dealt with, and there is a new state 3, as follows:

```
0  [0,1] done
1  [1] done
2  [1,3,11] done
3  [4,5,11]
```

The transition table is now

```
    + - .  0  1  2  3  4  5  6  7  8  9  E  e

0   1 1     2* 2* 2* 2* 2* 2* 2* 2* 2* 2*
1           2* 2* 2* 2* 2* 2* 2* 2* 2* 2*
2         3* 2* 2* 2* 2* 2* 2* 2* 2* 2* 2*
```

There are moves from DFA state 3 on **digit**, 'E' and 'e'. Move([4,5,11],digit) is [5], and E-closure([5]) is [4,5,11], which is state 3. Move([4,5,11],'E') and move([4,5,11],'e') both give [6], the E-closure of which is [6,7]. The tables are then

```
0  [0,1] done
1  [1] done
2  [1,3,11] done
3  [4,5,11] done
4  [6,7]
```

```
    + - .  0  1  2  3  4  5  6  7  8  9  E  e

0   1 1     2* 2* 2* 2* 2* 2* 2* 2* 2* 2*
```

	+	-	.	0	1	2	3	4	5	6	7	8	9	E	e
1				2*	2*	2*	2*	2*	2*	2*	2*	2*	2*		
2			3*	2*	2*	2*	2*	2*	2*	2*	2*	2*	2*		
3				3*	3*	3*	3*	3*	3*	3*	3*	3*	3*	4T4	

Next, there are moves from [6,7] on '+', '-' and **digit**. Both '+' and '-' yield [7], and **digit** yields [8], which closes to [8,11], adding an acceptance state and extending the tables to

0 [0,1] done
1 [1] done
2 [1,3,11] done
3 [4,5,11] done
4 [6,7] done
5 [7]
6 [8,11]

	+	-	.	0	1	2	3	4	5	6	7	8	9	E	e
0	1	1		2*	2*	2*	2*	2*	2*	2*	2*	2*	2*		
1				2*	2*	2*	2*	2*	2*	2*	2*	2*	2*		
2			3*	2*	2*	2*	2*	2*	2*	2*	2*	2*	2*		
3				3*	3*	3*	3*	3*	3*	3*	3*	3*	3*	4T4	
4	5	5		6*	6*	6*	6*	6*	6*	6*	6*	6*	6*		

State 5 has just the one possibility, E-closure(move([7],digit)), which is [8,11], state 6. State 6 also has just one move and gives E-closure([9]), which is [9,11], another acceptance state. There is then a further move from [9,11] on a digit, leaving the tables as follows:

0 [0,1] done
1 [1] done
2 [1,3,11] done
3 [4,5,11] done
4 [6,7] done
5 [7] done
6 [8,11] done
7 [9,11] done
8 [10,11] done

	+	-	.	0	1	2	3	4	5	6	7	8	9	E	e
0	1	1		2*	2*	2*	2*	2*	2*	2*	2*	2*	2*		
1				2*	2*	2*	2*	2*	2*	2*	2*	2*	2*		
2			3*	2*	2*	2*	2*	2*	2*	2*	2*	2*	2*		
3				3*	3*	3*	3*	3*	3*	3*	3*	3*	3*	4T4	

```
4  5  5     6* 6* 6* 6* 6* 6* 6* 6* 6* 6*
5           6* 6* 6* 6* 6* 6* 6* 6* 6* 6*
6           7* 7* 7* 7* 7* 7* 7* 7* 7* 7*
7           8* 8* 8* 8* 8* 8* 8* 8* 8* 8*
8
```

All that is required now is the transition table. The list of sets of states can be discarded.

The move and E-closure procedures, and using these, the Subset Construction, are quite amenable to translation into C++ functions. (See reference 2, which also describes an algorithm, Thompson's Construction, that can be used as the basis of a computer program to create a tabular representation of an NFA from a regular expression.)

There are some cautionary notes. Regular expressions can't represent all patterns, for example, balanced or nested constructs. Also, some DFAs can have a very large number of states compared to the number of states in the NFA from which they were derived. In such cases, extractors might need to be built by hand-coded methods.

19.12 Manipulators and Inserters

Remember that manipulators can be defined to help automate the output of complicated user-defined types. See the examples in Chapter 15.

19.13 Summary

In designing extractors or inserters for user-defined types, the following factors should be taken into account:

- High-level extractors and inserters will usually involve the least design effort and provide the least scope for errors. On the other hand high-level extractors and inserters may be relatively inefficient compared to their low-level counterparts. The high-level approach should be used for prototyping extractors and inserters.

- Extractors for data types with multiple parts, some of which are optional, will often require a mixed-level approach. The mixed-level approach might also provide noticeable efficiency benefits in inserters. Apply some low-level operations to extractors and inserters prototyped at high-level, where low-level operations could clearly improve efficiency.

- Where a mixed-level implementation appears to be necessary, and certainly in cases where a low-level approach is required, table-driven alternatives should be considered. A table-driven approach should also be considered in cases in which there is a wide diversity of representation of the target type.

- Table-driven inserters will generally be fast, possibly at the expense of memory. It will also usually be easier make them work correctly than it is with the hand-crafted alternative.

20

Inserters and Extractors for Class Hierarchies

We restricted the discussion in Chapter 19 to the design of inserters and extractors for discrete types. However, it's also necessary to consider the implications of derivation. Public derivation gives rise to hierarchies of related types and provides a programming mechanism that can deal with abstract concepts in a generalized way. Programs taking advantage of this capability will usually manipulate collections of related objects. Operations on individual objects will be invoked using a pointer or reference of a type corresponding to the base class of the hierarchy. The result of the operation then must reflect the nature of the individual object rather than the type of the pointer or reference that was used to invoke it.

Input and output are typical of such operations, and like other kinds of polymorphic behavior, they need to be designed into the class hierarchy. Accomplishing this requires that the IOStreams related facilities for derived classes be provided in a slightly different way than was described in Chapter 19.

20.1 Insertion and Extraction of the Base Class

IO operations on objects in the hierarchy must be able to be invoked through a pointer or reference of the base class type. To illustrate the design considerations, we use the simple class `Tuple`, which is a generalization of groups of integers of some particular size. We want to be able to input and output `Tuple` objects, so we will need

```
istream &operator>>(istream&, Tuple&);
ostream &operator<<(ostream&, const Tuple&);
```

However, because `Tuple` is an abstraction, there will be no objects whose actual type is `Tuple`. Therefore, the IO behavior of specific derived types must be provided by virtual functions. Since the extractor and inserter functions we have specified for `Tuple` are file scope functions, they can't be virtual; thus the `Tuple` class must provide virtual functions representing the operations `extract` and `insert`, as follows:

```
class Tuple {
public:
    ...
private:
    virtual void extract(istream&);
    virtual void insert(ostream&);
};
```

Notice that these functions can be private. As they are implementation details, they don't need to be visible to the user of `Tuple` type objects.

The implementation of the `Tuple` inserter and extractor functions can now be defined in terms of the virtual functions, as follows:

```
istream &operator>>(istream &is, Tuple &t)
{ return t.extract(is); }
ostream &operator<<(ostream &os, const Tuple &t)
{ return t.insert(os); }
```

20.2 Input and Output of Derived Types

Given the design presented in Section 20.1, we can consider what happens with a derived type, as shown in the following:

```
class Singleton : public Tuple {
public:
    Singleton(int);
    ...
private:
    void extract(istream&);
    void insert(ostream&);
    ...
};
```

An object of type Singleton can be used as an argument to the file scope Tuple inserter and extractor functions because they take a Tuple reference argument. A reference to a Singleton will be implicitly converted to a reference to Tuple, as in

```
Singleton s = 0;

cin >> s;
cout << s << endl;
```

So individual objects will behave as required. In a more general case, in which collections of Tuple objects must be manipulated, this can be done through a pointer to the base class, as follows:

```
Tuple *tp[SOMESIZE];
tp[0] = new Singleton(22);
tp[1] = new Pair(-1,1);
int a[] = { 1,2,3,4,5,6,7,8 };
tp[2] = new Octet(a);
for (int i = 0; i < 3; ++i)
    cout << *tp[i] << endl;
```

To demonstrate this approach, the Tuple class can be completely abstract and needs only the virtual extract and insert functions. The file scope inserter and extractor functions can be inlines. If they are, they should be defined in the same place, for example:

```
#include <iostream.h>

class Tuple {
friend istream &operator>>(istream&, Tuple&);
friend ostream &operator<<(ostream&, const Tuple&);
private:
    virtual istream &extract(istream&) = 0;
    virtual ostream &insert(ostream&) const = 0;
};

inline istream &operator>>(istream &is, Tuple &t)
{ return t.extract(is); }

inline ostream &operator<<(ostream &os, const Tuple &t)
{ return t.insert(os); }
```

Notice that we have relocated the input and output functions. In the case of the built-in types, these are member functions of classes istream and ostream with built-in type arguments. When we discussed extractors and inserters for discrete class types, we used file scope functions with a stream reference and a type reference argument. For derived types we use a member function of the type with a stream reference argument. The techniques discussed in Chapter 19 for the design of extractors and inserters are applicable in each case.

The demonstration's derived classes need only a constructor and an implementation of the `extract` and `insert` functions:

```
class Singleton : public Tuple {

public:
    Singleton(int n) : val(n) {}
private:
    istream &extract(istream&);
    ostream &insert(ostream&) const;

    int val;
};

class Pair : public Tuple {
public:
    Pair(int a, int b) : v0(a), v1(b) {}
private:
    istream &extract(istream&);
    ostream &insert(ostream&) const;

    int v0, v1;
};

class Octet : public Tuple {
public:
    Octet(int *);
private:
    istream &extract(istream&);
    ostream &insert(ostream&) const;

    int v[8];
};

Octet::Octet(int *ip)
{
    for (int i = 0; i < 8; ++i)
            v[i] = ip[i];
}
```

The extraction and insertion functions are about the simplest that can be devised for the demonstration. However, they are shown fully decorated with prefix and suffix functions. If you know that your IOStreams implementation doesn't perform any system dependent actions in these functions, these may be omitted.

```
istream &Singleton::extract(istream &is)
{
    if (is.ipfx(0))
            cin >> val;
    return is;
}

ostream &Singleton::insert(ostream &os) const
{
    if (os.opfx()) {
            os << val;
            os.osfx();
    }
    return os;
}

istream &Pair::extract(istream &is)
{
    if (is.ipfx(0))
            cin >> v0 >> v1;
    return is;
}

ostream &Pair::insert(ostream &os) const
{
    if (os.opfx()) {
            os << '(' << v0 << ", " << v1 << ')';
            os.osfx();
    }
    return os;
}

istream &Octet::extract(istream &is)
{
    if (is.ipfx(0))
            cin >> v[0] >> v[1] >> v[2]
                >> v[3] >> v[4] >> v[5] >> v[6] >> v[7];
    return is;
}
```

As an aside, notice a typical "pretty-printing" requirement in the `Octet` inserter, whereby the last integer in the group doesn't get a following comma and space. This sort of requirement is quite common.

```
ostream &Octet::insert(ostream &os) const
{
    if (os.opfx()) {
            os << '(';
            for (int i = 0; i < 8; ++i) {
              os << v[i];
              if (i < 7)
                os << ", ";
            }
            os << ')';
            os.osfx();
    }
    return os;
}
```

The test program follows the outline given in Section 20.2. It instantiates an isolated `Tuple` object, in this case an `Octet`, inputs a new value for it through `cin`, and then outputs it. Some mixed `Tuple` instances are then allocated dynamically to an array of `Tuple` pointers and their values displayed, as shown:

```
int a[] = { 1, 2, 3, 4, 5, 6, 7, 8 };

void main()
{
    Octet oc = 0;
    cout << "Octet: ";
    cin >> oc;
    cout << oc << endl;

    Tuple *p[3];
    p[0] = new Singleton(22);
    p[1] = new Pair(-1,1);
    p[2] = new Octet(a);
    for (int i = 0; i < 3; ++i) {
            cout << *p[i] << endl;
            delete p[i];
    }
}
```

The base class of the hierarchy doesn't have to be abstract. It could equally well be a concrete type with its own implementation of the `extract` and `insert` virtual functions.

20.3 A Broader Hierarchical Context

In some object-oriented environments all types are derived from a general-purpose base type, usually called `Object`. `Objects` are able to display themselves. C++ doesn't impose such a requirement. However, its users can benefit from this capability if class designers provide each discrete class with file scope inserter and extractor functions and give types in class hierarchies IOStreams IO capabilities using virtual functions as described in this chapter. Output capabilities of this sort contribute to the ease with which software components can be used and understood; they serve almost as built-in documentation. Input capabilities encourage users to become familiar with the data type through experimentation.

Nearly all types can be given some meaningful text representation that will make them more user friendly. (Also, if such a representation is provided by the class designer, users will be less likely to concern themselves with implementation detail.) For example,

`int`	->	1234
`class String`	->	The quick brown fox
`class Triplet`	->	(1, 2, 3)
`class Triangle`	->	Triangle ((12,3), (0,0), (8,8)) (possibly part of a shape hierarchy)
`class Secretary`	->	Jane Doe, Room 234b, Ext 2901, 100 wpm, fluent Spanish (possibly part of an employee hierarchy)

It's important in this context that an output sequence produced by an inserter function be acceptable to the corresponding extractor function as input.

20.4 Summary

Implementation of IO operations for data types that belong to families that exhibit polymorphic behavior does not pose any substantial new problems as far as IOStreams is concerned. The generic behavior is provided by global extractor and inserter functions taking an argument that is a reference to the base class type. The IO differentiation is then provided by virtual functions. It is suggested that if extractors and inserters are provided uniformly for all user-defined types, the C++ environment might be made more user friendly for all.

21

Cookbook 2– Investigative Examples

As noted in preceding chapters, the behavior required of IOStreams systems has not yet been comprehensively defined. Consequently different implementors have made slightly different interpretations. In this chapter, we check out many limiting conditions and areas where the system specification might be weak. In cases where the outcome of an example is not well defined, we review the various possibilities. By working through these example programs for a particular implementation of IOStreams, you should obtain a good grounding in IOStreams usage and should subsequently find few surprising aspects of that implementation's behavior.

Note that in many cases, the examples use `cin`, but they will make their point best with input redirected from a file. Such cases are noted.

21.1 State Checking

The following test performs basic checks on the state of the standard input and standard output streams. In doing this, it checks out the `operator!`, `operator void *`, `good`, `fail`, `bad`, and `eof` functions to some extent. It also makes use of the inserters for `int` and `const char*`.

```cpp
// t1.cpp
#include <iostream.h>

main()
{
    int tally = 0;

    if (cout)
        tally++;
    if (!cout == 0)
        tally++;
    if (cout.good())
        tally++;
    if (!cout.fail())
        tally++;
    if (!cout.bad())
        tally++;
    if (!cout.eof())
        tally++;
    cout << tally;
    if (tally == 6)
        cout << ", cout is ok\n";

    tally = 0;
    if (cin)
        tally++;
    if (!cin == 0)
        tally++;
    if (cin.good())
        tally++;
    if (!cin.fail())
        tally++;
    if (!cin.bad())
        tally++;
    if (!cin.eof())
        tally++;
    cout << tally;
    if (tally == 6)
        cout << ", cin is ok";
    return 0;
}
```

21.2 Character and String Output

The next program investigates the capability of ostream cout and ostream cerr to transfer character variables and strings. The values chosen for the char, signed char, and unsigned char variables should produce some character outside the range of the ASCII character set. (On a PC in native text mode, it's the double line graphics intersection character.)

   The program also investigates the endl manipulator, padding of character output within a field width, and the justification of strings. Each operation is performed to the standard output and to the standard error streams. The effect of this should be noticeable when the output of the program is redirected to a file. Only one set of output should then appear on the screen.

```
// t2.cpp
#include <iomanip.h>

const char a[] = "This string contains\0 an embedded zero";

main()
{
   char c = '\316';
   signed char sc = c;
   unsigned char uc = c;
   signed char *ss = (signed char *) "world ";
   unsigned char *us = (unsigned char *) "again";
   int w = sizeof(a)-1;
```

The next fragment tests the inserters for the various flavors of char*. Each should behave in the same way.

```
   cout << "Hello " << ss << us << endl;
```

The following section deals with individual characters using the inserters and the low-level put function:

```
   cout << "char " << c << " signed char "
        << sc << " unsigned char " << uc << endl;
   cout.put(c);      cout.put(' ');
   cout.put(sc);     cout.put(' ');
   cout.put(uc);     cout.put(' ');
   cout << endl;
```

The ostream::write function is now used to display a sequence of characters with an embedded 0. Just how this turns out will depend on the nature of the display device.

```
cout << a;
cout << '|' << endl;
cout.write(a,w);
cout << '|' << endl;
```

Finally, the insertion of strings and characters into a specified field width is investigated:

```
cout << setw(w) << "Default justification" << '['
     << setw(4) << '.' << ']' << endl;
cout.setf(ios::left,ios::adjustfield);
cout << setw(w) << "Left justified" << '['
     << setw(4) << '.' << ']' << endl;
cout.setf(ios::internal,ios::adjustfield);
cout << setw(w) << "Internally justified" << '['
     << setw(4) << '.' << ']' << endl;
cout.setf(ios::right,ios::adjustfield);
cout << setw(w) << "Right justified" << '['
     << setw(4) << '.' << ']' << endl;
```

The whole sequence is then repeated for the standard error stream `cerr`. The results should replicate those on `cout`.

```
cerr << "Hello " << ss << us << endl;
  // and so on
...

  return 0;
}
```

Depending on which character the value 0316 maps to and how a null byte gets displayed, the output should look something like the following for both `cout` and `cerr`:

```
Hello world again
char ✥ signed char ✥ unsigned char ✥
✥ ✥ ✥
This string contains|
This string contains an embedded zero|
              Default justification[   .]
Left justified                      [.   ]
              Internally justified[   .]
                    Right justified[   .]
```

However, don't be surprised to see some variation. Before the ANSI committee made any suggestions on IOStreams, some implementors disagreed with the

AT&T implementation and treated `signed char` and `unsigned char` as one-byte integral types. As a result it is possible that you might see

```
char % signed char -50 unsigned char 206
```

Also, some implementations might not apply padding in the single character inserters, so the output in square braces may simply be

```
[.]
```

Another example program in this general category exercises the inserter for a `streambuf` pointer. A `strstreambuf` is a convenient source for such a test, so this program exercises the constructor for a `strstreambuf` from a static string also:

```
// t3.cpp
#include <strstream.h>

char s[] =
"The quick brown fox jumped\nover the lazy dogs back.";

main()
{
  strstreambuf sb(s);
  cout << &sb << endl;
  cout << sb.sgetc() << endl;

  return 0;
}
```

The output should be

```
The quick brown fox jumped
over the lazy dogs back.
-1
```

Note that the last line of the output is -1. `sgetc` has returned `EOF` since the contents of the get area of `streambuf sb` were exhausted by the insertion into `cout`.

21.3 Character and String Input

The next program looks at character input through the standard input stream `cin`. As input, it is given a sequence of single characters like the following. The first line is a mixture of alphabetic characters plus spaces and tabs. After that, the sequence is arbitrary except that it contains two periods to serve as delimiters.

```
a b c d e f g h  i  j
now is the time
for all.
good men to
come
to the aid of
the party. etc
```

In the first instance, the test takes single characters using an unformatted `get`. This loop breaks when the first newline is encountered and the sequence of characters is echoed back exactly as they were entered. Subsequent characters are taken using the `char` extractor, which ignores the intervening whitespace characters. The loop terminates only when the required terminator, a period, is encountered. The output should cram the characters together.

Whitespace skipping is then turned off and further characters are taken using the `char` extractor until another delimiter or an `EOF` condition is encountered. However, `EOF` shouldn't happen unless the input was redirected. Once again the characters are echoed back as entered.

```
// t4.cpp
#include <iostream.h>

main()
{
  char c;
```

In the following, the tie between `cin` and `cout` is broken to improve the clarity of the output. Usually any use of `cin` causes `cout` to be flushed. In this case, the outcome of the program is easier to assimilate if all the output takes place after input is completed. With typical output buffer sizes, that will be the case here.

```
  cin.tie(0);
  for (;;) {
    cin.get(c);
    cout << c;
    if (c == '\n') break;
  }

  for (;;) {
    cin >> c;
    cout << c;
    if (c == '.') break;
  }
```

Unsetting the `ios::skipws` flag as follows causes the character extractor to behave in the same way as `cin.get`. Whitespace characters now become significant.

```
cin.unsetf(ios::skipws);
for (;;) {
  cin >> c;
  cout << c;
  if (c == '.') break;
}

  return 0;
}
```

With input like that suggested, the output should look as follows:

```
a b c d e f g h  i  j
nowisthetimeforall.
good men to
come
to the aid of
the party.
```

The previous example (`t4.cpp`) depended to some extent on the working of the tie mechanism. The standard input and the error output are both tied to the standard output. The following program demonstrates the effects of both ties:

```
// t5.cpp
#include <time.h>
#include <iostream.h>

main()
{
//   cin.tie(0);
//   cerr.tie(0);
  cout << "Press ENTER to continue:";
  cin.get();
  cout << "Pending";   // no flushing
  cerr << '.';
  sleep(5);   // pause for 5 seconds

  return 0;
}
```

If the ties are working correctly, the prompt "Press ENTER..." is displayed and the program then waits for input. The output stream `cout` is flushed by `cin.get()`. The string "Pending," followed by the period, is then displayed immediately. If the tie between cerr and cout isn't working, the period is displayed followed by a five-second pause before "Pending" appears. Try the program with the commented-out lines reinstated.

The next example looks at the unformatted get and getline functions for strings. These functions allow you to specify a maximum length and a delimiting character, defaulted to the newline character. The maximum length specified is understood as including a terminating null byte, which these functions should always add. The get function stops when it has extracted maximum length − 1 characters or when it encounters the delimiting character in the stream. The getline function behaves in the same way, except that it extracts the delimiting character from the stream and throws it away. These functions should set the error state only if they encounter EOF before extracting any characters. The following example needs to check that situation, so it should have its input redirected from a file, which can be as follows:

```
123456789\n
\n
123456789\n
\n
12345678\n
\n
12345678\n
\n
$\n
```

The newlines are shown explicitly so it's clear what is required in the last line of the source file. Of course, if this were an MS-DOS file, the newlines would be '\r\n' pairs, but cin should handle those transparently.

```
// t6.cpp
#include <iostream.h>

main()
{
  char c, buffer[10];
```

The first two uses of get and getline produce the same result, with the nine characters '1'–'9' stored in buffer. (In these cases, the newline character doesn't play a part.) Extraction stops when nine characters have been taken. The tenth position is needed for a terminating null byte. So in each of these cases, the example program reports two newlines found.

```
  cin.get(buffer,10);
  if (!cin) {
```

```
    cout << "Failed\n";
    return -1;
  } else
    cout << buffer << '.' << endl;
  for (int n = 0; cin && cin.peek() == '\n'; ++n)
    cin.get();
  cout << n << endl;

  cin.getline(buffer,10);
  if (!cin) {
    cout << "Failed\n";
    return -1;
  } else
    cout << buffer << '.' << endl;
  for (n = 0; cin && cin.peek() == '\n'; ++n)
    cin.get();
  cout << n << endl;
```

The next get/getline pair places the characters '1'–'8' in the buffer. In the get case, the newline character is left on the stream and two newline characters are reported. With getline, the newline character is thrown away and only one newline character is reported.

```
  cin.get(buffer,10);
  if (!cin) {
    cout << "Failed\n";
    return -1;
  } else
    cout << buffer << '.' << endl;
  for (n = 0; cin && cin.peek() == '\n'; ++n)
    cin.get();
  cout << n << endl;

  cin.getline(buffer,10);
  if (!cin) {
    cout << "Failed\n";
    return -1;
  } else
    cout << buffer << '.' << endl;
  for (n = 0; cin && cin.peek() == '\n'; ++n)
    cin.get();
  cout << n << endl;
```

The `cin.get()` removes the isolated '$' character that serves as a separator for this example. Then the next `get`/`getline` pair both leave an empty string in the buffer. A newline character is found immediately. Note, this is not a failure.

```
cin.get();

cin.get(buffer,10);
if (!cin) {
  cout << "Failed\n";
  return -1;
} else
  cout << buffer << '.' << endl;

cin.getline(buffer,10);
if (!cin) {
  cout << "Failed\n";
  return -1;
} else
  cout << buffer << '.' << endl;
```

In the last `get`/`getline` pair each function finds an EOF condition if a redirected source file is being used as suggested. No characters are extracted, and this is a failure condition.

```
cin.get(buffer,10);
if (!cin) {
  cout << "Failed as expected\n";
  cin.clear();
} else
  cout << buffer << '.' << endl;

cin.getline(buffer,10);
if (!cin) {
  cout << "Failed as expected\n";
  cin.clear();
} else
  cout << buffer << '.' << endl;

  return 0;
}
```

The output from the test program with the suggested input should be as follows:

123456789.

```
2
123456789.
2
12345678.
2
12345678.
1
.
```
.
```
Failed as expected
Failed as expected
```

We should also run a test at this stage to check that an unbuffered istream is behaving in the same way as the buffered istream cin. Both istream::get and the example program use lookahead. A cautious user will want to establish that such lookahead works properly during unbuffered operation. The tests just presented that used cin can be repeated along the following lines:

```
//t7.cpp
#include <fstream.h>

main()
{
  char buffer[10];

// Set up an unbuffered filebuf using the standard
// input file descriptor
  filebuf fb(0,0,0);
// Then set up an istream to use it.
  istream is(&fb);

  is.get(buffer,10);
    // and so on
  ...
}
```

The next example program in this group makes similar use of the formatted extractor for strings. In this case, control of the number of characters read is by the field width setting. The test input (which once again should be redirected from a file to achieve the effect described) is

```
batmobile\n
```

and the test is

```
// t8.cpp
```

```
#include <iostream.h>
#include <iomanip.h>

main()
{
  char buf1[4], buf2[80];

  cin >> setw(4) >> buf1 >> buf2 >> ws;
  cout << buf1 << '\n' << buf2 << endl;
  cin >> buf2;
  int s = cin.rdstate();
  if ((s & ios::failbit) && (s & ios::eofbit))
    cout << "Failed as expected" << endl;
  else {
    cerr << "Error\n";
    return -1;
  }

  return 0;
}
```

This program should split the word batmobile into bat and mobile. The width is reset automatically after each operation so the extractor, when used a second time, will extract characters until it encounters a whitespace character. The final use of the extractor finds the state of the stream already set to `ios::eofbit`, so it fails and sets the error state appropriately (`ios::eofbit | ios::failbit`). The output therefore should be

```
bat
mobile
Failed as expected
```

The last example in this group reads input strings into a `streambuf` using the appropriate extractor and the corresponding get function. The extractor is

```
istream &istream::operator>>(streambuf&);
```

It takes characters from the input stream until EOF is reached, so we can conveniently use a file-oriented stream, an `ifstream`, as a source for that part of the test. The get function into the `streambuf` is

```
istream &istream::get(streambuf &sb, char delim = '\n');
```

which can be exercised from a file redirected to `cin`.

Two source files are involved here, one each for the ifstream and redirected cin. The following test should be done twice: once with a combined string length that will fit in the streambuf and once with a combined length that won't. In either case, the redirected input source should have a final '!' character to match the delimiter specified by the get.

```cpp
// t9.cpp
#include <string.h>
#include <fstream.h>
#include <strstrea.h>

main()
{
  char buf[41];
  memset(buf,0,41);
  ifstream is("t9a.in");
  strstreambuf sb(buf,40,buf);   // "put only" strstreambuf

// get whatever is in t9a.in
  is >> sb;

// then as much as will fit from cin
// (redirected from t9b.in)
  cin.get(sb,'!');
  cout << sb.str();

  return 0;
}
```

Note the use of the strstreambuf::str function to get a char pointer to the contents of the strstreambuf after it has been filled. Also note that neither the strstreambuf::str nor strstreambuf::freeze functions terminate the array in question. In this example, such termination is ensured by zeroing the buffer to one beyond the specified strstreambuf length. With input file t9a.in

```
This is part one.
```

and redirected input file t9b.in

```
This is part two! It has a tail.
```

the output should be

```
This is part one. This is part two
```

If t9b.in is made longer, for example,

```
This is a longer version of part two!
```

then the output is chopped off at the specified strstreambuf length

```
This is part one. This is a longer versi
```

21.4 Raw (binary) Character Read/Write

The following example attempts to check that the low-level character transfer operations can deal with "difficult" characters, like '\0', other control characters, and characters with negative values. The first program creates a file with a block of such characters. The actual test then reads and writes this block, so that the input and output files can be checked for identity.

```cpp
// t10a.cpp
#include <stdio.h>

main()
{
  char buf[80];
  for (int i = 0; i < 5; ++i)
    buf[i] = i;
  for (i = 5; i < 40; ++i)
    buf[i] = '1'+i-5;
  for (i = 40; i < 70; ++i)
    buf[i] = 0xb0+i-30;
  buf[i++] = '\r';
  buf[i++] = '\r';
  buf[i] = '\n';

  FILE *f = fopen("t10.in","wb");
  fwrite(buf,1,73,f);
  fclose(f);

  return 0;
}
```

Notice the following example is written in a way that implies that cin is to use newline translation. We are asking for one less character than the file creation program actually wrote, since this block deliberately included a CR/LF pair ("\r\n") as well as an isolated CR ('\r'). On a UNIX-like system, increase the read count to 73, redirect the input for this program to use t10.in and redirect the output so that the result can be compared.

```cpp
// t10b.cpp
#include <iostream.h>

const int READ_COUNT = 72;
// READ_COUNT 73 for UNIX and other systems where text file
// line ends are plain '\n'.

struct Thing {
    char holds[80];
};

main()
{
  Thing x;
  cin.read((char*) &x, READ_COUNT);
  cerr << cin.gcount() << ' ';
  cout.write((char*) &x,cin.gcount());
  cerr << cout.pcount() << endl;

  return 0;
}
```

The input and output files should be identical.

21.5 IO of the Integral Types

This next group of examples covers a wide spectrum of the capabilities for input and output of integral values. The first test input consists of the limiting values of the various integral types—short, unsigned short, int, unsigned int, long, and unsigned long—with and without possibly extraneous sign characters. The input data are presented in decimal, octal, and hexadecimal forms.

Following are the values for an implementation with 16-bit int and 32-bit long. In a 32-bit implementation with 32-bit int values, the int values copy the long values rather than the short values.

```
0 0 0 0 0 0
-0 -0 -0 0 -0 -0
+0 +0 +0 +0 +0 +0
32767 65535 32767 65535 2147483647 4294967295
```

```
32768 65535 32768 65535 2147483648 4294967295
-32768 -65535 -32768 -65535 -2147483648 -4294967295
+32767 +65535 +32767 +65535 +2147483647 +4294967295
077777 0177777 077777 0177777 017777777777 037777777777
0100000 0177777 0100000 0177777 020000000000 037777777777
-0100000 -0177777 -0100000 -0177777 -020000000000 -037777777777
+077777 +0177777 +077777 +0177777 +017777777777 +037777777777
0x7fff 0xffff 0x7fff 0xffff 0x7ffffff 0xffffffff
0x8000 0xffff 0x8000 0xffff 0x80000000 0xffffffff
-0x8000 -0xffff -0x8000 -0xffff -0x80000000 -0xffffffff
+0x7fff +0xffff +0x7fff +0xffff +0x7ffffff +0xffffffff
```

The first integer example is as follows:

```
// t11.cpp
#include <iostream.h>

main()
{
  short s;
  unsigned short us;
  int i;
  unsigned ui;
  long li;
  unsigned long lu;

  for (int n = 15; n--;) {
    cin >> s >> us >> i >> ui >> li >> lu;
```

This is one of those places where it would be good to have a spacing manipulator to put a stream into a state in which it inserts a single space between other inserted items. It's very easy to make mistakes typing in item/space sequences.

```
    cout << s << ' ' << us << ' ' << i << ' '
         << ui << ' ' << li << ' ' << lu << endl;
  }
  return 0;
}
```

The output should be

```
0 0 0 0 0 0
0 0 0 0 0 0
0 0 0 0 0 0
32767 65535 32767 65535 2147483647 4294967295
```

```
-32768 65535 -32768 65535 -2147483648 4294967295
-32768 1 -32768 1 -2147483648 1
32767 65535 32767 65535 2147483647 4294967295
...
```

with the last four lines repeated three times.

In example t11.cpp, the input values were explicitly decimal, octal, or hexadecimal, that is, the octal input strings had a 0 prefix and the hex input strings a 0x prefix.

The next program uses input with nonexplicit strings and changes the integer conversion base setting for the istream instead. Once again the test input for this is shown in the form for 16-bit ints and 32-bit longs:

```
32767 65535 32767 65535 2147483647 4294967295
32768 65535 32768 65535 2147483648 4294967295
-32768 -65535 -32768 -65535 -2147483648 -4294967295
+32767 +65535 +32767 +65535 +2147483647 +4294967295
77777 177777 77777 177777 17777777777 37777777777
100000 177777 100000 177777 20000000000 37777777777
-100000 -177777 -100000 -177777 -20000000000 -37777777777
+77777 +177777 +77777 +177777 +17777777777 +37777777777
7fff ffff 7fff ffff 7fffffff ffffffff
8000 ffff 8000 ffff 80000000 ffffffff
-8000 -ffff -8000 -ffff -80000000 -ffffffff
+7fff +ffff +7fff +ffff +7fffffff +ffffffff
```

The program is:

```
// t12.cpp
#include <iostream.h>

main()
{
  short s;
  unsigned short us;
  int i;
  unsigned ui;
  long li;
  unsigned long lu;

  for (int n = 4; n--;) {
    cin >> s >> us >> i >> ui >> li >> lu;
    cout << s << ' ' << us << ' ' << i << ' '
         << ui << ' ' << li << ' ' << lu << endl;
```

```
  }

  cin >> oct;
  for (n = 4; n--;) {
    cin >> s >> us >> i >> ui >> li >> lu;
    cout << s << ' ' << us << ' ' << i << ' '
        << ui << ' ' << li << ' ' << lu << endl;
  }

  cin >> hex;
    // and so on

  ...

  return 0;
}
```

The output from this test on a 16-bit system should be the same as that from the previous test, excluding the lines of 0's.

The integer base flags also affect output, as does the showbase flag. Both also have an effect when padding to a field width is specified. The next example checks out these effects and exercises the manipulators with long parameters that can be used to modify the ios flags. Notice that to use these latter manipulators, the file iomanip.h needs to be included, as follows:

```
// t13.cpp
#include <iomanip.h>

void show(int w = 0)
{
  int zero = 0;
  int n = 27123;
```

The following repeated part of the example displays an integer value and 0 in some specified field width. The setiosflags and unsetiosflags manipulators are used to switch the display base. This assumes that the default base when none of the ios::basefield flags are set is decimal.

```
  cout << setw(w) << n << ".\n"
      << setw(w) << zero << '.' << endl;
  cout << setiosflags(ios::oct);
  cout << setw(w) << n << ".\n"
      << setw(w) << zero << '.' << endl;
  cout << resetiosflags(ios::oct)
      << setiosflags(ios::hex);
```

```
    cout << setw(w) << n << ".\n"
        << setw(w) << zero << '.' << endl;
    cout << resetiosflags(ios::basefield) << endl;
}
```

The show function then is called with 0 field width, first without base indication and then with base indication. It's then called with a specified field width and with left, internal, and right justification.

```
main()
{
    show();
    cout.setf(ios::showbase);
    show();
    show(12);
    cout.setf(ios::left,ios::adjustfield);
    show(12);
    cout.setf(ios::internal,ios::adjustfield);
    show(12);
    cout.setf(ios::right,ios::adjustfield);
    show(12);

    return 0;
}
```

The output should be as follows:

```
27123.
0.
64763.
0.
69f3.
0.

27123.
0.
064763.
0.
0x69f3.
0x0.

      27123.
          0.
      064763.
          0.
```

```
                  0x69f3.
                      0x0.

27123          .
0              .
064763         .
0              .
0x69f3         .
0x0            .

               27123.
                   0.
               064763.
                   0.
0x          69f3.
0x             0.

               27123.
                   0.
               064763.
                   0.
               0x69f3.
                  0x0.
```

Note here that when the base is shown, octal 0's don't get a leading 0 and only the hexadecimal representations get padded internally.

The next consideration for integers is the behavior of the extractors when badly formed input strings are encountered. The following program performs some tests in this area. The program loop breaks when a -1 is encountered. Otherwise an attempt is made to read one integer value from each line of input. The remaining characters on the line are displayed as a string. The test data for this program are

```
0x
-0x
0xx
-0xx
0x1gf
0778
-1
```

Not all of these are bad input. The first two are, they have no digits. The fail flag should be set but no characters should be lost. The third and fourth lines are acceptable input. The value read should be 0 in each case, and no characters should be lost. The fifth line produces the value 1. Scanning stops when the nondigit 'g' is encountered, and no error is flagged—the IOStreams system can't detect typos.

Finally, the octal number is read as decimal 63. The eight is not an octal digit, so scanning stops after the two sevens. No error should be flagged.

```cpp
// t14.cpp
#include <iostream.h>

main()
{
  int v = 5555;
  char waste[80];
  for (;;) {
    int rv;
    cin >> v;
    cout << v << "  cin state = "
          << (rv = cin.rdstate()) << endl;
    if (v == -1 && rv == 0) break;
    cin.clear();
    cin >> waste;
    cout << waste << endl;
  }
  return 0;
}
```

The required output is as follows:

```
5555  cin state = 2
0x
5555  cin state = 2
-0x
0  cin state = 0
xx
0  cin state = 0
xx
1  cin state = 0
gf
63  cin state = 0
8
-1  cin state = 0
```

The next group of errors investigated is caused by trying to read a character stream that represents a number too large to fit in the target variable, that is, when overflow occurs. Once again, the input data shown here are for the case when short and int are 16-bit and long is 32-bit. The data should be modified for 32-bit systems.

```
33000
33000
3333333333
70000
70000
9999999999
```

The test is as follows:

```
// t15.cpp
#include <iostream.h>

main()
{
  short s;
  int i;
  long l;
  unsigned short us;
  unsigned u;
  unsigned long ul;

  cin.clear();
  cin >> s;
  cout << cin.rdstate() << ' ' << s << endl;
  cin.clear();
  cin >> i;
  cout << cin.rdstate() << ' ' << i << endl;
  cin.clear();
  cin >> l;
  cout << cin.rdstate() << ' ' << l << endl;
  cin.clear();

  cin.clear();
  cin >> us;
  cout << cin.rdstate() << ' ' << us << endl;
  cin.clear();
  cin >> u;
  cout << cin.rdstate() << ' ' << u << endl;
  cin.clear();
```

```
cin >> ul;
cout << cin.rdstate() << ' ' << ul << endl;
cin.clear();

return 0;
}
```

It's not possible at the present state of standards development to say exactly what the output from this program should be. However, a plausible outcome is as follows:

```
0 -32536
0 -32536
0 -961633963
2 4464
2 4464
2 1410065407
```

In the case of the signed variables, the input data represents bit patterns that will fit within the receiving object. In the process, the sign bit gets set. In the remaining cases, the bit pattern overflows the receiving type; this should be detected as an error, as it would be by a compiler. The value left in the variables in this case is essentially garbage resulting from truncation.

21.6 IO of Floating-point Numbers

The first floating-point test accepts some input, then displays the values in the various available formats.

The input source for this program is

```
0.0
1.0
999999.999999
1.123457
1234567890.0
1e+20
```

and the program is

```
// t16.cpp
#include <iomanip.h>
```

```
double v1, v2, v3, v4, v5, v6;

void display()
{
  cout << v1 << endl;
  cout << v2 << endl;
  cout << v3 << endl;
  cout << v4 << endl;
  cout << v5 << endl;
  cout << v6 << '\n' << endl;
}
```

The reader is invited to implement the missing parameterless manipulators.

```
main()
{
  cin >> v1;
  cin >> v2;
  cin >> v3;
  cin >> v4;
  cin >> v5;
  cin >> v6;

  cout << fixed;
  display();

  cout << showpoint;
  display();

  cout << floating;
  display();

  cout << scientific;
  display();

  cout << setprecision(1);
  display();

  cout << showpoint;
  display();

  cout << setprecision(0);
  display();
```

```
  cout << floating << fixed;
  display();

  return 0;
}
```

The output (excluding the comments) should be

```
// Fixed - no showpoint, so trailing 0's omitted, standard
          precision of six places
0
1
999999.999999
1.123457
1234567890
100000000000000000000

// Fixed with showpoint

0.000000
1.000000
999999.999999
1.123457
1234567890.000000
100000000000000000000.000000


// The defaults, no showpoint, large values in scientific notation

0
1
1.0e+06
1.123457
1.234568e+09
1.0e+20


// Scientific

0e+00
1e+00
1e+06
1.123457e+00
1.234568e+09
1e+20
```

```
// Scientific with showpoint

0.0e+00
1.0e+00
1.0e+06
1.1e+00
1.2e+09
1.0e+20
```

```
// Scientific with 0 precision

0e+00
1e+00
1e+06
1e+00
1e+09
1e+20
```

```
// Fixed with precision 1, no showpoint

0
1
1000000
1.1
1234567890
100000000000000000000
```

The next floating-point test examines the behavior with badly formed representations in the input stream. One of many possible dubious-looking sequences is

```
1e
1e-
1e+
1e+a
1e-a
1.0e-a
1.0e-e
1e1234
+-1
-+1
++1
--1
1..
..1
```

```
1..1
.+1
.-1
0
```

The following program investigates what happens with these inputs, reporting the stream state and displaying the remainder of the input line:

```cpp
// t17.cpp
#include <iostream.h>

main()
{
  double v;
  char s[80];
  for (;;) {
    v = 6.555555;
    int rv;
    cin >> v;
    cout << v << "   cin state = "
         << (rv = cin.rdstate()) << ' ';
    if (v == 0.0 && rv == 0) break;
    cin.clear();
    cin.get(s,80);
    cout << s << endl;
  }

  return 0;
}
```

Not all the input strings cause errors. The output should probably be as follows:

```
1   cin state = 0 e
6.555555   cin state = 2 -
6.555555   cin state = 2 +
6.555555   cin state = 2 +a
6.555555   cin state = 2 -a
6.555555   cin state = 2 -a
6.555555   cin state = 2 -e
6.555555   cin state = 2
6.555555   cin state = 2 +-1
6.555555   cin state = 2 -+1
6.555555   cin state = 2 ++1
6.555555   cin state = 2 --1
```

```
1  cin state = 0 .
6.555555  cin state = 2 ..1
1  cin state = 0 .1
6.555555  cin state = 2 .+1
6.555555  cin state = 2 .-1
0  cin state = 0
```

Here, the first line is not an error. It's just the number 1 followed by the letter 'e,' and the extractor can recognize this with its limited lookahead capabilities. The next six lines cause errors, however. The extractor has already thrown characters away before it runs into trouble from encountering a nondigit as the first character of the exponent.

Line eight is not a representable value with conventional 8-byte IEEE floating-point real representations, since there are too many digits in the exponent. The current C++ language definition of a floating-point literal doesn't indicate how many digits may occur in the exponent. It would not be unreasonable for an extractor to stop reading digits when it became clear that the floating-point number could not be represented. A compiler would be expected to flag a similar literal as an error.

The next four lines illustrate the lack of discrimination in the currently defined stream error states. The lines cause failure, but no characters are lost. The following line (1..) is read as 1. followed by a period and doesn't provoke an error. The repeated decimal points in the next line are an error, however. The next line (1..1) is two floating-point numbers, the first of which is read without error. The two strings with a sign after the decimal point are errors.

This output is qualified as "probable" because of the uncertainty about the floating-point exponent and because it's possible that if an extraction fails and some characters are lost, some implementations might set `ios::badbit` as well as `ios::failbit`.

21.7 Pointer Representation

There is an inserter for type `void*` that is designed to show the value of pointer variables. The ANSI discussion document suggests that pointers be converted to integral values and then displayed as hexadecimal representations. However, this doesn't work out well with PC-style architectures, where a pointer may consist of a segment and an offset; therefore the representation produced by this inserter is markedly implementation dependent. Check out the following program under whatever compilation memory models are available:

```
// t18.cpp
#include <iostream.h>

main()
{
  double d;
  void *p = (void *) &d;
  cout << (void *) 0 << ' ' << p << endl;

  return 0;
}
```

The latest ANSI discussion document also specifies an extractor for type void*. In an implementation that provides this, we could test it by inserting a void* into a strstream, reading it back, and then checking that it was unchanged.

21.8 Examples for Class filebuf

Class streambuf is essentially an abstract base class. The most important of the buffer types derived from streambuf is the filebuf. The first example below looks at the difference in performance between the buffered and unbuffered cases. Here's the program for the buffered case:

```
// t19.cpp
#include <iomanip.h>
#include <fstream.h>

void wait(int n)
{
  volatile int v = 0;
  for (; n--;)
    for (int j = 1000; j--;)
      ++v;
}
```

```
main()
{
  filebuf f1(1);  // buffered filebuf on standard output file
  ostream x(&f1);
  for (int i = 50; i--;) {
    x << setw(3) << i << ' ';
    x << "The quick brown fox jumped over the lazy dog\n";
    wait(100);
  }

  return 0;
}
```

Only a small modification is required to check out the unbuffered behavior.

```
main()
{
    filebuf f1(1,0,0);   // unbuffered filebuf on
                         // standard output file
    ostream x(&f1);
    ...
}
```

These programs produce the same output, but the effects of buffering should be clear if a suitable argument is provided to the wait function in the loop in main. The buffered output will appear in chunks (possibly only one), after a pause corresponding to the sum of the waits.

To check out the speed difference between buffered and unbuffered input requires a brute force timing test. A large source file is also required.

```
// t20.cpp
#include <time.h>
#include <fstream.h>

main()
{
  long t = clock();
  filebuf fb;
  fb.open("bigfile.txt",ios::in);

// Include the next line to test unbuffered output
//  fb.setbuf(0,0);

  char c;
  for (long i = 100000; i--;)
```

```
      fb.sbumpc();
   cout << clock()-t << endl;

   return 0;
}
```

The following innocent-looking program is about the worst case for a read/write filebuf. The test file consists of lines like the following:

```
aaaaaaaaaaaaaaaaaaaaaaaaaaaaaaaaaaaaaaaaaaa\n
aaaaaaaaaaaaaaaaaaaaaaaaaaaaaaaaaaaaaaaaaaa\n
aaaaaaaaaaaaaaaaaaaaaaaaaaaaaaaaaaaaaaaaaaa\n
..........              // etc
```

Characters are alternately got from and put to the filebuf, as shown in the following. This alternation of purpose causes read/write context switching, and probably many calls to the synchronization function or functions.

```
// t21.cpp
#include <io.h>
#include <fcntl.h>
#include <fstream.h>

main()
{
   filebuf fb;
   if (!fb.open("t21.in", ios::in | ios::out))
      return -1;
   for (;;) {
      int c;
      c = fb.sbumpc();
      if (c == EOF) break;
      if (c == 'a') {
         int next = fb.sgetc();
         if (next != EOF && !(next == '\r' || next == '\n'))
            fb.sputc('b');
      }
   }

   return 0;
}
```

The program should modify the file to

```
abababababababababababababababababababab\n
abababababababababababababababababababab\n
```

```
abababababababababababababababababababab\n
abababababababababababababababababababab\n
.........              // etc
```

If your implementation is one that supports newline translation, the program should behave identically if the constructor line is altered to one that forces explicit untranslated operation:

```
main()
{
    filebuf fb;;
    if (!fb.open("t21.in",
        ios::in | ios::out | ios::binary))
      return -1;
    ...
}
```

Another heavy test of the `filebuf` implementation checks out the behavior when the `filebuf` is constructed in `append` mode. In this case, the get and put pointers become decoupled. Characters are read from one part of the file, but all output is tagged on to the file end. For the example, the starting contents of the file are a group of period characters:

```
.................................................
```

Once again, sufficient characters are added to the file to ensure the put area gets flushed out while the program is running.

```
// t22.cpp
#include <string.h>
#include <fstream.h>

char *source =
  "\naaaaaaaaaaaaaaaaaaaaaaaaaaaaaaaaaaaaaaaaaaaaaaaaaaaaaaaaa";

main()
{
  filebuf fb;
  if (!fb.open("t22.in", ios::in | ios:: out | ios::app))
    return -1;

  int n = strlen(source);
  for (;;) {
    int c;
    c = fb.sbumpc();
    if (c != '.') break;
```

```
    fb.sputn(source,n);
  }

  return 0;
}
```

The line of periods should be left intact, with multiple lines of 'a' appended.

A similar test can be written using an `iostream` — actually most conveniently, an `fstream` — rather than a naked `filebuf`:

```
// t23.cpp
#include <string.h>
#include <fstream.h>

main()
{
  fstream s("t23.in",
        ios::in|ios::out|ios::app);
  if (!s)
    return -1;

  char buffer[80];
  for (;;) {
    s >> buffer;
    s << " /" << buffer;
    if (strchr(buffer,'.'))
      break;  // stop at end of sentence
  }
  s.seekg(streampos(0));
  s.get(buffer,80);
  cout <<'*'<< buffer << endl;

  return 0;
}
```

This will change an input file from

`The quick brown fox jumped.`

to

`The quick brown fox jumped. /The /quick /brown /fox /jumped.`

The next test is aimed specifically at the implementation of `filebuf` that was shown in Chapter 18. That implementation, when operating in translated mode, had to provide for the case in which a `'\r'` was the last character read when the get area was filled, and more particularly, for the condition when that '\r' was followed by another '\r' character. This condition is bound to be met by a file containing a suitably large number of '\r' characters. There are two test programs, one (t24a.cpp) creates a "difficult" file and the other (t24b.cpp) reads it and copies the result to another file.

```cpp
// t24a.cpp
#include <fstream.h>

main()
{
   ofstream ofs("t24.in");
   for (int i = 10000; i--;)
     ofs.put('\r');
   ofs << "and so forth" << endl;

   return 0;
}
```

```cpp
// t24b.cpp
#include <fstream.h>

main()
{
    int c;
    for (;;) {
// cin redirected from t24.in
        c = cin.get();
        if (c == EOF) break;
// cout redirected to t24.out
        cout.put(c);
    }

    return 0;
}
```

The criterion for success is of course that t24.out be identical to t24.in.

No similar specific condition applies in the translation of newlines during output. The implementation described uses only half the allocated buffer for puts, so a buffer full of newline characters can be translated with no problem. However, we should check that the implementation can correctly convert files of random length lines from translated to untranslated and vice versa.

In this test, we create two files in parallel, one translated and the other untranslated. The untranslated file is then read in untranslated mode and output in translated mode and vice versa. The following program, which creates the files in the first place, doesn't use IOStreams at all:

```cpp
// t25a.cpp
#include <stdio.h>
#include <string.h>

int main()
{
  char buf[100];
  FILE *f1, *f2;
  f1 = fopen("t25u.in","wb");
  f2 = fopen("t25t.in","w");
  for (int i = 0, r = 0; i < 2000; ++i) {
    memset(buf,'x',r);
    buf[r] = '\n';
    fwrite(buf,1,r+1,f1);
    fwrite(buf,1,r+1,f2);
    r = rand()%80;
  }

  return 0;
}
```

The following program uses the generated files.

```cpp
// t25b.cpp
#include <fstream.h>

int main()
{
  ifstream is1("t25u.in", ios::in | ios::binary);
  ofstream os1("t25t.out", ios::out | ios::trunc);
  os1 << is1.rdbuf();  // untranslated in, translated out
  ifstream is2("t25t.in");
  ofstream os2("t25u.out",
      ios::out | ios::binary | ios::trunc);
  os2 << is2.rdbuf();  // translated in, untranslated out

  return 0;
}
```

Some implementations might require the newline translation mode be set after the stream has been constructed, for example,

```
ifstream is1("t25u.in");
is1.setmode(filebuf::binary);
ofstream os1("t25t.out",
...
ifstream is2("t25t.in");
ofstream os2("t25u.out");
os2.setmode(filebuf::binary);
```

21.9 Character Putback

The `filebuf` class guarantees four characters of putback; this, too, should be checked out under normal and worst-case circumstances. "Normal" circumstances are, for example, putting four characters back after four were just read from the get area. Unless you are working with a very small buffer, doing this should simply cause the get pointer to be backed up. Worst case is putting back characters before any have been fetched from the get area.

```
// t26.cpp
#include <string.h>
#include <fstream.h>

char pback[] = "  oY";

int main()
{
  int rv;
  char buf[10];
  filebuf fb(0);

// Put some characters back to a virgin filebuf,
// quitting on failure
  for (int i = 0; i < 4; i++) {
    rv = fb.sputbackc(pback[i]);
    if (rv == EOF) {
      cout << "failed to put back to empty buffer, i = "
           << i << endl;
      return -1;
    }
  }
}
```

```
// Now get those characters back, and some more
  for (i = 0; i < 10; ++i)
    buf[i] = fb.sbumpc();
  cout << endl;
  for (i = 0; i < 10; ++i)
    cout << buf[i];
  cout << endl;

// Try put the whole lot back
  for (i = 9; i >= 0; --i) {
    cout << "putback " << i << ' ' << buf[i] << endl;
    rv = fb.sputbackc(buf[i]);
    if (rv == EOF) {
      cout << "failed i = " << i << endl;
      break;
    }
  }

// See what we ended up with
  for (i = 0; i < 10; ++i)
    cout << char(fb.sbumpc());

  return 0;
}
```

The test input is a few more characters than are actually required by the program, as follows:

abcdefghijk

The output in the buffered case is as follows and should be implementation independent:

```
Yo  abcdef
putback 9 f
putback 8 e
putback 7 d
putback 6 c
putback 5 b
putback 4 a
putback 3
putback 2
putback 1 o
putback 0 Y
Yo  abcdef
```

Here, the four characters " oY" were successfully put back to the virgin filebuf and then these four characters, plus six more from the input stream, were transferred to buf. All these characters were then successfully put back and recovered.

The unbuffered case can be similarly tested. The output is likely to be implementation dependent, however, since the behavior of unbuffered streambuf is not particularly well defined in this respect.

21.10 File-oriented Translators

Various checks on the file-oriented streams have already been presented in Sections 21.8 and 21.9. These streams are ostreams and istreams that utilize a filebuf type streambuf and have specialized constructors and setup/shutdown functions. It's these latter functions that we check out next.

The first set of tests deals with the ifstream class. Within this set, the first test uses the constructor that takes a file descriptor argument:

```
// t27a.cpp
#include <io.h>
#include <fcntl.h>
#include <fstream.h>

int main()
{
  int fd = open("t27.in", O_RDWR);
  char buf[80];
  ifstream ifs(fd);
  ifs.getline(buf,80);
  cout << buf;

  return 0;
}
```

The second ifstream test uses the default constructor and attaches a file via an open file descriptor:

```
// t27b.cpp
#include <io.h>
#include <fcntl.h>
#include <fstream.h>

int main()
{
```

```
    int fd = open("t27.in", O_RDWR);
    char buf[80];
    ifstream ifs;
    ifs.attach(fd);
    ifs.getline(buf,80);
    cout << buf;

    return 0;
}
```

The third ifstream test uses the default constructor and then opens a named file:

```
// t27c.cpp
#include <fstream.h>

int main()
{
    ifstream ifs;
    ifs.open("t27.in");
    char buf[80];
    ifs.getline(buf,80);
    cout << buf;

    return 0;
}
```

The fourth ifstream test uses the constructor that opens a named file:

```
// t27d.cpp
#include <fstream.h>

int main()
{
    ifstream ifs("t27.in");
    char buf[80];
    ifs.getline(buf,80);
    cout << buf;

    return 0;
}
```

The last ifstream test uses the same constructor as the fourth did but overrides its default io_mode argument and explicitly opens the file without newline translation. In a UNIX environment, this is the default state of affairs and this test is superfluous.

```
// t27e.cpp
#include <ctype.h>
#include <fstream.h>

int main()
{
  ifstream ifs("t27.in", ios::in | ios::binary);
  char c;
  while (ifs.get(c))
    if (iscntrl(c))
      cout << hex << int(c) << ' ';

  return 0;
}
```

Some implementations might provide an extra function in class `filebuf` and in the `fstream` classes. This function allows streams set up in the default translation mode to be switched to some other behavior. In such a case, this test can be written as follows:

```
ifstream ifs("t27.in");
ifs.setmode(filebuf::binary);  // default was filebuf::text
```

Assuming the input to this program is a file that was created with newline translation, containing one or more newlines, the output from this test should be

d a

with the CR/LF pair read literally.

21.11 ofstream **Tests**

Five small programs test class `ofstream`. The first one uses the constructor that takes an open file descriptor as its argument, as follows:

```
// t28a.cpp
#include <io.h>
#include <fcntl.h>
#include <fstream.h>

int main()
```

```
{
  int fd = creat("t28.out",0644);
  ofstream of(fd);
  of << "t28a - OK";

  return 0;
}
```

The second test uses the default constructor, then attaches an open file descriptor:

```
// t28b.cpp
#include <io.h>
#include <fstream.h>

int main()
{
  int fd = creat("t28.out", 0644);
  ofstream of;
  of.attach(fd);
  of << "t28b - OK";

  return 0;
}
```

The third uses the default constructor, then the open function to associate the ofstream with a file:

```
// t28c.cpp
#include <fstream.h>

int main()
{
  ofstream of;
  of.open("t28.out");
  of << "t28c - OK";

  return 0;
}
```

The fourth test uses the constructor that takes a filename argument:

```
// t28d.cpp
#include <fstream.h>

int main()
```

```
{
  ofstream of("t28.out");
  of << "t28d - OK";

  return 0;
}
```

All the programs in the t28 series create a new file and produce numbered output. The next test uses the same constructor as the fourth one did, but overrides its defaulted second argument to create the ofstream in append mode:

```
// t28e.cpp
#include <fstream.h>

int main()
{
  ofstream of("t28.out", ios::out | ios::ate);
  of << ", OK don't hassle" << endl;

  return 0;
}
```

If this test is run immediately after the fourth one, it should produce the following output:

```
t28 - OK, OK don't hassle
```

21.12 fstream Tests

There are potentially many fstream tests. The first one roughly parallels the ifstream and ofstream tests. For fstream, however, all the tests are performed in one program. Pairs of functions create a file. The first function writes something to the file, then closes it; the second one opens it and reads it back.

The first pair of functions checks the case where an open file descriptor is provided. Notice that in these cases, the fstream destructor doesn't close the file. We provided it, so we must close it.

```
// t29.cpp
#include <stdlib.h>
#include <io.h>
#include <fcntl.h>
#include <string.h>
```

```
#include <fstream.h>

char *testphrase = "She sells sea shells.";

void create1()  // fstream from opened file descriptor
{
  int fd = creat("t29.out", 0644);
  fstream fs(fd);
  fs << testphrase << endl;
  close(fd);   // we provided the file descriptor
           // and must close it
}

void open1()
{
  int fd = open("t29.out", O_RDWR);
  fstream fs(fd);
  char buf[80];
  fs.getline(buf,80);
  if (strcmp(testphrase,buf)) {
    cerr << "Failed in open1\n";
    abort();
  }
  close(fd);
}
```

The second pair uses the default constructor and then attaches an open file. Once again the fstream destructor is not responsible for closing the file.

```
void create2()     // default fstream constructor then use attach
{
  int fd = creat("t29.out", 0644);
  fstream fs;
  fs.attach(fd);
  fs << testphrase << endl;
  close(fd);
}

void open2()
{
  int fd = open("t29.out", O_RDWR);
  fstream fs;
  fs.attach(fd);
```

```
  char buf[80];
  fs.getline(buf,80);
  if (strcmp(testphrase,buf)) {
    cerr << "Failed in open2\n";
    abort();
  }
  close(fd);
}
```

The third pair of functions uses the default constructor and the open function. This time the fstream object opens the file and is responsible for closing it.

```
void create3()
{
  fstream fs;
  fs.open("t29.out");
  fs << testphrase << endl;
}

void open3()
{
  fstream fs;
  fs.open("t29.out");
  char buf[80];
  fs.getline(buf,80);
  if (strcmp(testphrase,buf)) {
    cerr << "Failed in open3\n";
    abort();
  }
}
```

In the last of this group of functions, the succinct form of fstream instantiation is used. Again, the destructor closes the file.

```
void create4()
{
  fstream fs("fs.out");
  fs << testphrase << endl;
}

void open4()
{
  fstream fs("fs.out");
  char buf[80];
  fs.getline(buf,80);
```

```
  if (strcmp(testphrase,buf)) {
    cerr << "Failed in open4\n";
    abort();
  }
}
```

The next two functions open the existing file with an explicit mode, then try to perform an operation that conflicts with the mode:

```
void open5()
{
  fstream fs("fs.out", ios::in);
  fs << testphrase << endl;
  cout << "open5 - state = " << fs.rdstate() << endl;
}

void open6()
{
  fstream fs("fs.out", ios::out);
  char buf[80];
  fs.getline(buf,80);
  cout << buf << "open6 - state = " << fs.rdstate() << endl;
}
```

In main, the sequence of operations uses explicit unlink operations to ensure the same file is not simply carried through the first four tests:

```
int main()
{
  create1();
  open1();
  unlink("t29.out");
  create2();
  open2();
  unlink("t29.out");
  create3();
  open3();
  unlink("t29.out");
  create4();
  open4();
  open5();
  open6();

  return 0;
}
```

In this example, both open5 and open6 should fail.

The fstream class is an ideal vehicle for testing the behavior of the ios::open_mode flags. We started this process in the last two functions of the previous test, but there is more to do.

The following series of tests checks out the flags ios::nocreate, ios::trunc, ios::app, and ios::noreplace. The first one attempts to set up an fstream for both input and output but with the caveat that the file is not to be created if it doesn't exist. If the series of tests is run in sequence, the existence of the file should cause failure at t35.

```cpp
// t30.cpp
#include <fstream.h>

int main()
{
  fstream fs("t30_36.out",
           ios::in | ios::out | ios::nocreate);
  cout << "state = " << fs.rdstate();

  return 0;
}
```

The second test does the same thing without qualification and creates the required file with the specified output, as follows:

```cpp
// t31.cpp
#include <fstream.h>

int main()
{
  fstream fs("t30_36.out");
  fs << "Mary had a little lamb\n";

  return 0;
}
```

The third test opens the same file in ios::in | ios::out mode but also specifies by using ios::trunc that its existing contents are to be junked:

```cpp
// t32.cpp
#include <fstream.h>

int main()
{
```

```
fstream fs("t30_36.out",
   ios::in | ios::out | ios::trunc);
fs << "Mary had a substantial sheep\n";

return 0;
}
```

The fourth test checks the `ios::ate` specification, which requires that the file currency be set to EOF when opened. The attempt at input should fail and the new output then should be appended, as follows:

```
// t33.cpp
#include <stdlib.h>
#include <fstream.h>

int main()
{
  fstream fs("t30_36.out",
      ios::in | ios::out | ios::ate);
  char buf[80];
  fs >> buf;
  if (fs) {
    cerr << "Failed - should be positioned at EOF\n";
    abort();
  }
  fs.clear();
  fs << "that was covered in wool\n";

  return 0;
}
```

We next check that after these operations, the file can still be opened as a regular input file.

```
// t34.cpp
#include <fstream.h>

int main()
{
  ifstream fs("t30_36.out");
  cout << fs.rdbuf();
  return 0;
}
```

The last test in this series checks to make sure that it's possible to use the `ios::noreplace` flag to prohibit automatic truncation of a file opened for writing only. The stream should record an error, as follows:

```
// t35.cpp
#include <fstream.h>

int main()
{
  fstream fs("t30_36.out", ios::out | ios::noreplace);
  cout << "state = " << fs.rdstate();

  return 0;
}
```

The following test exercises, for an `fstream`, the file positioning functions `seekg` and `seekp` and the file position inquiry function `tellp`.

```
// t36.cpp
#include <fstream.h>

int main()
{
  char buffer[80];
  fstream f("t30_36.out");

// Get to the end of the file
  while (f >> buffer) ;

// Clear the EOF state
  f.clear(0);

// Append something
  f << "something";

// Search back to the start of what was appended,
// and note the position
  f.seekp(-9,ios::end);
  streampos sp = f.tellg();

// Seek to the start of the file and write something
  f.seekp(0);
  f << "Tony";
```

```
// Back to where we were, read and report
  f.seekg(sp);
  f >> buffer;
  cout <<
    "String at remembered position = " << buffer << endl;
  f.clear();

// Back to start, read and report
  f.seekp(0);
  cout << f.rdbuf();

  return 0;
}
```

Given the file t30_36.out as it was left by the previous tests, the new file contents should be

```
String at remembered position = something
Tony had a substantial sheep
that was covered in wool
something
```

The following and final test on the fstream class investigates the behavior when an attempt is made to construct an fstream with a file descriptor value of EOF, which is the value returned when an open or creat operation fails:

```
// t37.cpp
#include <io.h>
#include <fstream.h>

int main()
{
  int fd = -1;
  ifstream ifs;
  cout << ifs.rdstate() << endl;
  ifs.attach(fd);
  cout << ifs.rdstate() << endl;
  ifs.close();
  cout << ifs.rdstate() << endl;

  return 0;
}
```

The output from this test is not well defined by current standards. However, plausible output might be

```
4
6
6
```

Here, the first output after the default constructor (`ios::badbit`) indicates that the stream is unusable, but not that there has been a failure. The other two state reports (`ios::badbit | ios::failbit`) show that the stream is unusable and indicate that there was a failure.

21.13 **Streams Using a** `strstreambuf`

The following set of tests investigate the behavior of the translators for in-memory operations.

The first program tests the three constructor options of an `istrstream`. The first stream is set up to correspond to a chunk of the run-time heap. The constructor used indicates the stream continues "indefinitely." Characters are then extracted from this stream and the occurrences of null bytes counted. The same estimate of the number of null bytes also is made by scanning a pointer through the same memory in parallel.

```
// t38.cpp
#include <stdlib.h>
#include <string.h>
#include <limits.h>
#include <strstream.h>

char *source = "1234.5678E-07 And the rest";

int main()
{
  unsigned count1 = 0, count2 = 0;
  char *heap, *t;

// Establish approximate heap extent
  for (unsigned chunk = INT_MAX;
      (t = new char[chunk]) == 0; chunk >>= 1) ;
  heap = t;
  delete[] t;
```

```
// Now instantiate stream of indefinite length
// spanning the heap
  istrstream s1(heap,-1);
  t = heap;

// Count null bytes
  for (unsigned i = 0; i < chunk; ++i, ++t) {
    int c = s1.get();
    if (c == EOF) break;
    if (!c) count1++;
    if (!*t) count2++;
  }
  if (count1-count2) {
    cerr << "Pointer and strstream don't match\n";
    abort();
  }
  cout << (100.0*count1)/chunk << "% nulls" << endl;
```

A second instance is then set up using the default second argument. This causes the length of the string pointed at by the supplied char pointer argument to be used as the extent of the stream. Characters are then extracted from this string, as in the following:

```
  istrstream s2(source);
  double d;
  char buf[80];
  s2 >> d;
  s2.get(buf,80);
  cout << d << ' ' << buf << endl;
```

The third instance specifies both memory and actual length and reads a single character from it after whitespace has been skipped:

```
  t = new char[512];
  if (!t) return;
  memset(t,' ',512);
  t[511] = '#';
  istrstream s3(t,512);
  char c;
  s3 >> c;
  cout << c;

  return 0;
}
```

21.14 An `ostrstream` Test

The following test sets up first a dynamically allocated `ostrstream` and then a static (fixed-size) one. It writes enough to cause dynamic allocation to the first and as much as possible to the second.

```
// t39.cpp
#include <strstream.h>

char buf[128];

int main()
{
  ostrstream s1;             // dynamic stream
  for (int n = 1000, i = 1234; n--; i++)
    s1 << i <<'';
  s1 << ends;
  cout << s1.str() << endl;
  cout << "s1 state = " << s1.rdstate() << endl;

  ostrstream s2(buf,127);  // static (fixed size) stream
  for (; s2; ++i) {
    s2 << i << '';
  }
  cout << s2.str() << endl;
  cout << "s2 state = " << s2.rdstate() << endl;

  return 0;
}
```

The final states of the two streams should differ. The dynamic stream should indicate an EOF condition (`ios::eof`), since it has been frozen by the use of the `str` function. The static stream should indicate that a failure occurred and that it's at EOF (`ios::fail | ios::eof`).

21.15 A Static `strstream`

The first `strstream` test exercises a `strstream` with a static buffer, that is, one that doesn't indulge in dynamic allocation. Specifying `ios::ate` to the constructor implies that the put area is to begin after the null-terminated string contained in the nominated area of memory. The following strstream is created for reading and writing:

```
// t40.cpp
#include <string.h>
#include <strstream.h>

int main()
{

  char buf[512] = "The quick brown fox";
  strstream ss(buf,512,ios::in|ios::out|ios::ate);
  char buffer[80];
```

Next, we take words from the get area and place them in the put area, that is, we concatenate the words:

```
  ss >> buffer;
  ss << buffer << endl;
  ss >> buffer;
  ss << buffer << endl;
  ss >> buffer;
  ss << buffer << endl;
```

Then we seek the get pointer to a position close to the end of the get area, check the state, and report the get pointer position:

```
  ss.seekg(17,ios::beg);
  streampos t = ss.tellg();
  int st;

  cout << "state after seek " << ss.rdstate() << endl;

  cout << long(t) << endl;
```

Next, read a string from the new get pointer position and check the state again. It should still be good since we are now reading characters that have been put. Once again the string read is concatenated:

```
  ss >> buffer;
  cout << "state after read " << (st = ss.rdstate()) << endl;
  ss << buffer << ends;
```

The stream now is frozen and its contents displayed using the returned pointer value. The state is checked at this point. Note, available IOStreams descriptions don't say if freezing should effect the state of a strstream. However, an error state of `ios::eofbit` would not be unreasonable at this point. To be safe, the stream state is cleared, then the stream is unfrozen, as follows:

```
cout << ss.str() << endl;
cout << "state after freeze " << ss.rdstate() << endl;
ss.clear();
ss.rdbuf()->freeze(0);
```

Both get and put pointers are now repositioned to the original start of the put area, where a substitution is made. Remember, the output operation doesn't move the get pointer, so it should be possible to read back what was just written:

```
ss.rdbuf()->seekoff(19,ios::beg,ios::in|ios::out);
ss << "XXXX";
ss >> buffer;
cout << buffer << endl;
```

Finally we freeze the `strstreambuf` and look at the whole memory area contents again:

```
cout << ss.str() << endl;

    return 0;
}
```

The output should look as follows:

```
state after seek 0
get pointer at 17
state after read 0
The quick brown foxThe
quick
brown
oxThe
state after freeze = 1
XXXXquick
The quick brown foxXXXXquick
brown
oxThe
```

21.16 A Dynamic `strstream`

The following test for a dynamic `strstream` begins with an empty dynamic `strstreambuf` into which a string gets written. As in the previous test using a static buffer in Section 21.16, the contents of the stream are then snipped up and appended. The snipping process includes a seek of the get pointer.

```
// t41.cpp
#include <string.h>
#include <strstream.h>

main()
{

// Set up a dynamic strstream.
  strstream ss;
  char buffer[80];

  ss << "Now is the time for all good men";
// Take one word at a time and concatenate it
  ss >> buffer;
  ss << buffer << endl;
  ss >> buffer;
  ss << buffer << endl;
  ss >> buffer;
  ss << buffer << endl;

// Now seek the get pointer to a position close to
// the end of the get area
  ss.seekg(30,ios::beg);
  ss >> buffer;
  ss << buffer << ends;

// Freeze the stream, and get a pointer to its contents.
  cout << ss.str() << endl;
```

Freezing might have put the stream into an error state to prevent further use, so we need to clear the error state before anything else is attempted. If the stream is to be further extended it must also be unfrozen.

```
  ss.clear();
  ss.rdbuf()->freeze(0);
```

Both pointers are now positioned at the start of the stream. Characters are then read and overwritten up to a specified point:

```
// Seek put and get pointers to start
  ss.rdbuf()->seekoff(0,ios::beg,ios::in|ios::out);
```

```
    char c;
    for (;;) {
      c = ss.get();
      if (c == 'g') break;
      ss << 'a';
    }

// Look at the whole memory area contents again
    cout << ss.str() << endl;

    return 0;
}
```

The output should be as follows, provided our implementation permits get operations on characters present in the put area and we have arbitrary positioning of the get and put pointers as discussed in Chapter 14.

```
Now is the time for all good menNow
is
the
enNow
aaaaaaaaaaaaaaaaaaaaaaaaaaagood menNow
is
the
enNow
```

21.17 Checking `strstream` Cleanup

This test first creates a dynamic `strstream`, then writes a substantial number of characters to it to check its behavior over multiple reallocations. It's important we establish that all memory allocated is properly deallocated. We do that here by providing alternative versions of operators `new` and `delete` that report their operations as they happen. However, this approach will work only if the `strstreambuf` implementation uses the `new` and `delete` operators to allocate memory, and this won't necessarily be the case. It's quite possible the C library functions `malloc`, `realloc`, and `free` might be used, since `realloc` is apt to be more efficient than `new` - copy - `delete`.

```
// t42.cpp
#include <stddef.h>
#include <stdlib.h>
#include <string.h>
```

```
#include <strstrea.h>

const char *jabberwocky =
  "Twas brillig and the slithy toves.";

void *operator new(size_t s)
{
  void *p = malloc(s);
  cout << "allocated at " << p << endl;
  return p;
}

void operator delete(void *p)
{
  cout << "deleting " << p << endl;
  free(p);
}

void foo()
{
  strstream ss;
  for (int i = 0; i < 100; ++i)
    ss << jabberwocky << endl;
  char buffer[80];
  for (i = 0; i < 100; ++i) {
    ss.getline(buffer,80);
    if (strcmp(jabberwocky,buffer)) {
      cerr << "Mismatch at " << i << endl;
      abort();
    }
  }
}

int main()
{
  foo();

  return 0;
}
```

The output should be similar in form to the following:

```
allocated at :26B2
allocated at :2ED6
```

```
deleting :26B2
allocated at :2F38
deleting :2ED6
allocated at :305A
deleting :2F38
allocated at :33BC
deleting :305A
allocated at :3DDE
deleting :33BC
deleting :3DDE
```

Here, we have an initial allocation followed by five reallocations, that is, allocate/delete pairs. The destructor then deletes the block that was allocated last.

The replacement of operators new and delete by functions that use cout is an interesting test in itself. The standard streams like cin and cout are static and are initialized before execution of any function in the translation unit. If the standard streams use operator new in their construction, then operator new may use cout before it is initialized. Because we want an overload of operator new to be able to use cout without provoking a crash or a system error message, it follows that the constructors for the standard streams should provide any buffers they require in some other way, for instance using malloc().

If dynamic strstream allocation is done in some other way, the test must include checks on the state of the heap before and after the call to foo, as follows:

```
void main()
{
  heaptest();
  foo();
  heaptest();
}
```

The memory allocation/deallocation test can be modified as follows to test the behavior of the strstream when the str function is called. Calling the str function should inhibit the strstreambuf destructor from deleting the buffer area. The function is split into two separate parts—foo1 and foo2—and the allocated memory is deleted in main.

```
// t43.cpp
// same operator new and operator delete as previous
// test, then

char *foo1()
{
  cout << "foo1" << endl;
  strstream ss;
```

```
    for (int i = 0; i < 100; ++i)
      ss << jabberwocky << endl;
    char *s = ss.str();
    return s;
}

char *foo2(char *buf)
{
    cout << "foo2" << endl;
    istrstream ss(buf);
    char buffer[80];
    for (int i = 0; i < 100; ++i) {
      ss.getline(buffer,80);
      if (strcmp(jabberwocky,buffer)) {
        cerr << "Mismatch at " << i << endl;
        abort();
      }
    }
    return buf;
}

int main()
{
    delete[] foo2(foo1());
    return 0;
}
```

The output should resemble the following:

```
foo1
allocated at :2EB4
allocated at :2ED6
deleting :2EB4
allocated at :2F38
deleting :2ED6
allocated at :305A
deleting :2F38
allocated at :33BC
deleting :305A
allocated at :3DDE
deleting :33BC
foo2
deleting :3DDE
```

21.18 Using Streams with Assignment

Variants of istream, ostream, and iostream that support assignment are provided. The following examples check that such assignment works correctly.

A common requirement is to check if a filename was supplied on the command line, then to take input either from that file, if a name was specified, or from the standard input if not.

```
// t44.cpp
#include <fstream.h>

int main(int argc, char *argv[])
{
  char buffer[80];
  ifstream ifs;
  if (argc > 1) {
    cout << "reassigning" << endl;

    ifs.open(argv[1]);
    if (!ifs)
      return -1;
    cin = ifs;
  }
  cin >> buffer;
  cout << buffer;
  return 0;
}
```

Of course, this sort of assignment need not be done using an ifstream, since a streambuf pointer can be assigned to an istream_withassign. Therefore the following test also can be made:

```
// t45.cpp
#include <fstream.h>

int main(int argc, char *argv[])
{
  char buffer[80];
  filebuf *fbp;
  if (argc > 1) {
    cout << "reassigning" << endl;

    fbp = new filebuf;
    if (!fbp)
```

```
      return -1;
    fbp->open(argv[1],ios::in);
    cin = fbp;
  }
  cin >> buffer;
  cout << buffer;
  if (argc > 1)
    delete fbp;
  return 0;
}
```

The next two tests attempt the same thing with an istream_withassign object. In this case, the object is defined within the program, not in some "special" way like cin.

As before, the first test assigns an ifstream to an existing istream:

```
// t46.cpp
#include <fstream.h>

istream_withassign in;

int main(int argc, char *argv[])
{
  char buffer[80];
  ifstream *fsp;
  if (argc > 1) {
    cout << "reassigning" << endl;
    fsp = new ifstream(argv[1]);
    if (!*fsp)
      return -1;
    in = *fsp;
  } else
    in = cin;
  in >> buffer;
  cout << buffer;
  if (argc > 1)
    delete fsp;
  return 0;
}
```

The second test assigns a filebuf pointer to the existing istream:

```
// t47.cpp
#include <io.h>
#include <fcntl.h>
```

```
#include <fstream.h>

istream_withassign in;

int main(int argc, char *argv[])
{
  char buffer[80];
  filebuf *fbp;
  if (argc > 1) {
    cout << "reassigning\n";
    cout.flush();
    fbp = new filebuf;
    if (!fbp)
      return -1;
    if (!fbp->open(argv[1],ios::in))
      return -1;
    in = fbp;
  } else
    in = cin.rdbuf();
  in >> buffer;
  cout << buffer;
  if (argc > 1)
    delete fbp;

  return 0;
}
```

The last test in this group temporarily switches output to a file to output to the console and then back again, a switch that might be helpful during debugging:

```
// t48.cpp
#include <fstream.hpp>

void foo(ostream_withassign &s)
{
// temporarily divert from s to cout
  ostream_withassign temp;
  temp = s;
  s = cout;
  s << "Whatever we wanted to see\n";
  s = temp;
}

int main()
```

```
{
  filebuf fb;
  if (!fb.open("dummy.dat", ios::out))
    return -1;
  ostream_withassign dummy(&fb);
  dummy << "Something" << endl;
  foo(dummy);
  dummy << "Still here?";

  return 0;
}
```

Here, an `ostream_withassign` is set up using a `filebuf` in `main`. In function `foo`, the output to the file must be displayed, so a temporary `ostream_withassign` is used to hold the existing stream, which then has `cout` assigned to it. At the end of `foo`, the original stream is replaced.

21.19 Mixed `stdio` and IOStreams Output

If `stdio` style output via `printf`, `puts`, etc., is mixed with IOStreams `cout` output without any precaution, the output from the program will probably be garbled. This is because the order of appearance of the output is determined by two separate and unconnected buffering mechanisms. You can eliminate this effect by calling the function `ios::sync_with_stdio`. This static member function replaces the `filebuf` elements associated with the standard streams `cin`, `cout`, `cerr`, etc., with `stdiobuf` elements and sets flags in these streams to force appropriate flushing of the `stdio` streams.

   A test for this capability must take sufficient input from both sources and send sufficient output to both destinations to ensure that the associated buffers underflow and overflow, respectively. This requirement will vary from implementation to implementation.

   The source file can conveniently be of the form

```
aaaaaaaaaaaaaaaaa bbbbbbbbbbbbbbbbbbbbbbb\n
aaaaaaaaaaaaaaaaa bbbbbbbbbbbbbbbbbbbbbbb\n
```

The 'a' characters get read through `cin` and the 'b' characters through `stdin`.

```
// t49.cpp
#include <stdiostr.h>
const int ENOUGH = 100;   // see below

int main()
{
```

```
ios::sync_with_stdio();

char buf1[80], buf2[80];

for (int i = ENOUGH; i--;) {
  cin >> buf1;
  cout << buf1 << endl;
  fgets(buf2,79,stdin);
  printf("%s",buf2);
}

return 0;
}
```

An appropriate value for ENOUGH can be determined by compiling and running the test with the ios::sync_with_stdio() line commented out. Increase ENOUGH until the screen output gets mixed up, ensuring that the file from which test input is redirected has enough source lines. Replace the call to ios::sync_with_stdio. The output then should consist of the 'a' and 'b' characters on twice as many separate lines as was the input.

APPENDIX 1

An Example of a Table-driven, Floating-point Extractor

This example implementation doesn't modify any IOStreams class definitions, though that could easily be done. Also, it makes no attempt to provide an efficient translation function to go from the checked digit strings built by the extractor and translator helper functions to a floating-point number representation. The translator shown is intended only to be easily understood. Further, we note that the transition table used is not the same as that generated at the end of Chapter 19. The one used here was machine generated.

The supplementary information used in this example provides for separating the character stream into strings to represent the whole, fractional, and exponent parts and to note whether the number itself and its exponent are intended to be negative. It also has a scratch member to note the progress of the character scanning process.

```
#include <ctype.h>
#include <string.h>
#include <math.h>
#include <iostream.h>

#define BIG_ENOUGH 80

typedef void (*translate_t)(void *,const char *, void *);
```

```
typedef int (*helper_t)(int,char,void *);

static int tt[] = {
//  +    -    .   0   1   2   3   4   5   6   7   8   9   E   e
    2,   3,   0, -4, -4, -4, -4, -4, -4, -4, -4, -4, -4,  0,  0,
    0,   0,   0, -4, -4, -4, -4, -4, -4, -4, -4, -4, -4,  0,  0,
    0,   0,   0, -4, -4, -4, -4, -4, -4, -4, -4, -4, -4,  0,  0,
    0,   0,  -5, -4, -4, -4, -4, -4, -4, -4, -4, -4, -4,  6,  7,
    0,   0,   0, -8, -8, -8, -8, -8, -8, -8, -8, -8, -8,  6,  7,
    9,  10,   0,-11,-11,-11,-11,-11,-11,-11,-11,-11,-11,  0,  0,
    9,  10,   0,-11,-11,-11,-11,-11,-11,-11,-11,-11,-11,  0,  0,
    0,   0,   0, -8, -8, -8, -8, -8, -8, -8, -8, -8, -8,  6,  7,
    0,   0,   0,-11,-11,-11,-11,-11,-11,-11,-11,-11,-11,  0,  0,
    0,   0,   0,-11,-11,-11,-11,-11,-11,-11,-11,-11,-11,  0,  0,
    0,   0,   0,-12,-12,-12,-12,-12,-12,-12,-12,-12,-12,  0,  0,
    0,   0,   0,-13,-13,-13,-13,-13,-13,-13,-13,-13,-13,  0,  0,
    0,   0,   0,  0,  0,  0,  0,  0,  0,  0,  0,  0,  0,  0,  0
};

char *ok = "+-.0123456789Ee";
int charset[128];

struct _fp_translate_info {
  char whole[20];
  char frac[20];
  char exp[4];
  int neg, negexp;
  int stage;
};
```

The translation helper function makes notes in the supplementary information structure as scanning of characters proceeds:

```
int fhf(int n, char c, void *supplement)
{
  _fp_translate_info *info
      = (_fp_translate_info *) supplement;
  static char *p = info->whole;
```

A plus character is a notational convenience; it can be ignored. A minus sign can be used to give the complete number its sign, or alternatively the sign belonging to the exponent. The stage variable of the supplementary information structure allows us to determine which one.

```
  switch (c) {
```

```
case '+':
  return 0;
case '-':
  if (info->stage == 0) {
    info->neg = 1;
  else if (info->stage == 2)
    info->negexp = 1;
  return 0;
```

When the decimal point is encountered, the whole part digit string is terminated and stage progresses from 0 to 1. Then when a letter 'e' or 'E' arrives, the fractional part digit string is terminated, and stage progresses to 2.

```
case '.':
  info->stage = 1;
  p = info->frac;
  return  0;
case 'e':
case 'E'
  info->stage = 2;
  p = info->exp;
  return 0;
}
```

Otherwise, the character is a digit and gets copied into whatever string is appropriate for the current stage:

```
*p++ = c;
  return 0;
}
```

As noted, this translator doesn't pretend to be efficient. Review the coding of the atof function in your C standard library to see how it might be done better. In this case, all the information required to form the final value gets stored in the supplementary data structure, so the second argument, the pointer to the accepted string, doesn't get used:

```
void fxf(double *t, const char *, void * supplement)
{
  _fp_translate_info *info
        = (_fp_translate_info *) supplement;

// for the example, report progress
  cout << info->whole << ' ' << info->frac
              << ' ' << info->exp << endl;
```

```
   double f = 0.0, v = 0.0;

// assemble whole part
   for (char *p = info->whole; *p; ++p) {
     v *= 10;
     v += *p-'0';
   }

// assemble fractional part
   int lf = strlen(info->frac);
   p = info->frac+lf-1;
   for (; lf--; --p) {
     f += *p-'0';
     f /= 10;
   }
   v += f;

// assemble exponent
   int e = 0;
   for (p = info->exp; *p; ++p) {
     e *= 10;
     e += *p-'0';
   }
   if (info->neg) v = -v;               // add sign information
   if (info->negexp) e = -e;
   *t = v * pow(10.0,e);                // apply the exponent
}
```

The extract function is as described in Chapter 18, with the extensions to call the helper function and the translation function with a supplementary information pointer. If this method were built into IOStreams, the extract function would be a private member of class istream.

```
istream &extract(istream &is, void *t, int *charset,
                 int alphabet, int *tt, translate_t tf,
                 helper_t hf, void *supplement)
{
  if (!is.ipfx(0))
    return is;
  char buf[BIG_ENOUGH], *p = buf;
  int pc, c = is.rdbuf()->sgetc(), err = 0, state = 0,
    back2 = 0, back1 = 0, last = 0, accept = 0, n = 0;
  for (;;) {
    if (c == EOF) {
```

```
      err = ios::eofbit;
      break;
    }
  int col = charset[c];
  if (col == -1) {   // char not in Type's alphabet
    back2 = back1;
    back1 = last;
    last = 0;
    break;
  }
  state = tt[state*alphabet+col];
        // get next state from Type's transition table
  if (state < 0) {
    accept = 1;
    state = -state;
  }
  --state;
  back2 = back1;
  back1 = last;
  last = accept;
  accept = 0;
  pc = c;          // remember previous char for putback

  if (state < 0)  // character out of context
    break;
  hf(n,c,supplement);
  *p++ = c;
  c = is.rdbuf()->snextc();
  ++n;
}
*p = 0;
if (!(back2 || back1 || last)) {
  err |= ios::failbit;
  if (n) {
    is.rdbuf()->sputbackc(pc);
    --n;
  }
  cout << "failed " << n << endl;
} else {
  if (last)
    is.rdbuf()->stossc();
  else if (!back1) {
    *(--p) = 0;
```

```
      is.rdbuf()->sputbackc(pc);
    }
    tf(t,buf,supplement);

// for the example
    cout << buf << ' ' << back2 << ' '
         << back1 << ' ' << last << endl;
  }
  is.clear(err);
  return is;
}
```

The following is a test extractor function for double. If it were built-in to IOStreams, it would replace `istream &operator>>(double&);`.

```
istream &fp_extract(istream &is, double &a)
{
  _fp_translate_info info;
  memset(&info,0,sizeof(_fp_translate_info));
  return extract(is,&a,charset,15,tt,fxf,fhf,&info);
}
```

Because this extractor is for one of the built-in types, the transition table, the acceptable character set, and the supplementary information data structure are defined at file scope here. In an extractor for a user-defined type, these would all presumably be static members of the class, and the `charset[]` array could be set up dynamically by the first constructor call for an object of that type. For a built-in type, it can be set up by the first execution of an `istream` constructor.

```
void main()
{
  double d = 0.0;

  for (int i = 0; i < 128; ++i)
    charset[i] = -1;
  char *p = ok;
  for (i = 0; *p; ++p, ++i)
    charset[*p] = i;

  fp_extract(cin,d);
  cout << d << endl;
}
```

APPENDIX **2**

UNIX-like Low-level IO Operations

The `filebuf` implementation presented in Chapter 17 used some functions that are not part of the C standard library. The relevant header file is `io.h`.

The `open` function opens the file specified by `filename` in a mode specified by `open_mode`, with access specified by `protection`. The return value is either an `int` file descriptor that may be used in the other functions described below, or if an error occurs, −1. In the latter case the global error variable `errno` is set.

```
int open(const char *filename, int open_mode, int protection);
```

The `open_mode` argument will typically support the following values:

O_RDONLY	Read only
O_RDWR	Read write
O_WRONLY	Write only
O_CREAT	Create a file if one doesn't already exist.
O_EXCL	Return an error if O_CREAT and the file already exists.
O_TRUNC	Truncate an existing file.

These values represent flag bits that can be orred together. There will probably be other mode values, but they are likely to be system dependent.

The values required for the protection argument will be markedly system dependent. The protection argument may only be required if O_CREAT is specified as the open mode.

The `read` function inputs n bytes from the file nominated by `file_de-scriptor` and places them in the area of memory nominated by `destination`. It returns the number of bytes read, which may be 0 if the file currency is at EOF. If some error occurs, it returns −1 and sets the global error variable `errno`.

```
int read(int file_descriptor, void *destination, size_t n);
```

The `write` function outputs n bytes to the file nominated by `file_de-scriptor`, taking them from the area of memory nominated by `source`. It returns the number of bytes written, or if some error occurs, it returns −1 and sets the global error variable `errno`.

```
int write(int file_descriptor, void *source, size_t n);
```

The `lseek` function sets the currency of the file specified by `file_de-scriptor`. It sets the currency to the offset specified by the second argument from the file position specified by the `mode` argument. It returns the resulting offset from the start of the file, or if some error occurs, it returns -1 and sets the global error variable `errno`.

```
long lseek(int file_descriptor, long offset, int mode);
```

The `mode` value specifies the following:

Beginning of file	(Mode value SEEK_SET–usually 0)
Current file position	(Mode value SEEK_CUR–usually 1)
End of file	(Mode value SEEK_END–usually 2)

The `isatty` function returns nonzero if the device referred to by `file_de-scriptor` is in fact a terminal, printer, or some similar device. The principal inference will be that seeking on the device is an error. The `isatty` function returns 0 if the device is a file.

```
int isatty(int file_descriptor);
```

The `close` function closes the file referenced by `file_descriptor`. It returns 0, or if some error occurs, it returns -1 and sets the global error variable `errno`.

```
int close(int file_descriptor);
```

References

1. Aho, A. V., R. Sethi, and J. D. Ullman. 1986. *Compilers: Principles, Techniques, and Tools.* Addison-Wesley, Reading, Mass. (The Dragon book.)

2. Aho, A. V., J. E. Hopcroft, and J. D. Ullman. 1974. *The Design and Analysis of Computer Algorithms.* Addison-Wesley, Reading, Mass.

3. Coplien, James O. 1992. *Advanced C++ Programming Styles and Idioms.* Addison-Wesley, Reading, Mass.

4. Cox, Brad J. 1986, 1987. *Object Oriented Programming.* Addison-Wesley, Reading, Mass.

5. Ellis, Margaret A. and Bjarne Stoustrup. 1990. *The Annotated C++ Reference Manual.* Addison-Wesley, Reading, Mass. (The ARM.)

6. Lippman, Stanley. 1989, 1991. *A C++ Primer.* Addison-Wesley, Reading, Mass.

7. Liskov, Barbara and John Guttag. 1986. *Abstraction and Specification in Program Development.* MIT Press, Cambridge, Mass.

8. Schwarz, Jerry. 1990. ANSI Committee document no. X3J16/92-0059.

9. Sethi, Ravi. 1989. *Programming Languages Concepts and Constructs.* Addison-Wesley, Reading, Mass. (The Teddy Bear book.)

10. Vilot, Mike. 1990. ANSI Committee document no. X3J16/90-0078.

11. Vilot, Mike. 1990. ANSI Committee document no. X3J16/90-0078 Rev. 2/12/91.

Index

file-oriented translators, 154-158
mode control, 76, 83-84, 141-142, 146
operator! - see ios::operator!
operator, - see comma operator
operator= - see ios::operator=,
    iostream_withassign::op-
    erator=, istream_withas-
    sign::operator=,
    ostream_withassign::op-
    erator=
operator<< - see ostream::opera-
    tor<<, inserters
operator>> - see istream::opera-
    tor>>, extractors
operator delete, 336-338
operator new, 161, 196, 336-338
operator precedence, 100-101, 265
operator void* - see ios::opera-
    tor void*
opfx - see ostream::opfx
OS/2, 4-5, 18, 25, 83, 110, 115, 141
osfx - see ostream::osfx
ostream, 103-117
ostream::
  flush, 9, 105, 114, 150, 342
  operator<<, 104, 107-112, 237-247
  opfx, 104-107, 113, 179-180, 184, 222,
      228-231, 237, 240, 244, 246, 277-278
  osfx, 104-107, 113, 180-181, 185, 222,
      228-229, 231, 238, 242, 245, 247,
      277-278
  ostream, 104, 218, 310
  put, 8, 104, 113, 115-116, 231, 283, 314
  seekp, 105, 115-116, 328-329
  tellp, 105, 115-116
  write, 105, 113-114, 184, 284, 295
  ~ostream, 104
ostream_withassign, 136-138
ostream_withassign::
  operator=, 136-137
  ostream_withassign, 136-137
  ~ostream_withassign, 136
ostrstream, 27-28, 48, 50, 165-168,
    227, 332
ostrstream::
  ostrstream, 27-28,166, 227

pcount, 166, 168, 295
rdbuf, 166, 168
str, 28, 166
out - see ios::out
overflow - see filebuf::over-
    flow, streambuf::over-
    flow

padding, 10-11, 15-16, 85, 110-111, 238,
    240-241, 283, 285, 298
  character, 77, 88
parameterized manipulators - see manipu-
    lators with parameters
pbackfail - see filebuf::pback-
    fail, streambuf::pbackfail
pbase - see streambuf::pbase
pbump - see streambuf::pbump
pcount - see ostrstream::pcount
peek - see istream::peek
persistence
  ios state, 11, 14
  streambuf buffer, 51
plus sign, 15, 85, 109-110, 249, 266, 346
pointer
  extractors, 309
  inserters, 104, 107-110
  output, 18, 308-309
  representation, 110, 308
pointer to function, 111, 126
polymorphism, 31, 36, 38, 224, 273
portability, 79, 90, 131, 147, 160, 166
positive sign - see plus sign
pptr - see streambuf::pptr
precision - see ios::precision
prefix function
  see istream::ipfx, ostream::opfx
printer, 80, 352
printf, 2-3, 8, 10, 12-14, 16, 31,40, 87,
    94, 117, 183-186, 343-344
propagation - see error propagation
protected
  interface of streambuf, 192-196
pure virtual function, 61, 63. 69, 215
put - see ostream::put
putback - see istream::putback,
    character putback